Dinner showcases the inventive yet unfussy approach to cooking that will make anyone a better and more confident cook.

Dinner has the range and authority—and the author's trademark warmth—of an instant classic. With more than 200 all-new recipes, *Dinner* is about options: inherently simple recipes that you can make any night of the week.

Each recipe in this book is meant to be dinner—one fantastic dish that is so satisfying and flavor-forward it can stand alone—maybe with a little salad or some bread on the side. This is what Melissa Clark means by changing the game. Organized by main ingredient—chicken, meat, fish and seafood, eggs, pasta and noodles, tofu, vegetable dinners, grains, pizza, soups, and salads that mean it—*Dinner* covers an astonishing breadth of ideas about just what dinner can be. This is the kind of easy cooking that makes the most of a few ingredients and simple techniques. Many nights you'll need only a sheet pan or one pot, other times you'll have the benefit of a make-ahead dish that requires just a little time in the oven.

Melissa Clark's mission is to help anyone, whether a novice or an experienced home cook, figure out what to have for dinner without ever settling on fallbacks.

DINNER

CLARKSON POTTER
NEW YORK

DINNER

CHANGING THE GAME

MELISSA CLARK

PHOTOGRAPHS BY ERIC WOLFINGER

Published in the United States by
Clarkson Potter/Publishers, an imprint of
the Crown Publishing Group, a division of
Penguin Random House LLC, New York.
crownpublishing.com
clarksonpotter.com

CLARKSON POTTER is a trademark and POTTER
with colophon is a registered trademark of
Penguin Random House LLC.

Library of Congress Cataloging-in-Publication Data
Names: Clark, Melissa, author.
Title: Dinner / Melissa Clark.
Description: First edition. | New York :
Clarkson Potter/Publishers, [2017] |
    Includes index.
Identifiers: LCCN 2016013021 (print) | LCCN
2016017454 (ebook) | ISBN 9780553448238
(hardcover) | ISBN 9780553448245 (eISBN) | ISBN
9780553448245 (ebook)
Subjects: LCSH: Cooking. | LCGFT: Cookbooks.
Classification: LCC TX714 .C5535 2017 (print) |
LCC TX714 (ebook) | DDC
 641.5—dc23
LC record available at https://lccn.loc.gov/2016013021

ISBN 978-0-553-44823-8
eISBN 978-0-553-44824-5

Printed in China

Book design by Marysarah Quinn
Cover design by Marysarah Quinn

10 9 8 7 6 5 4 3 2 1

First Edition

TO DANIEL AND DAHLIA:

DINNER IS SERVED!

CONTENTS

THE GRIND

FISH & SEAFOOD

INTRODUCTION

One of the most thrilling moments of culinary discovery in my life was when, at age 16, a friend and I took ourselves out to dinner at a "fancy" restaurant with our babysitting money.

We were paying. We were without any grown-ups. And we could eat anything we wanted.

For the first time in my life, I didn't have to order a "proper meal." I didn't even have to get an entrée. What I craved was two appetizers, the crab salad and the rustic pâté. Then my friend and I split three desserts. It felt both rebellious and liberating, and very adult.

I think these days a lot of us eat this way at restaurants, putting meals together from a variety of small plates and side dishes and splitting entrées and desserts. We aren't afraid to mix it up to get what we really want.

But at home, dinner still often means a protein and two sides. A meat-and-two-veg. And this can make cooking dinner night after night a challenge because it ignores our evolution as a food culture. That's not how most of us eat—or want to eat—on a daily basis. Today's dinner can take a lot of different forms. But the conundrum for cooks is that we haven't defined what those forms are. So it's left many of us struggling in a void between what we *think* a proper meal should be, and what we actually *want* to cook and eat for dinner.

But the fact that our collective tastes have changed is a boon for the cook, an excuse to get creative. We've fallen love with all kinds of diverse ingredients: preserved lemons, kimchi, miso, quinoa, pork belly, panko. And now that these ingredients are becoming more available, they can become kitchen staples, expanding our horizons once we figure out how we like to use them.

And they're a path out of the tyranny of a perfectly composed plate with three distinct elements in separate little piles. The chicken, the carrots, the rice. The meatloaf, the mashed potatoes, the peas.

At least for me, even more pleasing is a giant salad filled with oozing, creamy Burrata cheese, ripe juicy tomatoes, and peaches (page 344). Serve it with a baguette you picked up on the way home or squirreled away in your freezer, and maybe some salami and that's all you need for a meal. Likewise, a grain bowl made from brown rice or red quinoa and topped with corn, black beans, and avocado, or fried tofu and kimchi. Or how about curried lentils with runny eggs and cool spiced yogurt? Or a simplified chicken pho with rice noodles and crispy chicken skin?

These are one-pot (or bowl) meals that reach a very high bar, both in terms of taste and also preparation. Less is more here. More flavor, less work.

That's what this book is about. It's designed to help you figure out what to make for dinner without falling back on what you've eaten before. It's about giving you options, lots of options. Are you a vegetarian or just a vegetable lover? I've got you covered. A die-hard meat lover? A fish enthusiast? A pasta aficionado? A culinary explorer ready to take on a challenge? Or the kind of cook who wants to revel in the comforting and familiar, but with a twist—a dash of Sriracha, a sprinkling of Turkish chile, a spoonful of minced preserved lemon or Indian lime pickle. Adding flavor in unexpected ways using condiments makes dinner better, but without any extra work once you've stocked your pantry (see pages 17 to 19). And the payoff is exponential.

In these pages, it's all here for you.

With the exception of the go-withs (which you can take or leave—or turn to when you're having friends over), each recipe in this book is meant to *be* your dinner—one fantastic dish that shines bright on the table. Maybe you'd prefer to round it out with a simple salad and some crusty bread. Or maybe that pizza with broccoli rabe and chile flakes is all you want and need.

It's up to you.

Giving you choices and helping you to expand the way you think about dinner is what I mean by changing the game.

It's about retooling one's mindset. It's about acquiring new muscle memory. This can be hard. But with more than 200 recipes and ideas from which to choose, it becomes at least a little less daunting.

Even better, once you get into the groove, cooking dinner can morph from a dreaded chore into a beautiful dance.

Case in point: the first time you make Cacio e Pepe with Asparagus and Peas (page 179), a springtime staple in my house, it might take 30 minutes. The second time, 25 minutes. And by the third time it will take you exactly 2 minutes longer than it took the pasta to cook. Along the way you'll have developed the skills necessary to make any pasta dish in this book—or to develop your own personalized recipe.

Here's what this kitchen choreography can look like:

First, you make a bold entrance. Eduoard de Pomiane, the great French chef and author of the famous *French Cooking in Ten Minutes,* first published in 1930, suggested that as soon as you walk in the house, before you've even taken your hat off (they all wore hats back then), you should put a pot of water on to boil. Chances are you will need it for something in your meal, and if not you can at least use it to make your coffee when you're done (they all drank coffee after dinner back then; I would make mint tea).

While the water comes to a boil, you're trimming and slicing your asparagus and heating up your skillet. Water boils, salt and pasta go in, butter goes in the skillet followed by plenty of coarsely ground pepper— enough to make you sneeze if you're sensitive like that. Sauté for a minute, then add your pasta and peas or asparagus. Stir in your cheeses and butter and a little more pasta water. Voilà, you're a Cordon Bleu chef in ten minutes.

Of course you're drinking wine and chatting with your loved ones while you do this. Or maybe you're rocking out to your favorite jams while you chop. Or you're enjoying a precious moment of serenity and quiet before dinner.

Engineer your cooking time so that it's one of the most satisfying and loveliest moments of the day. That sweet spot—the glass of wine, the conversation, the good food—is what I look forward to all day long. It's my daily equivalent of the weekend, when I can exhale and relax.

I've written this book to guide and inspire you to this happy and delicious place, but really, once you learn the basic dance, you can take the lead. After all, no matter what you read or what recipes you follow, it's you who is in command of your nightly meal. Take charge, go forth, and conquer. And, most of all, enjoy!

INGREDIENTS TO KEEP ON HAND

FOR GETTING DINNER TOGETHER EASILY

A well-stocked pantry is your key to dinner freedom. With a bevy of condiments, sauces, and spices to choose from, you will always have options. The next time you pick up a piece of chicken or fish or tofu on the way home from work without a plan, you'll know you've got what it takes to make it come out great. Below are the ingredients I like to keep on hand. Most are easy to find, and if you lay them in you'll be able to make pretty much any recipe in this book. And having them there will be an added enticement to try—or create—something new.

EXTRA-VIRGIN OLIVE OIL

You'll need two kinds: an inexpensive supermarket oil for cooking, and a more expensive high-quality oil to use for drizzling and salads. Use the cheaper oil when you're going to heat it up (which destroys some of the nuances) and the good stuff raw when its flavor really counts.

LEMONS AND LIMES

Keep citrus in the fridge for making salad dressings and also for adding brightness to any dish that needs a lift. If a dish seems to be lacking a little something but you aren't sure what, try a squeeze of lemon or lime and a pinch of salt. That should do it. Buy organic so you can use the zest as well as the juice.

GARLIC

Of course you should always have garlic on hand. Store it out of the light in a cool place. Mine is in a mesh basket tucked away in a kitchen drawer.

FRESH GINGER

I always keep some in the fridge in a sealed container for longer storage. It lasts for weeks if you buy it when it's fresh and plump.

MUSTARD

You need two types of mustard: smooth, sharp Dijon and crunchy, whole-grain mustard. For the Dijon, a bright, vibrant yellow indicates a higher quality and fresher mustard. I like extra-spicy Dijon for salad dressings, marinades, or just dipping and spreading. Grainy mustard is nice when you want texture and crunch.

VINEGARS

Vinegar adds acidic punch whenever you need to balance sweet and salty. There are many vinegars out there, but here are the essentials:

- **White wine vinegar** works well for adding a mild hit of acid to delicate dishes and baby lettuces.

- **Red wine vinegar** has more of a zing to it but also an underlying fruitiness. Use it where you want a more pronounced, wine-y flavor.

- There is a range of **balsamic vinegars** out there—some sweeter and richer, some brighter and more tart. The best come from Modena and tend to be more expensive. Use the higher-quality stuff when you're using a drizzle of balsamic to finish a dish. Inexpensive supermarket brands are fine for cooking. I always have one of each.

- **Cider vinegar** has a fruity, mild flavor. It goes well with mustard for salad dressing. And it's my favorite way to add sourness to a fruit-filled meat dish, like a roast pork with apples. Raw (unpasteurized) cider vinegar has more flavor than pasteurized and will last for months in your cupboard.

- **Rice vinegar** is a staple in Asian cuisine, but don't limit yourself there. It has a mild, citrusy flavor that works well with starches, vegetables, and meat.

- **Sherry vinegar** is nutty, oxidized, and a bit honeyed. It is sharper than red wine vinegar and deeper tasting, too.

- **Chinese black vinegar** Also known as Chinkiang vinegar after the Chinese province from which it comes, this tart, deep brown liquid is often served with soup dumplings at Chinese restaurants. It might look like soy sauce, but expect something totally different. Vaguely reminiscent of balsamic vinegar in its sweet/acid balance, it's also more pungent, with an earthy note. You can find black vinegar at specialty food stores or Asian markets. If you can't find it, substitute balsamic, though the dish won't be quite the same.

SOY SAUCE

There is light and dark soy sauce, and both are equally salty. Dark soy sauce is thicker and richer tasting, with more going on. Never buy reduced sodium soy sauce; it's just watered-down soy sauce, which you can do yourself if you're watching your salt intake. Japanese soy sauces tend to be a bit sweeter than Chinese soy sauces. Tamari is a dark and slightly thick Japanese soy sauce.

ASIAN FISH SAUCE

Fish sauce is the salty, funky key to Asian cooking. It is made by fermenting salted fish that have been packed into jars and left in the sun. The pungent liquid that collects in the jars after several months is what gets bottled and sold. A tablespoon or two adds an incredible depth to stocks, vinaigrettes, marinades, and sauces. You can find fish sauce at most supermarkets or specialty food stores. When shopping, look for *nuoc mam* or *nam pla* fish sauce. It should be a caramel-colored liquid made from fish, salt, and water alone (without preservatives).

POMEGRANATE MOLASSES

This is an intensely sour syrup with a fleeting, caramelized sweetness. It's made by cooking down pomegranate juice, water, sugar, and lemon juice or citric acid until the mixture turns dark brown and sticky. It's usually drizzled over salads, dips, and cooked dishes as a finishing condiment in Turkish and Middle Eastern cuisine, but you can also add it to pan sauces for a sweet tang. Balsamic vinegar can work as a substitute.

SUMAC

Sumac berries, which are grown on trees native to the Mediterranean, North Africa, and Asia, are dried and ground into a purplish powder that adds color and a subtle, fruity smack of flavor to all kinds of dishes. Sprinkle it on soup, grilled meats, roast vegetables, dips, and crostini. If you've ever tried za'atar, you've tried sumac, one of its key components.

TURKISH CHILE FLAKES

There are several varieties of chile flakes from Turkey and nearby Syria, including Aleppo, Ufra, and Maras. They are moister, stickier, and saltier than the standard chile flakes or powder we are used to, with a smoky, complex, and somewhat milder heat. **Urfa** is the richest and darkest of the three, with a bitter chocolate character, while **Aleppo** and **Maras** are redder and more fruity and bright. I like to use them as a garnish to add color and a gentle bit of heat to soups, stews, and dips (and eggs, they are wonderful on fried eggs). If you can't find them, substitute ground smoked paprika or cayenne pepper in smaller amounts.

SICHUAN PEPPERCORNS

This reddish-brown spice comes from the Sichuan province of China, and is not, in fact, related to true peppercorns or chiles, as they are from another variety of plant entirely. They pack an intense, mouth-numbing heat and an earthy, camphor-like taste that is indispensable in many Sichuan dishes. They will keep for years in your spice bin, as long as you don't grind or pound them until right before using.

HARISSA

Harissa paste combines chiles, caraway, coriander, cumin, garlic, and sometimes mint, lemon, and tomato, all in one tube (or jar, depending on the brand). It comes from North Africa, where it is used as a fiery condiment for tagines, couscous, and falafel, and as an ingredient in marinades, dips, soups, and sauces. Harissa is quite spicy and smoky, so use it sparingly when cooking.

SRIRACHA CHILE SAUCE

This is a bright red, smooth sauce of chile peppers, sugar, salt, garlic, and distilled vinegar. It's one of the most approachable sauces because it's not very spicy and has a mildly sweet undertone. Because it's pureed, it gives you an even heat so you don't have to fear biting into an incendiary hot pepper seed when you weren't expecting it. Sriracha is most popular as a condiment, but you can also use it as an instant marinade or add it to dips (Sriracha mayonnaise is one of my favorites; mix the two to taste).

CHILE GARLIC PASTE

Chunkier and more garlicky and pungent than Sriracha, chile garlic sauce also packs more heat because of chile pepper seeds throughout.

SAMBAL OELEK

Similar in texture to chile garlic sauce, *sambal oelek*, from Indonesia, lacks garlic—just chiles, vinegar, and salt. Use it in dressings, sauces, and marinades, or as a condiment on rice bowls or for soups.

THAI RED CURRY PASTE

This paste is meant to give you a head start on Thai red curry: mix it into hot coconut milk, add vegetables, and you've got dinner. The basic red curry paste you'll find at the supermarket is a blend of dried red chiles, lemongrass, galangal, kaffir lime, and spices like cumin, coriander, and black pepper. With one spoonful, you get all these flavors into your pot. An opened jar keeps for months in the fridge, especially if you top it with a layer of oil to help preserve it.

PRESERVED LEMONS

These are lemons that have been fermented in their own juice along with plenty of salt and often spices like peppercorns, bay leaves, and cardamom or dried chiles. They are a staple in Moroccan and Middle Eastern cooking but shouldn't be reserved for just that—they add a zesty, saline, and slightly musky flavor anywhere you use them. Always remove the lemon seeds before mincing up the flesh and peel altogether to add to dishes, or spoon off some of the pungent juices to stir in. They will last for years in the fridge once you get a jar. So don't be afraid to buy a big one.

INDIAN PICKLES

Funky, spicy, salty Indian pickles are an acquired taste, but if you're as hooked as I am, you'll want to keep a jar on hand in the fridge, where it will pretty much last forever. They are fermented in the same way as preserved lemons, but with added chiles and spices, making them much hotter and more pungent. Lime and lemon are the most popular kinds, but look for carrot, garlic, and mango pickles as well. You can find them at Indian markets or online.

KIMCHI

There are many types of kimchi in Korean cuisine (cucumber, radish, chive), but in this book when I call for kimchi, I mean pickle-y fermented cabbage, which is what you're most likely to find in supermarkets as well as Asian groceries. Most kimchis contain some kind of fishy element—dried shrimp or fish—that have been fermented along with the vegetables and chiles. If you're a vegetarian, look for jars specifically labeled as vegetarian kimchi. Use kimchi as a condiment alongside grain and rice dishes, or chopped up and added to soups and stews. Its slightly sour, fiery flavor adds depth, heat, and a little crunch.

ZA'ATAR

This is a Middle Eastern herb and spice blend that usually contains some combination of thyme, oregano, sesame seeds, and sumac. You can order it online from a spice market if you can't find it at your local (large) supermarket. Since your za'atar may or may not contain salt, taste it before using. If it's very salty, reduce the salt in the recipe.

If you can't find za'atar, combine equal parts of dried thyme, dried oregano, and sesame seeds in a small bowl, and then add a large pinch of ground sumac if you have that on hand.

CHICKEN

ROAST A CHICKEN AND YOU'LL ALWAYS HAVE DINNER

Roast chicken is the iconic home-cooked meal, what we picture when we think of Dinner with a capital D. Learning how to make an excellent roast chicken—from the simplest salt and pepper version on page 24, to more elaborate recipes—is the one surefire thing you can do to up your dinner game for the better.

SOME ROAST CHICKEN TIPS

CHOOSE A GOOD BIRD

Look for **air-chilled organic birds**. The air-chilling means they aren't processed with water after slaughter, which dilutes their flavor and makes the skin soggy. Organic ensures a better diet, which in turn makes the bird taste better.

PREP THE CHICKEN

I never a truss my chickens, but if you would like to, do so after seasoning the bird. I roast breast side up and never turn my chicken as it cooks. If your chicken comes with a bag of offal tucked inside the cavity, freeze the gizzard and neck for stock, and sauté the liver in butter with a rosemary branch for a snack if you like. Then pat the chicken down and trim off any large blobs of fat from the cavity. I leave the wing tips on my chickens because I like to eat them, but you can cut them off with kitchen shears if you prefer.

USE PLENTY OF SALT AND SEASON AHEAD

You need to make sure you add enough salt to season your chicken before you start roasting. You'll need approximately ½ to ¾ teaspoons coarse kosher salt per pound of chicken—or slightly less if you're using fine sea salt (this ratio works for any bone-in chicken recipe, by the way, not just for whole chickens). I prefer Diamond Brand, which is a bit fluffier and coarser in texture than other kosher salts. Ideally, before roasting you'd let your seasoned bird rest uncovered in the refrigerator overnight. The cold refrigerator air helps to dry out the skin, which in turn will crisp up more delightfully when you roast it.

But even letting your seasoned chicken rest for half an hour makes a difference. You can leave the salted bird on the counter at room temperature for up to 30 minutes. Any longer than that, stick it in the fridge.

CRANK UP YOUR OVEN

For the most gorgeously browned bird, roast it in a very hot oven. I generally call for 450°F, but if your oven has a tendency to smoke at high temperatures, you can roast at 425°F instead. The bird might need a few extra minutes, so watch it carefully. It's done when it's burnished and crisp all over, and an instant-read thermometer inserted into the thickest part of the breast reads between 145 and 155°F. I pull it at 150°F because the temperature continues to rise when the chicken rests, so don't go above 155°F. And if you don't have a thermometer, use a paring knife to make a small slit into a chicken thigh near the joint and look to make sure neither the juices nor the meat itself is pink.

GIVE IT A REST

Before carving, always let your bird rest for about 10 minutes. If you like you can tent it with foil to keep it warm. But that will diminish the crispness of the skin as the steam rising off the bird gets trapped by the foil. So I never cover it. I'd rather keep the crunch at the expense of some heat.

MAKE A ROASTING GAME PLAN

In this book, I give you my three favorite options for roasting a chicken: whole, spatchcocked, and splayed. Each option has its virtues and I recommend giving them all a try at least once.

WHOLE ROASTED

A **whole roasted chicken** is the most classic version and will give you an elegant and traditional looking bird. But it does take the longest to cook through, and can, if you're not careful, cook unevenly, with the breast reaching doneness, and drying out, before the thighs are finished. Always watch a whole bird carefully to catch the sweet spot when all the flesh is perfectly cooked.

SPATCHCOCKED

Spatchcocking your bird (also called butterflying), gives you particularly burnished crispy skin and cooks the bird more quickly, too, in under 45 minutes. You can ask your butcher to spatchcock your chicken for you, or you can do it yourself. It's actually not that hard, and it's a nifty and useful skill to possess.

To spatchcock a chicken, place the bird on a work surface, breast-side down. Using a sharp knife or kitchen shears and starting at the tail end, cut along one side of the backbone. Open up the chicken, flip it over, and press it down like an open book. Press firmly on the breastbone to flatten it; you'll feel it pop.

SPLAYED

Splayed chickens are my own personal twist on a skillet-roasted chicken, and the technique gives you succulent white meat and perfectly cooked dark meat all at once. The thighs, usually the last part of the chicken to finish cooking, get a jump start by being pressed into a preheated skillet. Then the breast cooks more slowly.

To splay a chicken, place the bird on a cutting board. Using a sharp knife, cut the skin connecting the legs to the body. Splay (or pull) the thighs open until you feel the joint pop on each side. Spread the thighs out so they can lie flat against the bottom of the pan when you put them in the skillet.

SALT & PEPPER ROASTED CHICKEN

Fancy roast chicken recipes come and go. This one is forever. It's one of the simplest, best roast chickens you can make, the kind of thing that—after whipping it up once or twice—will etch itself into your brain, so you'll never need to look at the recipe again. Flavored with nothing more than salt, pepper, and herbs, this recipe gives you the very essence of roast chicken— crisp-skinned, golden.

1 whole chicken (3½ to 4 pounds), patted dry with paper towels

2½ teaspoons kosher salt

1 to 2 teaspoons freshly ground black pepper, to taste

Small bunch mixed fresh herbs, such as rosemary, thyme, and sage (optional)

TOTAL TIME: 1¼ HOURS + AT LEAST 1 HOUR MARINATING
SERVES 4

1. Season the chicken inside and out with the salt and pepper. If you have time, refrigerate it, uncovered, for 1 hour or as long as overnight.

2. Heat the oven to 450°F.

3. Place the chicken, breast-side up, in a roasting pan, rimmed baking sheet, or oven-safe skillet. Stuff the cavity of the chicken with the herbs if using.

4. Roast the chicken for 50 minutes; then baste it with the pan juices. Continue roasting until the juices run clear when the thigh flesh is pierced with a knife, 5 to 10 minutes longer. Let the chicken stand for 10 minutes before carving and serving.

Roasted SUMAC CHICKEN
with Plums

Sumac—a spice ground from tart, dried berries grown in Mediterranean regions—adds a fruity hit of acid to dishes and a gorgeous red hue. Here, its gentle sourness contrasts with chicken that's been rubbed down with cinnamon and allspice before being roasted with sweet plums. The plums are pretty wonderful, caramelizing, condensing, and absorbing the spices and chicken juices as they roast, turning into a chutney-like sauce that you can spoon over the chicken for serving. If you can't get plums, try this with grapes or sliced peaches, nectarines, apples, or pears (use the same volume as you would plums). Or skip the fruit entirely. This fragrant, crisp-skinned chicken can stand alone.

1. **Prepare the chicken:** Grate the zest from the lemon and place it in a small bowl. Set aside the bald lemon.

2. Stir the sumac, salt, pepper, cinnamon, and allspice into the lemon zest until combined. Stir in 3 tablespoons of the olive oil and the garlic. The mixture should feel like wet sand. Rub it all over the chicken, including inside the cavity. Place the thyme in the chicken cavity. Place the chicken on a rimmed baking sheet and marinate, uncovered, in the refrigerator for at least 1 hour or up to 24 hours.

3. Heat the oven to 450°F.

4. Transfer the baking sheet to the oven, and roast the chicken for 30 minutes.

5. Meanwhile, **prepare the plums:** In a medium bowl, mix together the plums, shallots, honey, salt, cinnamon, allspice, and bay leaf. Set aside.

6. Squeeze 1 teaspoon juice from the reserved bald lemon into a small bowl, and mix it with the remaining 1 tablespoon olive oil; drizzle this over the chicken. Then add the plum mixture to the baking sheet and continue to roast until the bird is golden-skinned and cooked through, 20 to 35 minutes.

7. Let the chicken rest, covered lightly with aluminum foil, for 10 minutes. Then carve and serve it with the plums, garnished with thyme sprigs.

FOR THE CHICKEN

1 large lemon

1 tablespoon ground sumac

4 teaspoons kosher salt

1½ teaspoons freshly ground black pepper

½ teaspoon ground cinnamon

½ teaspoon ground allspice

4 tablespoons extra-virgin olive oil, plus more for drizzling

2 garlic cloves, grated on a Microplane or minced

1 whole chicken (4 to 5 pounds), patted dry with paper towels

½ bunch fresh thyme sprigs, about 6 sprigs, plus more for garnish

FOR THE PLUMS

5 medium plums, pitted and cut into 1-inch chunks (about 1⅔ cups)

2 shallots, very thinly sliced

2 to 4 teaspoons honey, to taste

¼ teaspoon kosher salt

¼ teaspoon ground cinnamon

⅛ teaspoon ground allspice

1 bay leaf, torn in half

TOTAL TIME: 1 HOUR 50 MINUTES + AT LEAST 1 HOUR MARINATING
SERVES 4 TO 6

Smoky PAPRIKA CHICKEN
with Crispy Chickpeas, Roasted Lemon, and Baby Kale

To get the crispiest chicken skin possible in this one-pan meal, roast the bird by itself in a very hot oven for the first hour. Then add cooked chickpeas and blanched slender lemon wedges seasoned with smoked paprika to the bottom of the roasting pan, where they sizzle and caramelize. Finally, while the chicken is resting, I fold tender baby greens into the hot chickpeas in the hot pan so they soften and absorb the chicken drippings. If you can get a Meyer lemon, use it here—it will be sweeter and milder and a bit more floral than a regular lemon. But either kind works.

1 whole chicken (4½ to 5 pounds), patted dry with paper towels

1 tablespoon kosher salt, plus more as needed

1 tablespoon freshly ground black pepper

Small bunch mixed fresh herbs, such as rosemary, thyme, and sage

1 lemon, preferably a Meyer lemon

1½ cups cooked chickpeas, homemade (see pages 232 to 233) or canned, rinsed and drained

2 tablespoons extra-virgin olive oil, plus more as needed

½ teaspoon sweet smoked paprika

½ teaspoon hot smoked paprika

6 cups baby kale or spinach

TOTAL TIME: 1¼ HOURS + AT LEAST 1 HOUR MARINATING
SERVES 4 OR 5

1. Season the chicken inside and out with the 1 tablespoon salt and the pepper. Refrigerate it, uncovered, for at least 1 hour or overnight.

2. Heat the oven to 450°F.

3. Place the chicken, breast-side up, on a large rimmed baking sheet. Stuff the cavity with the herbs.

4. While the chicken cooks, bring a small pot of salted water to a boil. Slice the lemon in half lengthwise, and reserve one half. Slice the remaining half lengthwise, and then slice the pieces crosswise into thin triangles. Drop the lemon triangles into the boiling water and cook for 1 minute; drain. If you are not using a Meyer lemon, you may want to repeat this blanching to eliminate some of the lemon's bitterness.

5. In a small bowl, toss the blanched lemon slices with the chickpeas, the 2 tablespoons oil, both paprikas, and a very large pinch of salt.

6. Baste the chicken with the pan juices, and scatter the lemon-chickpea mixture over the bottom of the baking sheet. Continue to roast until the chicken is just cooked through (the juices run clear when you pierce the thickest part of the thigh) and the chickpeas are crispy, about 20 minutes.

7. Transfer the chicken to a cutting board to rest. Scatter the kale over the hot baking sheet and toss it with the chickpeas and lemon slices, scraping up any browned bits from the bottom of the baking sheet. Top with the juice of the reserved lemon half, and sprinkle lightly with salt. If the mixture looks a little dry, drizzle with some olive oil. Serve the kale-chickpea mixture alongside the chicken.

CHILE-RUBBED *Spatchcocked* CHICKEN *with Avocado*

Ranch Dressing

In this recipe, lime zest, chile powder, and an avocado ranch dressing give the flattened bird a vaguely Southwestern appeal. But if you're looking for a more classic-tasting roast chicken, substitute lemon zest for the lime, and skip the chile powder and the dressing. A simple lemon-scented spatchcocked chicken is a wonderful thing. Serve this with tomato salad in summer or a nice green salad any other time of the year.

1 tablespoon plus ½ teaspoon kosher salt, plus more as needed

1 tablespoon grated lime zest

1 teaspoon freshly ground black pepper

½ teaspoon good chile powder, such as chipotle or New Mexico (optional)

1 spatchcocked chicken (4½ to 5 pounds), patted dry with paper towels (see page 23)

1 avocado, pitted, peeled, and cubed

1 cup mixed soft herb leaves, such as tarragon, parsley, mint, and basil

¼ cup buttermilk

3 tablespoons extra-virgin olive oil

1 teaspoon fresh lime juice

1 garlic clove, grated on a Microplane or minced

TOTAL TIME: 1¼ HOURS + 30 MINUTES MARINATING

SERVES 4 TO 6

1. In a small bowl, stir together 1 tablespoon of the salt, the lime zest, pepper, and chile powder if using. Rub this mixture generously over the chicken. Transfer the chicken, skin-side up, to a rimmed baking sheet. Let it stand at room temperature for 30 minutes, or refrigerate, uncovered, for up to 24 hours.

2. Heat the oven to 450°F.

3. Roast the chicken until it is just cooked through (the meat is no longer pink and the juices run clear), 40 to 55 minutes. Let the chicken rest on a cutting board for 10 minutes.

4. While the chicken is resting, prepare the dressing: In a blender, combine the avocado, herbs, buttermilk, olive oil, lime juice, garlic, and remaining ½ teaspoon salt. Puree until smooth. Taste, and add more salt, pepper, and/or lime juice as needed.

5. Serve the chicken with the dressing alongside.

VARIATION

In a small bowl, stir together 2 tablespoons Dijon mustard, 2 teaspoons light brown sugar, 1¾ teaspoons kosher salt, 1 teaspoon ground turmeric, ½ teaspoon good chile powder, such as chipotle or New Mexico, ¼ teaspoon ground cinnamon, ¼ teaspoon ground cardamom, ⅛ teaspoon cayenne, and a large pinch of cloves. Rub the mixture generously over a 3½- to 4-pound spatchcocked chicken. Transfer the chicken, skin-side up, to a small rimmed baking sheet. Let it stand at room temperature for 30 minutes, or refrigerate, uncovered, for up to 24 hours.

Roast the chicken in a 450°F oven until it is just cooked through (the meat is no longer pink and the juices run clear), 30 to 45 minutes. Let the chicken rest on a cutting board for 10 minutes before carving and serving.

CARAMELIZED LEMON CHICKEN

If I can lay claim to coming up with one great culinary technique, it's this. I take a classic skillet-roasted chicken one step further by splaying the bird's legs—popping them open so they can lie flat in the hot skillet. This allows the dark meat to cook more quickly, so it can finish at the same time as the breast. You'll get juicy, well-flavored meat all around, and you'll get it fast.

In this recipe I add thin, blanched lemon wedges to the bottom of the hot pan toward the end of cooking, letting them caramelize in the chicken drippings. But if you don't feel like dealing with them, leave them out and serve this with some Meyer or regular lemon wedges on the side for squeezing. It makes for a simpler dish, but no less delectable.

1. Season the chicken inside and out with the 2 teaspoons salt and ½ teaspoon black pepper. Let it rest uncovered at room temperature while the oven heats or uncovered in the fridge for up to 24 hours.

2. Heat the oven to 475°F.

3. Place a heavy 12-inch oven-safe skillet over high heat. Let it get very hot, 5 to 10 minutes.

4. While the skillet is heating, place 2 lemon quarters in the cavity of the chicken.

5. Carefully place the chicken, breast-side up, in the hot skillet. Press the legs flat on the bottom of the skillet. Drizzle the bird with the olive oil. Put the skillet in the oven and roast the chicken until the thigh meat is no longer pink when you cut into it, 30 to 40 minutes (depending on size of the bird).

6. While the chicken is roasting, bring a small pot of salted water to a boil. Thinly slice the remaining 2 lemon quarters crosswise to make triangle-shaped pieces. Drop the lemon pieces into the boiling water, cook for 1 minute to blanch them, and drain well. Set aside.

7. Using oven mitts, remove the hot skillet from the oven. Transfer the chicken to a cutting board to rest. Immediately place the skillet over medium-high heat (don't forget that the skillet handle will still be hot). Toss the lemon pieces into the skillet; they should sizzle and fry. Cook until golden brown, 3 to 5 minutes. Remove with a slotted spoon.

8. Carve the chicken and serve, topped with the skillet juices, fried lemon, and a sprinkling of Turkish red pepper.

1 whole chicken (about 3½ pounds), splayed (see page 23), patted dry with paper towels

2 teaspoons kosher salt, plus more as needed

½ teaspoon freshly ground black pepper

1 lemon, preferably a Meyer lemon, quartered lengthwise, seeds removed

1 tablespoon extra-virgin olive oil

Turkish red pepper or crushed chile flakes to taste

TOTAL TIME: 1¼ HOURS
SERVES 4

CHICKEN & GRAPES

with Sherry Vinegar

Spatchcocking chicken, also called butterflying, calls for cutting the bird along its backbone, then opening it up so that it can lie flat in the pan. Spatchcocked chickens cook quickly and evenly, turning gorgeously brown in the process. You can ask your butcher to spatchcock the chicken for you, but it's not a hard thing to do yourself (see instructions on page 23). Good, sharp poultry shears are all you need.

Roasting grapes with a sprinkle of sugar and some sherry vinegar is one of those culinary party tricks that I pull out whenever I want to seem impressively elegant without actually doing much work. Here it is with a golden spatchcocked chicken. This is company-worthy, weeknight easy, and exceedingly pretty if you use a combination of red and green grapes.

If you like, you can skip making the pan sauce and just serve the chicken with the grapes on top, drizzled with the sherry vinegar.

I love this with polenta (page 277) made with lots of butter, or nutty, plump farro (page 277) tossed with plenty of olive oil while still hot after cooking. In both cases, you want the fat to contrast with the vinegar in the grapes.

1 tablespoon kosher salt, plus more as needed

1½ teaspoons fennel seeds, lightly crushed in a mortar and pestle

1 teaspoon freshly ground black pepper, plus more as needed

Grated zest of 1 lemon

1 tablespoon plus 2 teaspoons extra-virgin olive oil

1 spatchcocked chicken (see page 23) (4½ to 5 pounds), patted dry with paper towels

12 ounces red seedless grapes, stemmed (1½ cups)

1 teaspoon sugar

1½ teaspoons sherry vinegar, or more to taste

1½ teaspoons unsalted butter

TOTAL TIME: 1¼ HOURS + AT LEAST 1 HOUR MARINATING
SERVES 4 TO 6

1. In a small bowl, combine the 1 tablespoon salt, fennel seeds, 1 teaspoon pepper, lemon zest, and 1 tablespoon of the olive oil. Rub this mixture generously over the chicken. Place the chicken, skin-side up, on a rimmed baking sheet and let it stand for at least 1 hour.

2. About 15 minutes before you are ready to cook the chicken, heat the oven to 475°F.

3. Transfer the chicken to the oven and roast it for 20 minutes.

4. In a small bowl, toss the grapes with the remaining 2 teaspoons olive oil, the sugar, and salt and pepper to taste. Scatter the grapes around the chicken, and roast until the chicken is just cooked through and the grapes are lightly caramelized, 20 to 25 minutes.

5. Transfer the chicken to a cutting board to rest. Spoon the grapes into a bowl. Place the baking sheet over two burners on medium-high heat. Add the vinegar to the pan juices and scrape up the browned bits from the bottom of the baking sheet. Pour the mixture into a small saucepan and warm it over medium heat. Whisk in the butter.

6. Carve the chicken and top it with the grapes and spoonfuls of the sauce.

SPEEDY ROASTED CHICKEN *with Garlic, Rosemary, and Mustard*

This is what to make when you crave the succulent, juicy flesh and bronzed skin of a roasted chicken but don't have the time to let it cook for an hour or more. This recipe gets you there by using parts, which cook in less than thirty minutes. Part of what makes this dish work is browning the chicken pieces, along with some garlic cloves, on top of the stove before adding a little bit of liquid to the pan and moving everything to the oven to finish cooking. You'll get juicy chicken with glistening skin, plus enough pan drippings to make a rich gravy seasoned with the soft, sweet roasted garlic. If you don't want to bother making the gravy, you can skip it and just serve the chicken and roasted garlic cloves with a dollop of good Dijon mustard on the side. If you have gravy, mashed potatoes are nice alongside.

1 whole chicken (3½ to 4 pounds), cut into 8 pieces (or use 3½ to 4 pounds of your favorite chicken parts), patted dry with paper towels

2 teaspoons kosher salt, plus more to taste

Freshly ground black pepper to taste

1 tablespoon extra-virgin olive oil

1 whole garlic bulb, halved through the equator to expose the cloves

4 sprigs fresh rosemary or thyme

1 cup chicken stock

½ cup good dry wine (any color is fine)

1 tablespoon all-purpose flour

Dijon mustard, for serving

Chopped fresh parsley, for garnish

TOTAL TIME: 50 MINUTES
SERVES 4

1. Heat the oven to 400°F.

2. Season the chicken pieces with the 2 teaspoons salt and black pepper to taste.

3. Heat a 12-inch oven-safe skillet over high heat. When the skillet is hot, add 1 tablespoon of the oil and toss in the garlic and half of the rosemary sprigs. Add the chicken pieces, skin-side down, and cook, without turning, until the skin is crisp and golden, 5 to 6 minutes.

4. Turn the chicken over and pour the stock and wine into the skillet without pouring it directly over the chicken skin. Place the remaining rosemary sprigs on top of the chicken, transfer the skillet to the oven, and roast until the chicken is cooked through, 15 to 25 minutes. (If the white meat is done first, remove it from the skillet and continue to cook the dark meat.) Arrange the chicken on a serving plate and tent it with foil to keep it warm.

5. Put the skillet over medium-high heat, and use a fork to fish the softened garlic cloves out of the skin, discarding the skin. Mash the garlic into the liquid in the skillet and bring everything to a boil (make sure you scrape all the sticky goodness off the bottom). Whisk in the flour. Reduce the heat and simmer for a few minutes, until thickened.

6. Serve the chicken with the gravy drizzled on top and dollops of mustard on the side, garnished with parsley.

SWEET GARLIC CHICKEN
with Wilted Chard

A garlicky, greens-laced version of my basic splayed chicken, this makes for a satisfying yet light one-pan meal. If you would rather use kale instead of chard, you can, but leave out their tough stems. Just skip that step and add the leaves as directed in step 6. I've also made this dish with ramps with great success. Treat the white bulbs like the chard stems and the greens just like the leaves.

1. Season the chicken inside and out with the salt and pepper. Let it rest uncovered at room temperature while the oven heats or uncovered in the fridge for up to 24 hours.

2. Heat the oven to 475°F.

3. Place a heavy 12-inch oven-safe skillet over high heat. Let it get very hot, 5 to 10 minutes.

4. Carefully place the chicken, breast-side up, in the hot skillet. Press the legs flat on the bottom of the skillet. Drizzle the bird with the oil. Roast the chicken in the skillet until the meat is not quite done (it should still be a little pink when a thigh is pierced with a knife), 25 to 35 minutes (depending on the size of the bird).

5. While the chicken is roasting, separate the chard stems from the leaves, tearing the leaves into bite-sized pieces. Cut the stems into ½-inch lengths.

6. Toss the chard stems (not the leaves) and the garlic into the skillet, and stir. Roast for 5 minutes more, and then stir again. Continue cooking until the stems are tender and the chicken is cooked through, 5 to 15 minutes more (for a total cooking time of 35 to 55 minutes).

7. Transfer the chicken to a cutting board to rest. Immediately place the skillet over medium-high heat. Toss in the chard leaves, olives if using, and the chile flakes, and cook until wilted, about 5 minutes. Serve the chicken with the chard mixture, seasoning everything with the pan juices and a sprinkling of juice from the remaining lemon wedges.

1 whole chicken (3½ to 4½ pounds), splayed (see page 23), patted dry with paper towels

2 teaspoons kosher salt

½ teaspoon freshly ground black pepper

1 lemon, quartered lengthwise, seeds removed

1 tablespoon extra-virgin olive oil

1 bunch Swiss chard or kale (about 12 ounces)

5 garlic cloves, smashed and peeled

¼ cup sliced pitted black or green olives (optional)

Large pinch of red chile flakes

TOTAL TIME: 1 HOUR
SERVES 4

GARLIC-CHILE CHICKEN BREASTS *with Cucumbers and*

Green Ginger Sauce

Fiery from green chiles, pungent with fresh ginger, and a little funky from the Asian fish sauce, this forceful, bold dish is a complete departure from meeker chicken breast recipes. To give it even more oomph, you can substitute boneless, skinless chicken thighs for breasts; just cook them for a few minutes longer. And be sure to save any extra ginger chile sauce in the fridge, where it will last for up to a week. Then slather it on anything that needs a spicy lift—plain broiled fish, stir-fried tofu, scrambled eggs, or any kind of roasted or steamed vegetable will blossom with even the smallest dab.

1. Cook the chicken: Combine the soy sauce, ginger, garlic, jalapeño, salt, and 4 cups of water in a 10-inch skillet. Bring to a simmer over medium heat; cook gently for 10 minutes. Add the chicken, cover the skillet, and remove from the heat. Let stand for 10 minutes, turning the chicken after 5 minutes. Then, if the chicken is not quite cooked through, return the skillet to low heat and simmer very gently until the meat is no longer pink, 1 to 2 minutes. Transfer the chicken to a plate and cover with aluminum foil to keep warm. Reserve the poaching liquid.

2. Prepare the cucumbers: While the chicken is cooking, combine the sliced cucumbers, garlic-chile sauce, sesame oil, fish sauce, and the ¼ teaspoon salt in a bowl. Toss well. Taste, and add more salt if needed.

3. Make the Green Ginger Sauce: Combine the ginger, garlic, jalapeños, lime juice, fish sauce, salt, and ¼ cup of the reserved poaching liquid in a blender, and pulse together; then blend well until smooth. Taste, and add more salt if needed.

4. To serve, slice the chicken and arrange the slices on top of the rice. Top with the cucumbers, warm Green Ginger Sauce, and fresh herbs. (If you like, you can moisten the rice with a little of the poaching liquid before arranging everything on top of it.)

FOR THE CHICKEN

3 tablespoons soy sauce

1½-inch piece fresh ginger, peeled and thinly sliced

1 garlic clove, thinly sliced

1 jalapeño, seeded and thinly sliced

1 teaspoon kosher salt

2 boneless, skinless chicken breasts (about 8 ounces each), halved crosswise

Cooked brown or white rice

Chopped fresh basil, cilantro, and/or scallions

FOR THE CUCUMBERS

8 ounces Persian or small Kirby cucumbers (2 to 3), halved lengthwise and thinly sliced crosswise

2 teaspoons garlic-chile sauce

1 teaspoon toasted sesame oil

1 teaspoon Asian fish sauce

¼ teaspoon kosher salt, plus more as needed

FOR THE GREEN GINGER SAUCE

1 3-inch piece fresh ginger, peeled and coarsely chopped

5 garlic cloves, coarsely chopped

2 jalapeños, seeded and coarsely chopped

2 teaspoons fresh lime juice

2 teaspoons Asian fish sauce

Fine sea salt to taste

TOTAL TIME: 35 MINUTES
SERVES 3 OR 4

COLOMBIAN-STYLE CHICKEN *with Corn,*
Avocado, and Lime

This dish is very loosely based on a traditional Colombian dish called *ajiaco*. Somewhere between a soup and a stew, it's made from short ribs and chicken slowly simmered with three different kinds of potatoes that practically melt into the broth, their starch thickening and enriching it.

My version is a more minimalist interpretation. I nix the beef and potatoes to create a cleaner, deeper, and more focused chicken flavor, then dress that up with nubby corn, juicy tomatoes, and creamy avocado bobbing in a spicy, tangy, lime-scented broth. It's still a bountiful and richly diverse meal, but a little more manageable—even on a weeknight.

1. Season the chicken breasts with 1 teaspoon of the salt and let them stand while you prepare the remaining ingredients.

2. Using a sturdy knife, cut the ears of corn into 1½-inch-thick rounds. Divide the cilantro into stems and leaves; coarsely chop both, but keep them separate.

3. Slice two-thirds of the onion into thick rounds, and finely dice the remainder (you should have about ½ cup diced).

4. Place a 12-inch skillet over medium-high heat. Add the sliced onion to the hot dry skillet and cook without moving until the undersides are well browned, 3 to 5 minutes. Carefully flip the onions over and repeat on the other side.

5. Stir the cilantro stems, oregano, garlic, bay leaf, and jalapeño into the onions. Pour in the stock and 1 cup water, and season with 1 teaspoon of the salt. Bring to a

simmer. Then lower the heat and cook gently for 15 minutes.

6. Lower the chicken into the poaching mixture. Cover the skillet and cook on low heat until the chicken is no longer pink, 7 to 10 minutes. Add the corn pieces during the last 3 minutes of cooking.

7. While the chicken cooks, combine the reserved diced onion, chopped cilantro leaves, tomato, lime zest and juice, and the remaining ½ teaspoon salt in a bowl.

8. Transfer the chicken and corn from the broth to a cutting board. Strain the hot broth into soup bowls; discard the aromatics. Slice the chicken and divide it among the bowls. Top each portion with corn, a spoonful of salsa, some diced avocado, capers if using, and a sprinkling of lime juice.

2 boneless, skinless chicken breasts (6 to 8 ounces each)

2½ teaspoons kosher salt

2 ears corn, shucked

1 bunch fresh cilantro (about 3 ounces)

1 large white onion

1 tablespoon dried oregano

4 garlic cloves, smashed and peeled

1 bay leaf

1 jalapeño or serrano chile, seeded and sliced

1 quart chicken stock

⅓ cup diced fresh tomato

Grated zest of ½ lime

1½ teaspoons fresh lime juice, plus more for serving

Salsa, for serving

Diced avocado, for serving

Drained, brined capers (optional)

TOTAL TIME: 50 MINUTES
SERVES 4 TO 6

THAI CHICKEN BREASTS
with Coconut Milk and Lemongrass

This gently flavored dish has the classic Thai flavors of lemongrass, lime, and coconut milk but no chiles, because not everyone likes things to be super spicy (my small child in particular). Feel free to garnish your portion with a sliced Thai or serrano chile if you'd like to remedy that. With or without the chiles on the side, this fragrant dish is perfect to serve to a mixed group of kids and adults when you want chicken that's out of the ordinary (i.e., not a classic roast chicken) but still crowd-pleasingly accessible. Added bonus: the lack of chiles makes this very wine friendly. A dry Riesling or sauvignon blanc would be a fine match.

1 13.5-ounce can unsweetened coconut milk

3 tablespoons Asian fish sauce

Juice of 1 lime

1 lemongrass stalk, trimmed, outer layers removed, inner core finely chopped

1 garlic clove, minced

2 boneless, skinless chicken breasts (8 ounces each)

Fine sea salt, as needed

8 ounces fresh shiitake mushrooms, stemmed and sliced (about 4 cups)

2 scallions (white and green parts), trimmed and cut into 2-inch pieces, plus sliced scallions for garnish

Cooked jasmine rice, for serving (optional)

TOTAL TIME: 20 MINUTES
SERVES 4

1. In a 12-inch skillet, combine the coconut milk, fish sauce, lime juice, lemongrass, and garlic. Bring this poaching liquid to a boil over medium-high heat; then reduce it to a simmer.

2. Season the chicken with salt, lower it into the simmering poaching liquid, and cook for 5 minutes. Then turn the breasts over and add the mushrooms and scallions; cook, covered, until the breasts are just cooked through, 3 to 4 minutes.

3. Transfer the chicken to a plate and tent with aluminum foil to keep warm. Return the skillet to the stove and simmer the sauce until it is slightly reduced, 2 minutes. Spoon the sauce over the chicken, and garnish with sliced scallions. Serve over cooked jasmine rice if desired.

MUSTARD CHICKEN BREASTS *with Ginger and Tangerine*

Chicken with lemon, mustard, and garlic is a weeknight staple—delicious, though nothing out of the ordinary. But add some fresh ginger and herbs, swap tangerine juice for the lemon and whole-grain mustard for the usual smooth Dijon, and you'll have shifted your dinner into a new and exciting space. Deeply flavored and sophisticated, it's a meal for white-meat lovers who want to get dinner on the table FAST. (Dark-meat lovers can substitute boneless chicken thighs here and add a few minutes to the cooking time.) Serve these with roasted sweet potatoes or regular potatoes and Simplest Green Salad (page 371) for an after-work meal with a little extra pizzazz.

1. Place the chicken breasts between two sheets of parchment paper or plastic wrap. Using a mallet or a rolling pin, pound each one to an even thickness of ½ inch. (Do not make them any thinner or they might dry out.)

2. In a large bowl, combine the mustard, thyme, garlic, salt, pepper, tangerine zest and juice, and ginger. Add the chicken breasts and toss to coat. Drizzle in the olive oil. Cover and refrigerate for 1 to 2 hours if you've got time; otherwise let them sit at room temperature for at least 10 minutes and up to 30 minutes.

3. Arrange a rack in the position closest to the heat source and heat the broiler.

4. Line a rimmed baking sheet with aluminum foil, and spread the chicken out on it in a single layer. Broil until the tops of the chicken breasts are cooked, 2 to 3 minutes. Flip the breasts over and broil until they are cooked through, 2 to 3 minutes more. (These may only brown a little bit, depending on the strength of your broiler, so don't necessarily look for browning. Cooking them through but not overcooking them is what you're after.)

5. Transfer the chicken to a platter. Garnish with more tangerine zest if you like, a drizzle of olive oil, some parsley, and a sprinkling of flaky sea salt.

4 boneless, skinless chicken breasts (6 to 8 ounces each)

2 tablespoons whole-grain mustard

2 tablespoons chopped fresh thyme leaves

4 garlic cloves, crushed

1 teaspoon kosher salt

½ teaspoon freshly ground black pepper

Grated zest and juice of 1 tangerine, plus more grated zest for garnish (optional)

1 teaspoon grated peeled fresh ginger

2 tablespoons extra-virgin olive oil, plus more for drizzling

Chopped fresh parsley, for garnish

Flaky sea salt to taste

TOTAL TIME: 25 MINUTES +
AT LEAST 10 MINUTES MARINATING
(UP TO 2 HOURS)
SERVES 4

Crispy CHICKEN CUTLETS
with Kumquats and Cranberries

FOR THE CRANBERRY-KUMQUAT CHUTNEY

4 ounces fresh or frozen cranberries (1 cup)

4 ounces kumquats, thinly sliced and seeded (½ cup)

⅓ cup sugar

1 serrano or jalapeño chile, seeded and finely chopped

FOR THE CITRUS DRESSING

1 teaspoon cumin seeds

1 orange

Grated zest and juice of 1 lime

1 teaspoon ground cumin

½ teaspoon kosher salt, plus more to taste

Freshly ground black pepper

3 tablespoons extra-virgin olive oil, plus more as needed

FOR THE CHICKEN

1½ pounds thinly sliced chicken cutlets

½ cup all-purpose flour

1 teaspoon kosher salt, plus more as needed

¾ teaspoon freshly ground black pepper, plus more as needed

2 large eggs, beaten

1½ cups panko bread crumbs

1 teaspoon ground cumin

Olive or grapeseed oil, for frying

Dill sprigs, for garnish

TOTAL TIME: 45 MINUTES
SERVES 4 TO 6

A fried, breaded chicken cutlet is a wonderful thing—crunchy, golden, juicy within. Universally adored even when served simple and plain, they also take well to embellishment. This slightly fancier version is scented with cumin and citrus, and served with a sweet-tart cranberry chutney spiked with a little jalapeño. If you're pressed for time, skip the cranberry-kumquat chutney and serve this with a spoonful of mango chutney, or a dollop of lingonberry jam if you've got some in the fridge from a recent IKEA excursion (that's where I always stock up). You're just looking to add something tangy-sweet to the plate to offset the richness of the fried cutlet.

This is a great dish all year-round, but if you swap turkey cutlets in for the chicken, it's particularly apropos for a small Thanksgiving gathering.

1. Prepare the chutney: In a medium pot, combine the cranberries, kumquats, sugar, and chile. Cook over medium heat, stirring frequently, until the sugar has dissolved and the cranberries have begun to pop, 7 to 10 minutes. Remove from the heat.

2. Prepare the citrus dressing: Heat a small skillet over medium heat, and toast the cumin seeds in it until fragrant, about 1 minute. Transfer them to a medium bowl. Holding a Microplane over the bowl, grate the zest of half the orange into the bowl. Then juice the orange and add the juice as well. Grate in the lime zest and squeeze in the juice. Add the ground cumin, salt, and a few grinds of black pepper. Whisk in the olive oil. Set aside.

3. Cook the chicken: Pat the chicken cutlets dry. Place the flour in a wide shallow bowl and season it with ¼ teaspoon of the salt and ¼ teaspoon of the pepper. Place the eggs in another wide shallow bowl and season them with ¼ teaspoon salt and ¼ teaspoon pepper. Place the panko in a third wide shallow bowl and season it with the ground cumin, remaining ½ teaspoon salt, and remaining ¼ teaspoon pepper.

4. Season the chicken cutlets lightly with salt and pepper. Dip each cutlet first in the flour, then in the eggs, and then in the panko, turning them in each mixture to make sure they are well coated.

5. Heat about ¼ inch of oil in your largest skillet over medium-high heat. Add the chicken cutlets (in batches, if necessary) and fry until they are deep golden brown and cooked through, 3 to 5 minutes, turning once. Transfer the cutlets to paper-towel-lined plates to drain; season them lightly with salt while they are still hot. Serve the cutlets topped with the chutney and drizzled with the citrus dressing.

VIETNAMESE GINGER CHICKEN

Heady and gingery, with a salty-caramel flavor from the soy sauce and slightly sweet note from a touch of brown sugar, this is midweek cooking at its best. If you tend to keep fresh ginger and lime on hand, you'll be able to whip this up with pantry staples, except maybe for the chicken. I call for boneless chicken thighs here because they have a rich enough flavor to stand up to the complexity of the marinade. But if it's white meat or bust at your house, go ahead and substitute thin chicken cutlets, reducing the broiling time to two to three minutes per side. This versatile marinade also works on full-flavored fish such as salmon or tuna, and it's terrific on pork tenderloin. Make it once and you'll want to find lots of ways to keep using it. It's that tasty and that convenient. Serve this with Smashed Sichuan Cucumber Salad (page 379) for crunch.

1½ pounds boneless, skinless chicken thighs

½ teaspoon kosher salt

1 tablespoon Asian fish sauce

1 tablespoon soy sauce

1 tablespoon light brown sugar

2 teaspoons peanut oil

Grated zest and juice of 1 lime, plus ½ lime, for serving

1 1-inch piece fresh ginger, peeled and finely chopped

2 garlic cloves, finely chopped

Pinch of red chile flakes

Cooked rice or rice noodles, for serving

Fresh cilantro, for serving

TOTAL TIME: 15 MINUTES + AT LEAST
30 MINUTES MARINATING
SERVES 4

1. Pat the chicken thighs dry with paper towels, and season them with the salt.

2. In a large bowl, stir together the fish sauce, soy sauce, brown sugar, peanut oil, lime zest and juice, ginger, garlic, and red chile flakes. Add the chicken and mix well to coat. Cover the bowl loosely with plastic wrap and let it stand for 30 minutes, or refrigerate for as long as overnight.

3. Arrange a rack in the position closest to the heat source and heat the broiler.

4. Line a rimmed baking sheet with aluminum foil, and spread the chicken out on it in a single layer. Broil the chicken, turning the pieces over halfway through cooking, until well colored and charred in spots, 5 to 7 minutes per side. Serve over rice or rice noodles, topped with a squeeze of lime and some cilantro leaves.

POMEGRANATE CHICKEN BREASTS

with Walnut Butter

Back in the '80s, my mother used to make Circassian chicken—a Turkish walnut-studded chicken-breast salad creamy with mayonnaise and rosy from paprika. It was the kind of thing she'd put out for an extravagant buffet between the poached side of salmon and the cold grilled lamb—elegant and, most important, good even at room temperature.

This recipe is only fleetingly based on hers, mostly because I've paired chicken and walnuts and thought about Turkey while I was making the dish. That's how I came up with the idea of adding pomegranate molasses, a near ubiquitous seasoning in the country, where it's drizzled over salads, meats, and dips to add a fruity-tangy note. Here, I make it into a sauce for roasted chicken breasts stuffed with a lemon- and thyme-flecked walnut butter. It's slightly fancier than the usual weeknight meal, but not hard to do. Or double it and serve it to company—hot from the pan and not on a buffet. Unlike my mother's dish, this one demands your attention as soon as it's ready.

Serve this with Pan-Fried Asparagus (page 376) for an elegant side dish.

1. Heat the oven to 425°F.

2. Pat the chicken breasts dry and cut a deep horizontal pocket through the meat of each one. Season each breast all over (including inside the slit) with ½ teaspoon of the salt and ½ teaspoon of the pepper.

3. In a mini food processor or with a mortar and pestle, blend together the walnuts, bread, butter, thyme, lemon zest, garlic, allspice, 1 teaspoon of the salt, and 1 teaspoon of the pepper until a paste forms. (You can also try this in a larger food processor, but since the quantity of ingredients is small, you may have to scrape down the sides of the machine every few pulses.)

4. Spread some of the paste under the skin of each breast and stuff the remaining paste inside each pocket. Arrange the breasts on a rimmed baking sheet, skin-side up. Place the baking sheet in the oven and roast until the meat is just cooked through, about 25 minutes.

5. Meanwhile, in a small bowl, whisk together the pomegranate molasses, olive oil, and a large pinch each of salt and pepper. If the mixture is too thick to drizzle, whisk in a little water.

6. Drizzle the pomegranate molasses over the chicken before serving. Garnish with chives and pomegranate seeds if you've got them.

4 bone-in, skin-on chicken breasts (12 ounces each)

3 teaspoons kosher salt, plus more as needed

3 teaspoons freshly ground black pepper, plus more as needed

⅔ cup toasted walnuts

¼ cup torn pieces of soft bread

4 tablespoons (½ stick) unsalted butter

2 teaspoons fresh thyme leaves, chopped

1 teaspoon finely grated lemon zest

2 garlic cloves, grated on a Microplane or minced

⅛ teaspoon ground allspice

2 tablespoons pomegranate molasses

4 teaspoons extra-virgin olive oil

Fresh chives, for garnish (optional)

Pomegranate seeds, for garnish (optional)

TOTAL TIME: 40 MINUTES
SERVES 4

SESAME CHICKEN
with Cashews and Dates

In the classic Taiwanese dish, three cups chicken, a sauce of toasted sesame oil, dark soy sauce, and honeyed rice wine give morsels of chicken and scallions an extraordinary depth of flavor, while chiles and fresh ginger add verve. In my version, I also toss in slivers of dates and roasted cashews to add both a sugary depth and a substantial crunch. It makes a great dish ever so slightly more interesting, both texturally and flavor-wise. Even better, it comes together in minutes, making it faster than takeout and so much more delicious.

1. Heat a 12-inch skillet or wok over high heat until it's very hot, at least 2 minutes. Add 2 tablespoons of the sesame oil to the wok and swirl it around; the oil should thin on contact. When the oil is hot, add the ginger, garlic, scallions, and chiles. Stir-fry until the garlic is golden at the edges, 2 to 3 minutes.

2. Add the remaining 2 tablespoons sesame oil, the cashews, and the chicken, and stir-fry until the chicken starts to brown, 4 to 5 minutes (reduce the heat if the cashews are browning too quickly). Add the rice wine, soy sauce, and dates; simmer until the sauce has reduced to a syrupy consistency and the chicken is cooked through, 5 to 7 minutes.

3. Stir in the basil, sprinkle with rice vinegar, and serve over rice.

4 tablespoons toasted sesame oil

1 2-inch piece fresh ginger, peeled and sliced into 12 thin coins

8 garlic cloves, smashed and peeled

1 bunch (about 8) scallions (white and green parts), cut into 2-inch lengths

3 to 4 dried red chiles, or ½ teaspoon red chile flakes

½ cup unsalted roasted cashews

6 boneless chicken thighs (about 2 pounds; preferably with skin on, but off is okay), cut into 2-inch chunks

⅓ cup rice wine or dry sherry

3 tablespoons dark soy sauce or tamari

4 pitted dates, thinly sliced

3 cups fresh basil or cilantro leaves, or a combination

Rice vinegar or fresh lime juice to taste, for serving

Cooked rice, for serving

TOTAL TIME: 20 MINUTES
SERVES 4 TO 6

ANCHOVY CHICKEN
with Lemon and Capers

There's nothing wrong with a simple dinner of pan-seared chicken with lemon and garlic. But there's everything right with the same chicken when you add capers and plenty of anchovies to the pan. What was once timid and expected turns vibrant, savory, and impossible to stop eating.

In this dish, the cut of chicken is less important than the pungent, garlicky pan sauce that goes with it. Since I love the full, rich flavor of dark meat, I call for boneless thighs. But if you prefer, substitute boneless, skinless breasts and subtract a few minutes from the cooking time; just watch them carefully so they don't dry out on you.

Although you could make this dish entirely on the stovetop, I take a cue from chefs and finish it in the oven. It cooks more evenly there, and you don't need to stand over it while it does. This frees you up to toss a salad and slice a crusty loaf of bread for mopping up the juices. If you love anchovies and garlic, you won't want to leave even a drop behind.

1¼ pounds boneless, skinless chicken thighs (4 to 5 thighs)

1 teaspoon kosher salt

Freshly ground black pepper

6 garlic cloves, smashed and peeled

¼ cup extra-virgin olive oil

5 oil-packed anchovy fillets

2 tablespoons capers, drained and patted dry

Large pinch of red chile flakes

1 lemon, halved

Chopped fresh parsley, for serving

Crusty bread, for serving

TOTAL TIME: 30 MINUTES
SERVES 4

1. Heat the oven to 400°F.

2. Season the chicken thighs with the salt and pepper. Mince one of the garlic cloves and set it aside for later.

3. Heat a 12-inch oven-safe skillet over medium-high heat, and then add the olive oil; it should thin out on contact. When the oil is hot, add the 5 smashed garlic cloves and the anchovies, capers, and chile flakes. Lower the heat to medium. Cook, stirring with a wooden spoon to break up the anchovies, until the garlic browns around the edges and the anchovies dissolve, 3 to 5 minutes.

4. Add the chicken thighs and cook until nicely browned on one side, 5 to 7 minutes. Flip the thighs over, transfer the skillet to the oven, and cook until the chicken is cooked through, 5 to 10 minutes.

5. When the chicken is done, transfer the thighs to a plate (be careful—the skillet handle will be hot, so use a pot holder or oven mitt). Place the skillet over medium heat, and add the reserved minced garlic and the juice of one of the lemon halves. Cook for about 30 seconds, scraping up the browned bits on the bottom of the skillet. Return the chicken to the skillet and warm it in the sauce for 15 to 30 seconds.

6. Squeeze the remaining lemon half over the chicken, and garnish with chopped parsley. Serve with crusty bread for mopping up the delicious pan sauce.

SAKE-STEAMED CHICKEN

Steaming chicken breasts over sake not only perfumes the meat with a heady, rice-wine scent, it also gives you a pan full of savory sake-spiked chicken broth. Then, for serving, you've got options. You can carve the soft meat into slices and drizzle it with a pungent, gingery soy-based sauce as I call for below. Or, shred the chicken and serve it in its own broth as a soup, using the ginger-soy mixture for seasoning (just stir it to taste into the broth). If you don't use the broth immediately, freeze it for future soups or, even better, pan sauces, where its built-in wine-y flavor will be an incredible asset.

Also of note: steaming skinless chicken breasts on the bone keeps them particularly juicy and moist and gives the broth a deeply meaty flavor. If you can find only bone-in breasts with the skin still attached, just pull it off and save it for another use—stock perhaps, or you could render it and sprinkle on top of either the sliced meat or the soup for a crunchy, salty garnish.

1. Place a steamer basket in the bottom of a large stockpot. Pour in the sake and add 1¼ cups water. If it's not enough liquid to reach the bottom of the steamer basket, add equal parts sake and water until it is. Bring to a boil.

2. Generously salt the chicken breasts on both sides, and set them in the steamer basket. Reduce the heat to low and cover the pot. Steam the chicken until the juices run clear when the flesh is pierced with a knife, 25 to 35 minutes. Remove the pot from the heat and allow to cool for about 10 minutes.

3. Meanwhile, prepare the sauce: In a small bowl, whisk together the soy sauce, orange juice, rice vinegar, lime zest and juice, mirin, ginger, and garlic. If desired, add some of the cooking broth to the sauce, to taste.

4. Remove the chicken breasts from the pot and put them on a large cutting board; slice the meat off the bones, and set the pieces on a platter. Spoon some of the sauce over the meat, and sprinkle with the scallions and sesame seeds. Serve extra sauce on the side for dipping.

1¼ cups dry sake, or as needed

1¼ teaspoons kosher salt

4 bone-in, skinless chicken breasts, patted dry with paper towels

2 tablespoons soy sauce

2 tablespoons fresh orange juice

2 teaspoons rice vinegar

¼ teaspoon grated lime zest

1½ teaspoons fresh lime juice

1½ teaspoons mirin or sweet sherry

1 tablespoon grated peeled fresh ginger

1 large garlic clove, grated on a Microplane or minced

3 scallions (white and green parts), thinly sliced

2 tablespoons sesame seeds, preferably black

TOTAL TIME: 35 MINUTES
SERVES 4

Sticky TAMARIND CHICKEN
with Crisp Lettuce

Sticky, zesty, and ridiculously easy to make, part of the pleasure of this dish is how the juicy tamarind-glazed chicken contrasts with the cool, crisp lettuce and, for chile lovers, the zingy heat of a sliced jalapeño. It's got a sweet-and-spicy appeal similar to eating chicken wings, but the chicken thighs make it more knife-and-fork friendly for your dinner plate.

If you want to make this with skinless, boneless breasts or thighs instead of bone-in meat, you can; just reduce the cooking time by five to ten minutes. Or use the tamarind glaze on wings, and, after roasting, run them under the broiler to crisp the skins.

3 tablespoons Asian fish sauce

2½ tablespoons soy sauce

3 tablespoons honey

1 tablespoon toasted sesame oil

½ tablespoon tamarind paste or concentrate

½ teaspoon red chile flakes

Grated zest of 1 lime

1 garlic clove, grated on a Microplane or minced

3 pounds bone-in, skinless chicken thighs

Freshly ground black pepper to taste

1 jalapeño, sliced (optional)

Crisp lettuce leaves, such as Bibb or romaine, for serving

TOTAL TIME: 40 MINUTES + OPTIONAL
24 HOURS MARINATING
SERVES 6

1. Heat the oven to 425°F.

2. In a large bowl, whisk together the fish sauce, soy sauce, honey, sesame oil, tamarind, chile flakes, lime zest, and garlic.

3. Pat the chicken dry with paper towels. Add the chicken to the sauce in the bowl, and turn to coat the pieces well. Arrange the chicken on a rimmed baking sheet, and pour the sauce over it. (If you like, you can refrigerate the chicken at this point, covered, for up to 24 hours.) Roast, turning the chicken occasionally, until it is cooked through and caramelized, 25 to 30 minutes.

4. Top the chicken with plenty of black pepper and jalapeño slices if desired. Serve over lettuce leaves.

HARISSA CHICKEN

with Leeks, Potatoes, and Yogurt

One of my all-time favorites, this sheet-pan supper has it all—spicy harissa-laced roasted chicken; sweet, browned leeks; crunchy potatoes; plus a cool garnish of salted yogurt and plenty of fresh bright herbs. It's a little lighter than your average roasted chicken and potatoes dinner, and a lot more profoundly flavored.

The key here (and with all sheet-pan suppers) is to make sure the ingredients can all cook together on the same pan. This means cutting sturdy, denser things into smaller chunks that will cook at the same rate (chicken, potatoes), and adding the more delicate ingredients (here, the leeks) toward the end so they don't burn. Another important note: don't overpopulate the pan. You need to leave space between things so ingredients can brown and crisp rather than steam. If you want to double the recipe to feed six, you can, as long as you spread everything out in two pans rather than crowding them in one.

1. Combine the chicken and potatoes in a large bowl. Season them with 2½ teaspoons of the salt and ½ teaspoon of the pepper. In a small bowl, whisk together the harissa, cumin, and 3 tablespoons of the olive oil. Pour this mixture over the chicken and potatoes, and toss to combine. Let it stand at room temperature for 30 minutes.

2. Meanwhile, in a medium bowl, combine the leeks, lemon zest, ¼ teaspoon of the salt, and the remaining 1½ tablespoons olive oil.

3. Heat the oven to 425°F.

4. Arrange the chicken and potatoes in a single layer on a large rimmed baking sheet, and roast for 20 minutes. Then toss the potatoes

lightly, and scatter the leeks over the baking sheet. Roast until the chicken is cooked through and everything is golden and slightly crisped, 20 to 25 minutes longer.

5. While the chicken cooks, place the yogurt in a small bowl. Grate the garlic clove over the yogurt, and season with the remaining ¼ teaspoon salt and ¼ teaspoon pepper.

6. Spoon the yogurt over the chicken and vegetables in the baking sheet (or you can transfer everything to a platter if you want to be fancy about it). Scatter the herbs over the yogurt, drizzle some olive oil and lemon juice over the top, and serve.

1½ pounds bone-in, skin-on chicken thighs and drumsticks

1¼ pounds Yukon Gold potatoes, peeled and cut into 1 × ½-inch chunks

3 teaspoons kosher salt

¾ teaspoon freshly ground black pepper

2 tablespoons harissa

½ teaspoon ground cumin

4½ tablespoons extra-virgin olive oil, plus more as needed

2 leeks, white and light green parts, halved lengthwise, rinsed, and thinly sliced into half-moons

½ teaspoon grated lemon zest

⅓ cup plain yogurt, preferably whole-milk (if using Greek, thin it down with a little milk to make it drizzle-able)

1 small garlic clove

1 cup mixed soft fresh herbs such as dill, parsley, mint, and/or cilantro leaves

Fresh lemon juice, as needed

TOTAL TIME: 1 HOUR +
30 MINUTES MARINATING
SERVES 3

CORIANDER SEED CHICKEN *with*

Caramelized Brussels Sprouts

In this wintry and warming sheet-pan supper, Brussels sprouts take the place of the usual potatoes cozied up next to the chicken. When blasted with enough heat, Brussels sprouts get intensely sweet, losing the mustardy, cabbage-like bite they have when cooked to a lesser degree. Both sprouts and chicken caramelize and brown, getting soft in the middle and crisp at the edges. Coriander seeds add a citrus spiciness to the pan that I intensify with grated lemon zest, while garlic and crushed red chile just make everything else even more delicious in that inimitable, garlicky-fiery way.

I really like this dish with polenta (page 277), which is buttery, gentle, and soft next to the vibrancy of chicken and sprouts.

1 lemon

2 teaspoons whole coriander seeds

3 pounds bone-in chicken pieces (use your favorite parts)

1¼ pounds Brussels sprouts, trimmed, halved if large

1½ teaspoons ground coriander

2½ teaspoons kosher salt

½ teaspoon red chile flakes

5 garlic cloves, smashed and peeled

¼ cup plus 2 teaspoons extra-virgin olive oil

1 tablespoon Dijon mustard

TOTAL TIME: 50 MINUTES + AT LEAST 30 MINUTES MARINATING
SERVES 3

1. Grate the lemon zest, and then quarter the bald lemon, seed the quarters, and set them aside.

2. In a small dry skillet set over medium heat, toast the coriander seeds until fragrant, about 2 minutes. Crush the seeds lightly in a mortar and pestle or with the flat of a heavy knife blade.

3. Pat the chicken pieces dry, and place them in a large bowl along with the Brussels sprouts. Add the crushed coriander seeds, ground coriander, lemon zest, salt, chile flakes, garlic, and the ¼ cup olive oil. Toss well. Marinate at room temperature for at least 30 minutes, or up to overnight in the refrigerator.

4. Heat the oven to 425°F.

5. In a small bowl, whisk the mustard with the remaining 2 teaspoons olive oil. Arrange the chicken pieces on a large rimmed baking sheet and brush the mustard mixture over them. Scatter the Brussels sprouts around the chicken.

6. Roast until the breast pieces are just done, 20 to 25 minutes. Transfer the breast meat to a plate and tent it with aluminum foil to keep warm while the dark meat and Brussels sprouts finish cooking, another 5 to 10 minutes. Serve with the reserved lemon wedges on the side.

BLOOD ORANGE CHICKEN
with Scotch Whiskey and Olives

A little more involved than the other sheet-pan suppers in this book, there are several steps necessary to create this lively, pretty, Mediterranean-flavored dish—including caramelizing pans of sliced blood oranges, marinated chicken, and roasted fennel and onion under the broiler in quick succession. It's not at all hard, and the layering of flavors—briny olives, smoky, garlicky meat, and juicy-sweet citrus—is worth the extra attention.

2 small blood oranges, or 1 large Cara Cara or navel orange

¼ cup smoky Scotch whiskey or Pernod

2 tablespoons light brown sugar

1 tablespoon whole-grain mustard

Juice of 1 lemon

2 teaspoons fennel seeds, lightly crushed

3 sprigs fresh thyme

1 garlic clove, grated on a Microplane or minced

2 teaspoons kosher salt

1 teaspoon freshly ground black pepper

Pinch of red chile flakes

1 small red onion

1 small fennel bulb, trimmed, fronds chopped for garnish

1 whole chicken (3½ pounds), cut into 8 pieces and patted dry

Extra-virgin olive oil, for drizzling

⅓ cup pitted green olives, quartered lengthwise

½ teaspoon granulated sugar

TOTAL TIME: 1 HOUR + AT LEAST
30 MINUTES MARINATING
SERVES 4

1. Finely grate the zest of one blood orange (or half of a large orange), and place in a large bowl.

2. Slice the ends off the oranges. Stand each orange up on a cut end and use a paring knife to slice off the peel and pith. Slice oranges crosswise into ¼-inch-thick rounds and set aside.

3. Stir the whiskey, brown sugar, mustard, lemon juice, fennel seeds, thyme sprigs, garlic, salt, pepper, and chile flakes into the bowl containing the orange zest.

4. Cut the onion in half lengthwise, through the root. Cut each half into ¼-inch-thick wedges, keeping the root end intact. Do the same with the fennel bulb. Add the onion, fennel, and chicken pieces to the bowl. Toss the entire mixture well to combine. Let it stand, covered, at room temperature for 30 minutes, or refrigerate it overnight.

5. Position a rack in the center of the oven, and heat the oven to 475°F.

6. Remove the chicken and vegetables from the marinade, leaving as much liquid behind as possible (discard the liquid). Arrange the meat and vegetables in a single layer on a large rimmed baking sheet, and drizzle with the olive oil. Transfer the baking sheet to the oven and roast until the chicken is just cooked through, about 30 minutes.

7. Turn the oven to broil, and broil the chicken until it is blistery, 1 to 2 minutes (watch it carefully). Transfer the chicken to a platter and tent it with aluminum foil to rest. Sprinkle the olives over the vegetables. If the vegetables look pale, run the sheet quickly under the broiler until the vegetables brown and caramelize; watch them carefully so they don't burn. (If they don't need broiling, just toss the vegetables and olives together in the baking sheet to warm up the olives.)

8. Arrange the reserved orange slices in a small roasting pan, sprinkle the slices with sugar, and broil until browned in spots, 5 to 10 minutes. Scrape the vegetable mixture and the pan juices over the chicken, and serve topped with the oranges and fennel fronds.

FAUX-TANDOORI CHICKEN

I started making faux-tandoori chicken in my tiny oven in the East Village back when I had my own one-woman catering business. It was great party food because most of the work was done ahead. I marinated small chunks of chicken in a spiced, aromatic yogurt puree, lined them up on skewers, then broiled everything just before serving as an hors d'oeuvre to be nibbled with cocktails. It was good hot, cold, and at room temperature, with mango chutney or Indian pickle for serving.

In this version, I use bigger pieces of chicken still on the bone, roasting them instead of broiling. It makes for a highly aromatic, heady dinner that's more appropriate as an entrée than a party snack (though it's still excellent with mango chutney or Indian pickle for dipping). Serve it with basmati rice and dollops of yogurt, and maybe sliced cucumbers and tomatoes. Just make sure to plan ahead because the chicken needs to marinate for at least six hours or overnight.

1. To make the marinade, combine the yogurt, cilantro, lime zest and juice, turmeric, cumin, salt, coriander, garam masala, black pepper, cayenne pepper, onion, jalapeño, ginger, and garlic in a food processor or blender, and puree until smooth.

2. With a sharp knife, slash each piece of chicken to the bone in one or two places (this helps the marinade penetrate the meat). Place the chicken in a large bowl and pour the marinade over it, turning the pieces to coat them well. Cover the bowl with plastic wrap and refrigerate for at least 6 hours or overnight.

3. Heat the oven to 450°F.

4. Line a rimmed baking sheet with aluminum foil, transfer the chicken pieces from the marinade to the prepared baking sheet, and drizzle with oil. Roast, turning the pieces after 15 minutes and basting occasionally, until the juices run clear and the meat is just cooked through, 25 to 30 minutes total. Serve the chicken with the Indian pickle, mango chutney, and lime wedges, as well as with yogurt and basmati rice alongside if you like.

1 cup plain yogurt, preferably whole-milk, plus more for serving (optional)

½ cup fresh cilantro leaves

Grated zest and juice of 1 lime, plus lime wedges for garnish

1 teaspoon ground turmeric

1 tablespoon ground cumin

2 teaspoons kosher salt

1 teaspoon ground coriander

1 teaspoon garam masala

½ teaspoon freshly ground black pepper

¼ teaspoon cayenne pepper

1 small onion, cut into chunks

1 jalapeño, stemmed and seeded if desired

1 1½-inch piece fresh ginger, peeled and sliced into thin coins

4 garlic cloves

3½ to 4 pounds chicken drumsticks and bone-in thighs, skinned

Grapeseed or safflower oil, for drizzling

Indian pickle, such as lime, lemon, mango, or carrot pickle, for serving

Mango chutney (store-bought), for serving

Cooked basmati rice, for serving (optional)

TOTAL TIME: 50 MINUTES + AT LEAST 6 HOURS MARINATING
SERVES 6

ZA'ATAR CHICKEN
with Lemon Yogurt

Intensely garlicky and lemony, this Middle Eastern–inspired dish gets an earthy, herbal character from za'atar, a mix of dried herbs, sumac, and sesame seeds that's rubbed all over the boneless thighs along with garlic, olive oil, and plenty of fresh parsley. Don't be surprised at the number of garlic cloves called for here. Grated into a puree, they melt into the chicken flesh, thoroughly perfuming it without making it overwhelmingly pungent.

These thighs work best cooked on the grill for maximum blackening at the edges. But they are still excellent under the broiler—just as long as you can get a deep, smoky char on the meat.

Serve this with the Citrus Salad with Olives on page 375.

1. In a large bowl, combine the chicken with all but 1 teaspoon of the grated garlic (save that for the yogurt sauce), half of the lemon zest and juice, and the za'atar, parsley, olive oil, and 1½ teaspoons of the salt. Cover and refrigerate for at least 2 hours and up to 8 hours.

2. Heat a grill, or arrange a rack in the position closest to the heat source and heat the broiler.

3. Remove the chicken from the bowl, reserving the marinade. If you are grilling, grill the chicken over high heat until it is charred in spots, 4 to 7 minutes. Baste the chicken with some of the reserved marinade, flip the pieces over, and continue cooking until they are just cooked through, another 4 to 7 minutes. If you are broiling, line a rimmed baking sheet with aluminum foil and spread the chicken out on it in a single layer. Broil the chicken, basting it with some of the reserved marinade and turning the pieces over halfway through, until well colored and charred in spots, 4 to 7 minutes per side. Be careful that the chicken doesn't burn.

4. While the chicken cooks, place the yogurt in a small bowl. Stir in the reserved grated garlic, the remaining lemon zest, the pepper, and the remaining ¼ teaspoon salt. To serve, drizzle olive oil and the remaining lemon juice, to taste, over the chicken. Sprinkle with parsley and ground sumac if using. Pass the yogurt for dipping.

6 boneless, skinless chicken thighs (about 2 pounds)

8 garlic cloves, grated on a Microplane or minced

Grated zest and juice of 2 lemons

1 tablespoon za'atar

3 tablespoons minced fresh parsley, plus more for serving

3 tablespoons extra-virgin olive oil, plus more for serving

1¾ teaspoons kosher salt

⅔ cup plain Greek yogurt, preferably whole-milk

¼ teaspoon freshly ground black pepper

Parsley leaves, for garnish (optional)

Ground sumac, for garnish (optional)

Pomegranate seeds, for garnish (optional)

Mint leaves, for garnish (optional)

TOTAL TIME: 30 MINUTES + AT LEAST 2 HOURS MARINATING
SERVES 4 TO 6

PIZZA CHICKEN

with Pancetta, Mozzarella, and Spicy Tomatoes

This "pizza chicken" has the same melting mozzarella and tomato deliciousness that you'd usually find on your slice, layered onto a pan of succulent browned pieces of chicken.

It's a recipe with a big personality, though the number of ingredients is rather small. To make the most of them, they are cooked in stages, allowing the flavors to build in the skillet. Pancetta goes in first, sautéed until golden and crisp. Next, the chicken is seared in the rendered fat, taking on its porky aroma. Tomatoes, garlic, anchovies, and capers follow, cooked down into a sauce in the very same pan, gloriously awash in a mix of chicken drippings, pancetta fat, and olive oil. All of these flavors season the chicken as it bakes. And as a final touch, chunks of fresh mozzarella are melted on top, dissolving into milky, gooey puddles.

You'll probably want to serve this with some kind of green vegetables to lighten the meal. Either a leafy salad (page 371) or perhaps Green Beans with Caper Vinaigrette (page 377) would do so nicely. And some crusty bread wouldn't hurt, either.

3½ pounds bone-in chicken pieces

2 teaspoons kosher salt, plus more to taste

1 teaspoon freshly ground black pepper

1 tablespoon extra-virgin olive oil

5 ounces pancetta, diced

3 garlic cloves, thinly sliced

4 oil-packed anchovy fillets (optional)

1 tablespoon capers, drained

¼ teaspoon red chile flakes

1 pint ripe cherry tomatoes, halved (a mix of colors is nice)

3½ cups diced ripe tomatoes

1 large sprig fresh basil, plus chopped basil leaves for serving

8 ounces bocconcini, halved (or use 1-inch cubes of fresh mozzarella)

TOTAL TIME: 1 HOUR
SERVES 4

1. Pat the chicken dry and season the pieces with 1½ teaspoons of the salt and ½ teaspoon of the pepper.

2. Heat a 10- or 12-inch oven-safe skillet over medium-high heat, and add the olive oil. Let the oil heat up for a few seconds, and then add the pancetta. Cook, stirring frequently, until it's well browned and crisp, about 3 minutes. Use a slotted spoon to transfer the pancetta to a paper-towel-lined plate.

3. Add the chicken to the skillet. Sear, turning the pieces only occasionally, until well browned on all sides, about 10 minutes. Transfer them to a large plate. Pour off all but 1 tablespoon of the oil in the skillet.

4. Add the garlic, anchovies if using, capers, and chile flakes to the skillet, and sauté for 1 minute.

Stir in all the tomatoes, the basil sprig, and the remaining ½ teaspoon salt and ½ teaspoon pepper. Cook and break up the tomatoes with a spatula, until the sauce thickens somewhat, about 10 minutes.

5. While the sauce is cooking, heat the oven to 400°F.

6. Return the chicken to the skillet, transfer the skillet to the oven, and cook, uncovered, until the chicken is no longer pink, about 30 minutes. Remove the skillet from the oven and scatter the bocconcini over the chicken.

7. Turn on the broiler, place the skillet under the heat source, and broil until the cheese is bubbling, 1 to 3 minutes (watch it carefully). Garnish the chicken with the pancetta and basil before serving.

COCONUT CURRY
CHICKEN *with Sweet Potatoes*

In this creamy stew, a cut-up chicken is braised with deeply aromatic Thai red curry, spices, green chiles, and rich coconut milk until the meat practically melts right off its bones. Cubes of sweet potato add a velvety texture to the sauce along with their wonderful plush sweetness, and a hit of lime juice at the end keeps things from turning cloying. Then, for a little crunch and heat, I garnish the stew with fat coconut chips toasted with piquant mustard seeds. It may seem like one step too many, but it adds a lot in terms of texture and taste. Serve this over barley (page 277) or rice (page 276).

1. Heat the oven to 325°F.

2. Pat the chicken dry with paper towels and season with the 2½ teaspoons salt and with black pepper to taste.

3. Heat a large Dutch oven over medium-high heat. When it is hot, add the oil; it should thin on contact. Once the oil is hot, brown the chicken pieces, in batches if necessary, until golden all over, 6 to 8 minutes per batch. Transfer the chicken to a plate.

4. Add the scallions, ginger, garlic, lemongrass if using, and chiles to the Dutch oven, and reduce the heat to medium. Cook, stirring, until soft, 1 to 2 minutes. Stir in the curry paste and cook for 1 minute. Then stir in the coconut milk and sweet potatoes.

5. Arrange the chicken pieces on top of the potatoes, placing the breast meat on top. Pour in enough water for the liquid to reach

halfway up the sides of the chicken (about ½ cup). Bring to a boil. Cover the pot and bake until the chicken is cooked through, about 40 minutes.

6. While the chicken cooks, heat a 9- or 10-inch skillet over medium heat. Add the coconut flakes to the dry skillet and toast until golden, 2 to 3 minutes. Add the mustard seeds and toast until they begin to pop, 1 minute more. Transfer the mixture to a small bowl and season with a pinch of salt.

7. Transfer the chicken and sweet potatoes to a platter. Return the Dutch oven to the stove and simmer the cooking liquid over medium-high heat until it has thickened to a sauce-like consistency, 5 to 10 minutes. Pour the sauce over the chicken and potatoes, and sprinkle the coconut-mustard seed mixture and the cilantro on top. Serve with lime wedges alongside.

1 whole chicken (3½ pounds), cut into 8 pieces

2½ teaspoons kosher salt, plus more as needed

Freshly ground black pepper to taste

2 tablespoons peanut, safflower, or vegetable oil

¼ cup finely chopped scallions (white and green parts)

1½ tablespoons grated peeled fresh ginger

4 garlic cloves, finely chopped

1 lemongrass stalk, trimmed, outer layers removed, inner core finely chopped (optional)

1 to 2 jalapeño or serrano chiles, to taste, seeded and finely chopped

2 tablespoons Thai red curry paste

1 13.5-ounce can unsweetened coconut milk

2 medium sweet potatoes (1 pound total), peeled and cut into 1½-inch chunks

¾ cup unsweetened coconut flakes

1 tablespoon black or brown mustard seeds

Fresh cilantro leaves and stems

Lime wedges, for serving

TOTAL TIME: 1¼ HOURS
SERVES 4

MEAT
PORK, BEEF, VEAL, LAMB, DUCK & TURKEY

HERB-MARINATED STEAK

with Lemon

Marinated steak is the foundational recipe of all my summer grilling. Flexible and forgiving, it doesn't matter what aromatics go into the marinade or which type of steak I use. As long as there's enough salt in the mix to bring out the flavor of the meat, I know it's going to taste amazing. For boneless steaks, I usually use about a teaspoon of coarse kosher salt per pound of meat—or a bit less if there are other salty ingredients going into the marinade (mustard, anchovies, soy sauce, fish sauce, miso, and the like). Bone-in steaks need about one-half teaspoon-ish salt per pound. Sprinkle on some pepper (either black or crushed red), a handful of fresh minced herbs, and some sliced garlic, and you are all set, especially if you're starting with excellent-quality meat.

In this recipe, I also add some chiles, scallions, and lemon to the mix, pureeing everything into a paste to extract as much flavor as possible. If you have time, let the meat sit in its herby coating overnight for the deepest flavor. Or, if you're starting this after work on a weeknight, leaving it for as little as thirty minutes is fine, too.

1 cup fresh basil leaves, plus torn basil leaves for garnish

3 scallions (white and green parts), thinly sliced, plus more for garnish

2 tablespoons fresh lemon thyme or regular thyme leaves, plus more for garnish

2 tablespoons fresh mint or dill leaves

2 fat garlic cloves

1 jalapeño, seeded (optional)

2½ teaspoons kosher salt

Finely grated zest of 1 lemon

Juice of ½ lemon

¼ cup extra-virgin olive oil

2½ pounds boneless steak, such as skirt, strip, ribeye, flank, or London broil

TOTAL TIME: 30 MINUTES + AT LEAST 30 MINUTES MARINATING
SERVES 8

1. In a blender or food processor, combine the basil, scallions, thyme, mint, garlic, jalapeño if using, salt, lemon zest, and lemon juice. Pour the olive oil over the mixture, and blend until it turns to a paste.

2. Pat the steak dry with paper towels, and place it in a wide bowl. Slather the paste all over the meat, cover the bowl, and refrigerate for at least 30 minutes or as long as overnight.

3. When you are ready to cook the steak, heat a grill or broiler to high.

4. Use a paper towel to gently pat the meat dry, leaving as much paste as possible on the meat. Grill the meat over direct heat or under the broiler on a rimmed baking sheet or broiler pan until it is nicely browned on both sides (see below for cooking times). Then transfer the steak to a cutting board and let it rest for 5 to 10 minutes.

5. Slice the steak against the grain and serve, garnished with basil, scallions, and thyme.

Cooking Times

- Skirt steak and other ½-inch-thick steaks: 2 to 4 minutes per side

- Strip, flank, filet mignon, ribeye, and other 1- to 1¼-inch-thick steaks: 3 to 6 minutes per side

- London broil and other 1½- to 2-inch-thick steaks: 6 to 9 minutes per side

VIETNAMESE-STYLE SKIRT STEAK

with Herb and Noodle Salad

The marinade for this juicy steak is based on *nuoc cham*, a classic Vietnamese dipping sauce. It hits all the major taste centers on the tongue—salty and funky/umami from fish sauce, sour from limes, fiery hot from fresh green chile, and sweet from a touch of brown sugar and tangerine juice. It works just as well as a salad dressing as it does as a marinade, so here I use it for both. After a thirty-minute soak, the marinade brings out the mineral brawny qualities of the meat, imbuing it with flavor. And as a dressing, it beautifully seasons the slippery noodles, crisp radishes and cucumbers, and peanuts with complex spicy sweetness. Although you do need to plan ahead so the meat can marinate, this dish otherwise comes together quickly and easily, and makes a complete meal with protein, veg, and carb all in the same bowl. Add a bottle of chilled white wine, a cold beer, or some lemonade, and dinner is served.

1. In a measuring cup, mix together the fish sauce, lime zest and juice, orange juice, garlic, brown sugar, and chile. Set aside half of this mixture to dress the noodles. Place the steak in a shallow bowl or in a heavy-duty sealable plastic bag, pour the remaining marinade over it, and seal the bag or cover the bowl with plastic wrap. Refrigerate for at least 30 minutes or up to 12 hours.

2. Heat a grill or broiler to high.

3. Remove the steak from the marinade, wipe off the excess marinade, and grill over direct heat or under the broiler until the steak reaches the desired doneness, 2 to 4 minutes per side for rare (the broiler might take a few minutes longer). Let the steak rest, lightly covered with aluminum foil, for 10 minutes.

4. In a large bowl, toss the noodles, cucumbers, radishes, mint leaves, and peanuts with the reserved marinade. Slice the steak very thin. Divide the noodle mixture among individual serving plates, and top each portion with slices of steak. Garnish with additional mint leaves if desired.

½ cup Asian fish sauce

Finely grated zest and juice of 2 limes

3 tablespoons fresh orange or tangerine juice

3 garlic cloves, grated on a Microplane or minced

1 tablespoon dark brown sugar

1 jalapeño or serrano chile, seeded and minced

1½ to 2 pounds skirt steak

8 ounces dried rice noodles (any shape), cooked according to the package directions

1½ cups thinly sliced Persian, Asian, or Kirby cucumbers

1½ cups thinly sliced radishes

1 cup torn fresh mint leaves, plus more for garnish (optional)

½ cup unsalted roasted peanuts, finely chopped

TOTAL TIME: 25 MINUTES + AT LEAST 30 MINUTES MARINATING
SERVES 4 TO 6

JALAPEÑO-HONEY STEAK
with Cilantro and Lime

Sweet and caramelized from the honey, sharp from the lime, and with a sting from the chiles, this is a simple-to-make recipe with a profoundly complex taste. And while you do need to plan ahead here in terms of marinating time (this really does benefit from at least two hours in the fridge), the ingredients are all supermarket-available, yet they come together in a dazzling, transcendent kind of way.

1. Season the steak with the 1 teaspoon salt and with pepper to taste. Separate the cilantro stems from the leaves. Finely chop enough stems to make ½ cup, and add them to a shallow bowl large enough to hold the steak. Stir in the honey, lime zest and juice, soy sauce, minced jalapeños, and olive oil. Add the steak and turn it to coat with the marinade. Cover and refrigerate for at least 2 hours and up to 24 hours.

2. Heat a grill or broiler to high.

3. Place the meat on a broiler pan or rimmed baking sheet if you are broiling it. Grill the meat over direct heat or under the broiler until it is nicely browned on both sides and done to your taste (see page 62 for cooking times). Then transfer the steak to a cutting board and let it rest for 5 to 10 minutes.

4. Slice the steak against the grain and serve, topped with the reserved cilantro leaves, sliced jalapeño if you like, and additional salt if needed.

1½ pounds boneless steak, such as skirt, strip, ribeye, flank, or London broil

1 teaspoon kosher salt, plus more as needed

Freshly ground black pepper to taste

1 bunch fresh cilantro (about 3 ounces)

2 tablespoons honey

Finely grated zest and juice of 1 lime

1 teaspoon soy sauce

2 jalapeños, seeded if you like it milder and minced, plus more sliced jalapeño for garnish if desired

2 tablespoons extra-virgin olive oil

TOTAL TIME: 30 MINUTES + AT LEAST 2 HOURS MARINATING
SERVES 4

CUBAN FLANK STEAK
with Lime and Fresh Mango

Using ingredients in several ways is one of my favorite methods for getting as much flavor as possible into a recipe without any extra effort. Here, I make a vaguely Cuban-inspired dressing out of limes and oranges spiked with garlic, oregano, and cumin. I save some to drizzle on fresh, ripe mangoes to serve, salsa-like, next to the meat; the rest becomes the marinade. You get to experience different aspects of the flavors: pungent and bright when fresh, mellow and caramelized after cooking. The marinated meat absorbs it all, each slice glistening with salty-sweet, wonderfully citrusy juices. It's excellent served hot from the grill or broiler, or cold and made into sandwiches the next day.

If you can't get good mangoes, substitute orange segments.

Finely grated zest and juice of 1 lime

½ teaspoon finely grated orange zest

¼ cup fresh orange juice

2 tablespoons olive oil

2 fat garlic cloves

1½ tablespoons packed fresh oregano leaves

1½ teaspoons ground cumin

1¼ teaspoons kosher salt

½ teaspoon freshly ground black pepper

1 flank steak (about 1½ pounds)

2 ripe mangoes, pitted and sliced, for serving

Lime wedges, for serving

TOTAL TIME: 20 MINUTES
SERVES 4 TO 6

1. In a blender, combine the lime zest and juice, orange zest and juice, olive oil, garlic cloves, oregano, cumin, salt, and pepper; blend until smooth.

2. Reserve 2 tablespoons of the marinade for serving. Place the steak in a wide, shallow bowl and pour the remaining marinade over it. Let it sit, uncovered, at room temperature while you heat the grill or broiler. (Or you can cover the bowl and refrigerate it for several hours or overnight.)

3. Heat the grill or broiler to high.

4. Remove the steak from the marinade, brushing off any solid bits. Grill over direct heat or under the broiler, turning it once, until done to your taste, about 3 minutes per side for rare.

5. Thinly slice the steak across the grain. Arrange the slices on individual plates, with the mango slices and lime wedges alongside. Drizzle the reserved marinade over the mangoes, and serve.

KOREAN-STYLE STIR-FRIED BEEF *(Bulgogi)*

Has our newfound love of kimchi been the gateway to the broadened appreciation for Korean food in this country? Or is it Korean-American star chefs like David Chang, Roy Choi, and Danny Bowien who are responsible for the fact that not only can I now buy half a dozen different kinds of kimchi at my local Brooklyn market, they've also got the Korean staple ingredients *gochujang* (red chile paste) and *doenjang* (fermented soybean paste) stocked on the shelves? However it happened, I'm in full favor, because once you have these ingredients on hand, making Korean food at home is a simple pleasure.

This recipe for bulgogi is Korean home cooking at its most accessible. The marinated beef is quickly cooked over very high heat. Because of the liquid content of the marinade, the meat won't necessarily brown very much. The aim is to just cook it through and to let the marinade bubble and evaporate until it's fully imbued in the meat. The gingery, garlicky beef is then served with an array of crisp vegetables, lettuce, and herbs to wrap everything up into little bundles. It's traditional to pop each bundle into your mouth with your fingers, devouring it in one bite. But sometimes it takes me two bites. And if you are more comfortable serving this with a fork and knife, go for it.

1. Prepare the beef: Combine the garlic, onion, ginger, soy sauce, sesame oil, honey, and black pepper in a blender or mini food processor, and blend until the mixture forms a smooth paste. Place the beef in a bowl and spread the paste over the slices. Stir in the scallions and sesame seeds. Cover and refrigerate for at least 1 hour or as long as overnight.

2. When you are ready to cook the beef, **make the sauce:** Combine the *doenjang*, sesame oil, garlic, scallion, honey, vinegar, and 1 teaspoon of water in a small bowl. Stir, and add the *gochujang* chile paste to taste.

3. Heat the largest skillet you have over high heat until it is smoking hot, about 5 minutes.

4. Pour the beef and its juices into the skillet and stir-fry until the juices have evaporated and the meat is cooked through and browned in spots, 2 to 5 minutes.

5. Serve the beef on a platter with the garnishes and the sauce on the side. Guests can wrap meat, grated carrots, sliced chiles, and/or herbs to taste in lettuce leaves. Pass the sauce for dipping.

NOTE: It's easiest to slice the steak when it's semi-frozen. Chill the meat in the freezer for 30 minutes before slicing.

FOR THE BEEF

4 large garlic cloves

1 small onion, thickly sliced

1 1-inch-thick slice peeled fresh ginger

2 tablespoons soy sauce

1 tablespoon toasted sesame oil

1 tablespoon honey

½ teaspoon freshly ground black pepper

1 pound beef sirloin, cut into ⅛-thick slices (see Note)

1 scallion (white and green parts), chopped

½ teaspoon sesame seeds, plus more for garnish

FOR THE SAUCE

¼ cup *doenjang* (Korean fermented soybean paste)

2 teaspoons toasted sesame oil

1 garlic clove, grated on a Microplane or minced

1 scallion (white and green parts), thinly sliced

1 teaspoon honey

½ teaspoon rice vinegar

1 to 2 teaspoons *gochujang* (Korean red chile paste) to taste

FOR SERVING

Grated carrots

Sliced green or red fresh hot chiles such as serrano, jalapeño, or fresno

Fresh herbs such as mint, basil, cilantro, and/or shiso leaves

Crisp romaine or Bibb lettuce

TOTAL TIME: 50 MINUTES + AT LEAST 1 HOUR MARINATING
SERVES 4

TURKISH LAMB CHOPS
with Sumac, Tahini, and Dill

Given my very high regard for a grilled naked lamb chop, all juicy and charred, when I do go for something more elaborate, it's got to be worth it. This dish is. Here, the meat is coated in toasted whole spices—fennel, coriander, and cumin seeds—that have been very lightly crushed. The seeds retain their texture, giving the meat both a heady scent and a good crunch. For serving, a tahini-lemon sauce adds a rich nuttiness, while a dash of sumac provides its berrylike tartness.

Serve this with Green Beans with Caper Vinaigrette (page 377) or Citrus Salad with Olives (page 375).

FOR THE LAMB
1 tablespoon Turkish red pepper or Aleppo pepper (or use red chile flakes)

2 teaspoons fennel seeds

2 teaspoons coriander seeds

2 teaspoons cumin seeds

2 teaspoons kosher salt, plus more to taste

½ teaspoon freshly ground black pepper

3 pounds bone-in loin lamb chops, the thicker the better

Extra-virgin olive oil, for grilling

FOR THE TAHINI SAUCE
⅓ cup fresh lemon juice (from about 2 lemons)

2 to 3 garlic cloves, grated on a Microplane or minced

1¾ teaspoons kosher salt

1 cup tahini

½ teaspoon ground cumin

4 to 6 tablespoons ice water

FOR SERVING
Fresh dill sprigs

Ground sumac (optional)

TOTAL TIME: 35 MINUTES + AT LEAST 30 MINUTES MARINATING
SERVES 4 TO 6

1. Prepare the lamb: Combine the Turkish red pepper, fennel seeds, coriander seeds, and cumin seeds in a small bowl. Heat a small skillet over medium-low heat, add the spice mixture, and toast until fragrant, 1 to 2 minutes. Pour the mixture into a mortar or spice grinder, add the salt and black pepper, and either pound or briefly grind until you get a coarse-textured spice mix. Don't overdo it if you've gone electric here—the coarse texture is an essential part of the dish.

2. Pat the spice mixture all over the lamb chops, and let them marinate at room temperature for at least 30 minutes, or uncovered in the fridge for up to 24 hours.

3. Make the tahini sauce: While the lamb is marinating, in a food processor, blend the lemon juice, garlic, and salt. Let the mixture sit for 10 minutes. Then add the tahini and ground cumin, and blend until a thick paste forms. With the processor running, gradually add the ice water, 1 tablespoon at a time, until the sauce is smooth enough to drizzle.

4. Heat a grill or broiler to high.

5. Drizzle the chops lightly with olive oil. Grill the chops until they are charred on the outside and cooked to taste within (or broil the chops on a broiler pan or rimmed baking sheet). Cooking time will depend on how thick your chops are, so watch them carefully: 2-inch-thick bone-in chops will take at least 3 to 5 minutes per side for rare. You'll need less time for thinner chops, and more time if you like them cooked medium rare or beyond. Let the lamb rest for 5 minutes before serving.

6. To serve, drizzle the tahini sauce over the chops, and garnish them with the dill sprigs. Add a dusting of the red sumac if you like.

GEORGIAN LAMB KEBABS
with Dill Sauce

My friend Alice Feiring, esteemed wine writer and champion of natural wines, also happens to be the foremost American expert on wines made in Georgia (the country, not the state). Because of her, not only have I developed a taste for the nutty, concentrated wines of the region, but I've also fallen for the food—at least what I can sample of it in New York City. I particularly love the juxtaposition of sweet spices—cinnamon, allspice—with cayenne and black pepper to give dishes both a haunting fragrance and a heated kick. Here, I rub that combination onto cubes of lamb, which, after grilling or broiling, are served with a chunky, dill-flecked cucumber relish spiked with red wine vinegar and sweetened with bell peppers. It's an unusual and powerful set of flavors that will make everyone wonder what you did to make these lamb kebabs taste so darn good.

1. Marinate the lamb: In a large bowl, combine the garlic, salt, cinnamon, paprika, cayenne, allspice, and black pepper. Add the lamb and the 2 tablespoons oil, toss to coat it well, and marinate for at least 30 minutes at room temperature or for up to 24 hours, covered, in the refrigerator. If you will be using wooden or bamboo skewers, soak them in water for 30 minutes while the lamb marinates.

2. Prepare the sauce: In a large bowl, mix together the red bell pepper, cucumber, dill, cilantro, chile, and garlic; season with sea salt and black pepper to taste. Add the oil and vinegar, and toss well. Taste, and season with more salt, pepper, oil, and/or vinegar if needed.

3. Heat a grill or broiler to high.

4. Thread the lamb cubes onto skewers, shaking off the pieces of garlic that cling to the meat. Brush the lamb generously with olive oil. Grill or broil (on a broiler pan or rimmed baking sheet) until the cubes are charred at the edges but still rare inside, 2 to 4 minutes per side (or cook a little longer if you like). Serve with the dill sauce.

FOR THE LAMB

1 garlic clove, minced

1 teaspoon kosher salt

1 teaspoon ground cinnamon

1 teaspoon hot paprika

¼ teaspoon cayenne pepper

¼ teaspoon ground allspice

¼ teaspoon freshly ground black pepper

1 pound boneless lamb, preferably from the leg, cut into 1½-inch cubes

2 tablespoons extra-virgin olive oil, plus more for grilling

FOR THE DILL SAUCE

1 red bell pepper, seeded and finely chopped

½ cup finely chopped cucumber

⅓ cup chopped fresh dill leaves

¼ cup chopped fresh cilantro leaves

1 red or green chile, seeded and minced

1 garlic clove, minced

Fine sea salt and freshly ground black pepper to taste

2 tablespoons extra-virgin olive oil, plus more to taste

2 teaspoons red wine vinegar, plus more to taste

TOTAL TIME: 20 MINUTES + AT LEAST 30 MINUTES MARINATING
SERVES 4

ANCHOVY LAMB CHOPS
with Capers and Garlic

If you like lamb but have never had a lamb shoulder chop, you should remedy that ASAP. Although slightly less tender than the usual rib or loin chops, they are also a lot less expensive. And they have a deeper, gamier flavor—in a very good way if you already love the mineral, herbal taste of lamb. The key with shoulder chops is to cook them either fast and furiously or low and slow—searing them quickly and serving them medium rare, or braising them until they fall apart. Anything in between leaves them chewy.

In this easy, weeknight-friendly recipe, I take the fast-and-furious route, giving the lamb just a few minutes in the blistering pan. For a sauce, I rely on my preferred flavor trifecta—anchovies, garlic, and capers—which combines with the pan drippings to form a rich, savory mixture brightened by a squeeze or two of lemon.

If you're serving this to company, feel free to substitute loin or rib chops if you want to make it a bit more swank.

Serve this with Pan-Fried Asparagus with Lemon Zest (page 376).

4 bone-in lamb shoulder chops, patted dry with paper towels

Kosher salt and freshly ground black pepper to taste

2 tablespoons extra-virgin olive oil

8 oil-packed anchovy fillets, coarsely chopped

1½ tablespoons drained capers

4 garlic cloves, minced

Juice of 1 lemon

Fresh basil or parsley sprigs, for garnish (optional)

TOTAL TIME: 20 MINUTES +
10 MINUTES MARINATING
SERVES 4

1. Season the lamb chops generously with salt and pepper. If you have time, let them rest at room temperature for 10 minutes.

2. Heat a large skillet over high heat for 30 seconds. Then add the oil and let it heat until it slides easily around the skillet, about 20 seconds. Add the chops and sear them until they are well browned on the first side, about 3 minutes. Flip the chops over, and add the anchovies and capers to the skillet. Cook for another 3 to 5 minutes. The anchovies will have disintegrated into the oil in the skillet; the lamb should be well browned on the second side and cooked to rare to medium rare in the center.

3. Transfer the lamb chops to serving plates and let them rest for 5 minutes.

4. In the meantime, add the garlic to the hot skillet and cook until it is fragrant, about 1 minute; then add the lemon juice. If the skillet looks very brown, you can also add 1 tablespoon or so of water to help release these browned bits. Pour all of the pan juices over the meat, and serve with basil or parsley sprigs for garnish if you like.

LAMB STEW
with Barley and Leeks

This thick, nubby stew is the essence of coziness. Based on a Scotch broth, it's got chunks of lamb, root vegetables, and barley, all slowly stewed together until they easily yield to your spoon, almost collapsing but not quite. Because you don't need to brown the meat or sauté the onions or bloom any spices, it's a fairly simple dish to put together: Just combine all your ingredients in a pot, add water and salt, and let it simmer gently and slowly. Then, at the very end of cooking, I stir in some sliced leafy greens to add color and texture, making this a lamb-y yet vegetable-rich one-pot meal.

Because the technique here is so basic, the variations are vast. Substitute beef or pork for the lamb; spinach, chard, or mustard greens for the kale; farro, wheat, or rye berries for the barley. Just make sure to use excellent ingredients since you're not actually doing very much to them. Then in the end, you'll be rewarded with a humble, homey, and utterly soulful dish. It's not the kind of thing that will stop conversation when you serve it, but will likely be gone to the very last barley grain by the time the party is over.

1. Season the meat generously with salt and pepper. Let it rest for 5 minutes.

2. In a medium Dutch oven or sturdy soup pot, combine the meat, 2 teaspoons salt, ½ teaspoon pepper, and the potato, carrot, turnip, leek, barley, and celery. Drop in the bundle of thyme sprigs and the bay leaf. Pour in 6 cups of water, bring to a boil, and then reduce the heat. Simmer gently, skimming off any foam that rises to the surface, until the meat is tender and beginning to fall apart, 1 to 1½ hours, depending upon the cut of meat used (the more sinewy it is, the longer it will take to break down, but the richer the resulting stew will be). If the stew looks too thick, add a little more water.

3. Fifteen minutes before the stew is completely done, stir in the kale.

4. Taste, and adjust the seasonings as needed. Ladle the stew into individual bowls, and garnish each one with chopped parsley, celery leaves, and a sprinkling of vinegar if desired.

1 pound boneless lamb stew meat, preferably from the shoulder, cut into 2-inch chunks

Kosher salt and freshly ground black pepper

1 medium potato, peeled and diced (1 cup)

2 large carrots, diced (¾ cup)

½ cup diced peeled turnip

1 leek (white and light green parts only), sliced

⅓ cup pearl barley

1 large celery stalk, diced (½ cup), and leaves for garnish

4 sprigs fresh thyme, tied together with kitchen twine

1 bay leaf

5 ounces baby kale (5 cups; or use chopped mature kale leaves)

Chopped fresh parsley, for serving

Cider vinegar or malt vinegar, for serving (optional)

TOTAL TIME: 2 HOURS
SERVES 4

CUMIN LAMB

Stir-fried cumin lamb, a dish from northwestern China, is a relatively recent addition to the Chinese restaurant circuit. At its most intense, there's a near equal ratio of fiery red chile pods to the browned bits of lamb, while the scents of toasted cumin and Sichuan peppercorns waft over your palate and thrum through every bite. Some kind of vegetable (bell peppers, onion, celery) is usually added to break up the meaty heat. Here, I use onions and scallions for their contrasting sweetness to the peppercorns and chiles.

My version is slightly less punishingly spicy than some of the cumin lambs I've had in restaurants, but if you're prone to sweating when you eat spicy foods, it ought to still make you damp at the temples. This is especially the case if you've sought out the Sichuan peppercorns and whole red chile pods, which pack the most heat. But even with regular black peppercorns and crushed red chile flakes, it makes a bracing, meaty dinner.

1 tablespoon cumin seeds

2 teaspoons Sichuan or regular peppercorns

1 teaspoon ground cumin

¾ teaspoon kosher salt

4 to 8 dried red chiles (or substitute ½ teaspoon or more crushed red chile flakes)

1 pound boneless lamb (preferably cut from the leg), sliced across the grain into ½-inch-thick strips

2 tablespoons peanut oil

1 large white onion, halved through the root end (vertically), ends trimmed, cut lengthwise into ½-inch-thick slices

1 bunch (about 8) scallions, white and light green parts cut into 2-inch lengths, dark green parts thinly sliced for garnish

3 large garlic cloves, finely chopped

1½ tablespoons soy sauce

1½ tablespoons Chinese cooking sherry (*xiao xing*) or dry sherry

2 cups fresh cilantro sprigs

TOTAL TIME: 25 MINUTES
SERVES 4

1. In a small dry skillet set over medium heat, toast the cumin seeds and peppercorns together until fragrant, 1 to 2 minutes. Transfer the spices to a mortar and pestle and crush them lightly.

2. In a large bowl, stir the crushed spices, ground cumin, salt, and dried chiles together. Add the meat and toss to coat it with the seasoning.

3. Turn on your stove hood fan, if you've got one, or open the windows. Heat a very large skillet over high heat until it is screaming hot, about 5 minutes. Then add the peanut oil and be prepared for it to smoke. Toss in the onion and the scallion pieces. Cook, tossing occasionally, until the vegetables are lightly charred but still crisp, about 2 minutes. Transfer them to a bowl.

4. Add the lamb strips and the chiles to the skillet. Cook, tossing them quickly, until the meat begins to brown (again, there could be more smoke from the chiles). Add the garlic, soy sauce, and sherry. Cook until most of the liquid has evaporated and the lamb is cooked through, about 2 minutes. Toss the onion and scallions back into the skillet. Remove the skillet from the heat and mix in the cilantro sprigs and the sliced scallion greens. Serve hot.

SEARED PORK OR VEAL CHOPS
with Peas, Scallions, and Pancetta

Make this quick one-pan dinner in late spring or early summer when you can get really good sweet peas at the market. You can use either sugar snap peas or regular peas here. The former will be juicy and crisp; the latter, sweeter and softer. Or use a combination to get the most out of pea season. The peas, along with some scallions, are quickly braised with pancetta-browned pork or veal chops, giving the vegetables an extremely deep, brawny flavor while the meat stays nice and juicy.

Both pork chops and veal chops will work in this recipe. Pork is more savory; veal is more sweetly delicate. A note about the veal—be sure to look for humanely raised meat. This is good practice in general, but it's especially important when buying veal so you know you're not supporting a famously abusive branch of the meat industry. Added bonus: humanely raised veal is usually pinker than traditionally raised veal, with a richer and better flavor.

1. Season the chops with salt and pepper, and set aside.

2. Heat the oil in a large skillet over medium-high heat until it is shimmering. Add the pancetta and cook until it is crisp and browned on both sides, about 3 minutes total. Transfer the pancetta to a paper-towel-lined plate.

3. Add the pork chops to the skillet and sear, without moving them, until dark golden on the first side, 2 to 3 minutes. Then flip them over and sear the other side, 2 to 3 minutes. Transfer the chops to the plate holding the pancetta.

4. Reduce the heat under the skillet to medium. Melt the butter in the skillet, add the scallions, and cook until they are golden all over, about 5 minutes. Pour in the stock. Toss in the sliced sugar snap peas, coating them lightly with the pan sauce. Nestle the pork chops on top of the peas. Cover, and braise over low heat until the chops are just cooked through, 7 to 10 minutes.

5. Sprinkle lemon juice over the dish, to taste. Garnish with the pancetta and chives, and serve.

2 center-cut bone-in pork or veal chops, about 1½ inches thick

Kosher salt and freshly ground black pepper to taste

2 tablespoons extra-virgin olive oil

2 ¼-inch-thick slices pancetta (3 to 4 ounces total)

1 tablespoon unsalted butter

1 bunch (about 8) scallions, halved or quartered lengthwise (depending upon thickness)

¼ cup chicken stock or water

2 cups sugar snap peas, sliced ¼ inch thick (or use shelled English peas or a combination)

Lemon juice to taste

Chopped fresh chives, for garnish

TOTAL TIME: 25 MINUTES
SERVES 2

PEACHY PORK OR VEAL

*with Pomegranate Molasses
and Charred Onion*

This incredibly easy sheet-pan supper combines thick pork or veal chops with sweet peaches and caramelized onions, all topped with a drizzle of pomegranate molasses for a fruity tang. The technique here is to start roasting the chops and onions so they begin to brown before adding the sliced peaches to the same pan. Then everything is broiled together until charred at the edges, with meat juices and peach juices condensing into a syrupy sauce. If you want to double the recipe, use two sheet pans, and make sure to rotate them so they both have time directly under the broiler.

2 bone-in pork or veal chops
(1½ inches thick)

1 medium red onion, sliced ½ inch
thick and separated into individual
rings

1 tablespoon plus 1 teaspoon
extra-virgin olive oil

1 teaspoon kosher salt, plus more
as needed

1 teaspoon freshly ground black
pepper, plus more as needed

8 ounces peaches or nectarines,
pitted and cut into thick wedges

Pomegranate molasses, for serving

Chopped fresh basil, for serving

TOTAL TIME: 20 MINUTES
SERVES 2

1. Heat the oven to 475°F.

2. In a large bowl, toss the chops and onions with the 1 tablespoon olive oil and salt and pepper. Arrange the chops and onions on a rimmed baking sheet, keeping the meat on one side and the onions on the other, and leaving space for adding the peaches later. Roast for 8 minutes.

3. Meanwhile, in a large bowl, toss the peaches with the remaining 1 teaspoon olive oil, and sprinkle them with a generous pinch each of salt and pepper.

4. Turn the oven to broil. Add the peaches to the cleared space on the baking sheet, and broil until everything is lightly charred and the chops are just cooked through, 3 to 5 minutes. (If your chops are thinner than 1½ inches, pull them from the broiler when they are cooked through, and then return the baking sheet to the broiler to finish the onions and peaches.)

5. Divide the chops, onions, and peaches among individual serving plates, drizzle them with pomegranate molasses to taste, and sprinkle with chopped basil.

CRISPY SALT & PEPPER PORK

Most recipes involving pork shoulder (aka the butt) call for it to be cooked low and slow until all the fat renders out and the meat falls to shreds with a nudge from your fork. This recipe, inspired by Nigel Slater, is entirely different. Here, the rich cubes of pork are stir-fried quickly over high heat until they caramelize. Instead of dissolving, the fat stays intact, turning pale golden and a little crisp in spots, like floppy bacon. And the meat becomes juicy and springy, absorbing the fiery, mouth-numbing flavors of Sichuan peppercorns, black peppercorns, and red chile flakes. If you don't have Sichuan peppercorns, use more black peppercorns. The dish won't have the camphor quality that makes the Sichuan spice so distinct, but you'll still get the muskiness and the heat.

Another point to note: you don't often see recipes that call for cooking with flaky sea salt such as Maldon. Most of the time, it's used to finish a dish when both a salty flavor and a crunchy texture are required. But here the pan is so hot and the meat cooked in such a dry environment without any added liquid that the flakes retain their identity, adding a brittle saltiness to the dish. Don't skimp on the crisp lettuce and cucumbers for serving. Not only do they add freshness, they also help tame the fiery heat. You could serve this with white rice (page 276) or Coconut Rice (page 381) if you like.

1. In a large bowl, toss the pork cubes with the fine sea salt. Using a spice mill or a mortar and pestle, coarsely grind together the black peppercorns, Sichuan peppercorns, and the red chile flakes. If you've gone electric, be careful not to overdo it; you want some texture here. Add the spices to the pork, tossing well. Let it rest for 20 minutes at room temperature.

2. Heat a large skillet over high heat until it is very hot. Add the oil and let it heat until it is shimmering. Then add the pork and sprinkle it with the flaky sea salt. Stir-fry until the pork cubes are golden brown all over, 5 to 7 minutes.

3. Transfer the pork to a platter and top it with the cilantro sprigs and jalapeño. Serve with lettuce and/or cucumbers, and with lime wedges on the side.

1 pound boneless pork shoulder (butt), cut into 1-inch cubes

½ teaspoon fine sea salt

1 tablespoon black peppercorns

2 teaspoons Sichuan peppercorns

Pinch of red chile flakes

1 tablespoon peanut, grapeseed, or safflower oil

1 teaspoon flaky sea salt

½ cup soft herbs, such as cilantro, mint, chives, and/or basil

1 small jalapeño or other chile, seeded and sliced or chopped

Crisp lettuce leaves, torn and/or sliced cucumbers, for serving

Lime wedges, for serving

TOTAL TIME: 15 MINUTES +
20 MINUTES MARINATING
SERVES 4

KIMCHI PORK CHOPS
with Kale

What could potentially be a rather ho-hum meal of seared pork chops and kale gains vibrancy here and heat from some chopped kimchi added to the pan. The kimchi has pretty much all of the savory, umami flavors necessary to elevate the protein and vegetables without you having to do very much, other than stir in a touch of sugar, some fish sauce, and a bit of sake to round out the pan sauce. These days there are many brands of kimchi on the market, and they vary widely from mild and funky to fiery and pungent. If you have this kind of kimchi access, sample a few, then choose one that you'll be happy to return to often.

1 bunch kale, about 12 ounces, stems removed, leaves torn into bite-sized pieces

2 tablespoons peanut or safflower oil

2 pork rib chops, 1 to 1½ inches thick

Kosher salt and freshly ground black pepper to taste

¼ cup sake

1 tablespoon brown sugar

½ tablespoon Asian fish sauce

¾ cup kimchi, chopped

3 large scallions (white and green parts), chopped, plus more for garnish

TOTAL TIME: 25 MINUTES
SERVES 2

1. Bring a large pot or kettle of water to a boil. Place the kale in a large colander in the sink, and pour the boiling water over the kale (this blanches it and drains it at the same time). Let the kale cool in the colander.

2. While the kale is cooling, heat a large skillet over medium-high heat and add the oil. Season the pork chops with salt and pepper, add them to the skillet, and sear on both sides, about 3 minutes per side. Transfer the chops to a plate.

3. Add the sake to the skillet, scraping up any pork bits that are stuck to the bottom. Let the sake reduce until it starts to turn syrupy, about 1 minute; then add the brown sugar and the fish sauce. Squeeze any remaining water out of the kale, and add it to the skillet along with the kimchi and scallions, stirring to combine. Nestle the pork chops into the greens, cover the skillet, and cook over medium heat until the chops are cooked through, 3 to 6 minutes per side.

4. Divide the pork chops and the kale mixture among individual plates. Garnish with chopped scallions, and serve.

DUCK SATAY
with Peanut Sauce

This recipe shows off the leaner, cleaner side of duck. Before cooking, all of the visible white fat is cut away from the pink meat, so you're left with just the quick-cooking muscle. Save the trimmings to render (see Note), then marinate the meat in a Thai-inspired mix of coconut milk, fish sauce, and lemongrass before grilling or broiling. It's a flavorful enough dish to serve on its own, maybe with some Coconut Rice (page 381) on the side. But if you have the time and inclination to make the dipping sauce, it's luscious, nutty, and well worth the work. And if you love satay but not duck, substitute boneless chicken or pork.

1. In a blender or mini food processor, combine the lemongrass, coconut milk, peanut oil, fish sauce, soy sauce, brown sugar, coriander, turmeric, lime zest and juice, garlic, scallions, and chile. Puree until smooth. Transfer the puree to a large bowl, add the duck, and turn to coat. Cover and refrigerate for at least 2 hours or as long as overnight.

2. If you will be using wooden or bamboo skewers, soak them in water for 30 minutes while the duck marinates.

3. When you are ready to cook the duck, heat a grill or broiler to medium-high.

4. Thread the duck cubes onto metal or wooden skewers, and drizzle some peanut oil over them. If you are using the broiler, place the skewers on a rimmed baking sheet. Grill or broil until the duck is just cooked through (but still slightly pink), 3 to 5 minutes per side. Serve the skewers sprinkled with lime juice, chopped scallions, and cilantro leaves. Pass the Spicy Coconut Cashew Dip if desired.

NOTE: To render duck fat, cut all the visible white fat and skin off the duck breasts and place them in a small, cold pan sprinkled with just a little water. Heat slowly over the lowest possible heat until the fat melts and the skin crisps. This could take anywhere from 15 to 40 minutes depending upon how much fat you are rendering at once and how hot your flame is. What you want to end up with is liquid fat bobbing with crunchy pieces of golden skin, which you should remove with a slotted spoon, sprinkle with salt, and eat. Save the fat in a jar in the fridge for up to 3 months or in the freezer for up to 6 months.

1 stalk lemongrass, trimmed, outer layers removed, inner core finely chopped

3 tablespoons unsweetened coconut milk

2 tablespoons peanut oil, plus more as needed

2 tablespoons Asian fish sauce

1½ tablespoons soy sauce

1 tablespoon dark brown sugar

1 teaspoon ground coriander

1 teaspoon ground turmeric

Finely grated zest and juice of 1 lime, plus more juice for serving

3 garlic cloves, finely chopped

2 scallions (white and green parts), chopped, plus more for garnish

1 serrano chile, seeded and coarsely chopped

2 pounds boneless duck breasts, skin removed, excess fat trimmed, meat cut into 1½- to 2-inch chunks

Fresh cilantro or basil leaves, for garnish

Spicy Coconut Cashew Dip (page 366), for serving (optional)

TOTAL TIME: 20 MINUTES + AT LEAST 2 HOURS MARINATING
SERVES 6

SEARED DUCK BREASTS
with Plums and Garam Masala

Duck breasts are not much harder to cook than chicken breasts, but they are a lot richer as well as more flavorful, plus you also get a pan full of rendered duck fat to save for future feasts. Store the fat in the fridge for up to three months and use it to sauté potatoes, green vegetables, or even salmon fillets or shrimp, where it adds its inimitable gamey, meaty flavor.

In this dish, the duck is rubbed down with a spice blend of garam masala, black pepper, and allspice, which gives it a sweet-spicy complexity. After rendering much of the fat, plums (or cherries) are added to the pan to create a chutney-like sauce spiked with wine and vinegar. Then the duck is finished in the oven, which helps it cook evenly and allows it to take on the flavors of the sauce.

This recipe calls for large duck breasts weighing ½ pound each. If you have smaller pieces, be sure to reduce the cooking time. Duck breasts are at their juiciest best served rare to medium rare, while they are still dark pink at the center. And if it's not plum season, try this with pitted sweet cherries instead.

2 pounds boneless duck breasts (4 large breast halves)

2 teaspoons garam masala

1 teaspoon kosher salt

½ teaspoon freshly ground black pepper

¼ teaspoon ground allspice

1 cup diced pitted plums

2 tablespoons dry rosé or dry white wine

1 bay leaf

Good-quality balsamic vinegar to taste

Handful of chopped fresh basil leaves

TOTAL TIME: 35 MINUTES + 30 MINUTES MARINATING
SERVES 4

1. Use a sharp knife to score the skin of each duck breast in a crosshatch pattern, spacing the cuts about ½ inch apart. Take care not to cut all the way through the fat into the flesh.

2. In a small bowl, stir together the garam masala, salt, pepper, and allspice. Rub the mixture all over the duck, cover the duck loosely with plastic wrap, and let it stand for 30 minutes.

3. Heat the oven to 350°F.

4. Heat a large skillet over medium heat. Add the duck breasts to the skillet, fat-side down. Cook, without moving the breasts, until much of the fat has rendered and the skin is mahogany colored, 4 to 5 minutes.

5. Spoon off all but a thin slick of fat from the skillet. Toss the plums into the skillet, and then add the wine and the bay leaf. Flip the duck breasts over and transfer the skillet to the oven. Cook until an instant-read thermometer inserted into the duck meat registers 125°F, 3 to 5 minutes.

6. Transfer the duck breasts to a cutting board to rest for 5 minutes.

7. Meanwhile, return the skillet to medium-high heat and simmer the pan juices and plums until they form a nice sauce, 2 to 3 minutes. Stir in a drizzle of balsamic vinegar and basil leaves. Thinly slice the duck breast and serve it with the sauce spooned on top.

FIVE-SPICE DUCK BREASTS
with Crisp Potato Cakes

Cooking potatoes in duck fat is a classic, and for good reason. The potatoes take on the meaty flavor of the fat, crisping and turning brown. Usually the potatoes are fried in duck fat that's been rendered separately in advance. Here, I streamline things so you get rosy slices of duck breast and golden, fat-fried potatoes, all prepared in stages in the same pan. It's a very thrifty way to cook, enhanced by fragrant five-spice powder rubbed into the duck before cooking. Serve this with something green and vegetable-y to lighten things up. Smashed Sichuan Cucumber Salad (page 379) or the Winter Vegetable Salad with Kale, Cabbage, and Thai Lime Dressing (page 369) would add a lively freshness to this ultra-rich dish.

2 pounds duck breasts (4 large breast halves)

1½ teaspoons kosher salt, plus more as needed

2 teaspoons Chinese five-spice powder

1 pound Yukon Gold potatoes, peeled and cut into 1½-inch-thick wedges

1 bay leaf

1 large garlic clove, smashed and peeled

Pinch of red chile flakes

Freshly ground black pepper to taste

TOTAL TIME: 1 HOUR + AT LEAST
30 MINUTES MARINATING
SERVES 4

1. Using a sharp knife, score the skin of each duck breast in a crosshatch pattern, spacing the cuts ½ inch apart. Take care not to cut all the way through the fat into the flesh.

2. Rub the duck with the salt and the five-spice. Let it stand at room temperature for 30 minutes, or cover and refrigerate overnight.

3. Bring a large pot of salted water to a boil. Add the potatoes, return to a boil, and cook until tender, 15 to 20 minutes. Drain the potatoes well and then spread them out on a baking sheet lined with a clean cloth to dry out a bit (this helps crisp them).

4. Heat the oven to 350°F.

5. Heat a large skillet over medium heat. Once the skillet is hot, add the duck breasts, skin-side down. Drop in the bay leaf. Cook, without moving the breasts, until the duck has rendered much of

its fat and the skin is uniformly browned, about 6 minutes. Flip the breasts over, and add the garlic and chile flakes to the skillet. Transfer the skillet to the oven and bake until the duck reaches 125°F on an instant-read thermometer, 3 to 5 minutes.

6. Transfer the duck to a cutting board to rest.

7. Meanwhile, remove the garlic from the skillet but leave in the bay leaf. Return the skillet to medium-high heat. Smash the potato wedges lightly; they should be somewhat flattened to increase their surface area, but not broken apart. Fry the potatoes in the hot rendered duck fat, in batches if necessary, until golden brown, 3 to 4 minutes per side. Sprinkle the potatoes with salt and pepper.

8. Slice the duck and serve it with the potatoes alongside and any juices spooned on top.

ROASTED TURKEY
BREAST *with Rosemary and Anchovies*

If it's not Thanksgiving or Christmas, people tend to forget about turkey beyond a club sandwich or a substitute for ground beef in burgers and the like. Turkey parts, either legs or breast, make robust meals any time of the year. And when you cook the bird's parts separately, you don't need to worry about drying out the white meat while the dark meat cooks through— the scourge of many a Thanksgiving dinner.

Here, I roast a boneless whole turkey breast that's been rubbed down with a potent paste of anchovies, garlic, rosemary, and lime zest, then plopped right on top of a thicket of rosemary needles for roasting. The breast emerges moist and very fragrant, ready to be sliced and served hot, maybe with some mashed potatoes and Green Beans with Caper Vinaigrette (page 377) on the side. Leftovers are excellent, of course, in sandwiches. I like to slather mine with aioli (page 141) *and* tapenade (page 337) to hit both creamy and salty-pungent notes. But the combination of good old mayo and mustard will achieve the same effect without any added work from you.

Serve this with Quick-Roasted Broccoli or Cauliflower (page 382).

1. If the turkey breast is pre-tied, untie it. Pat the meat dry with paper towels. Finely chop enough rosemary leaves to make 1 tablespoon; reserve the remaining rosemary.

2. Using a mortar and pestle, or a bowl and the back of a wooden spoon, mash together the anchovies, chopped rosemary, garlic, lime zest, salt, and pepper. Stir in the oil. Spread this mixture all over the turkey, place the turkey in a bowl, and cover it loosely with plastic wrap. Marinate at room temperature for at least 30 minutes, or refrigerate for up to 24 hours.

3. Heat the oven to 400°F.

4. Place the reserved rosemary sprigs on a small rimmed baking sheet. Roll the turkey breast up into a nice, even roast and tie it with kitchen twine so it keeps its shape and doesn't unroll as it cooks. Put the turkey, skin-side up, on top of the rosemary.

5. Roast the turkey for 25 minutes. Then reduce the heat to 350°F and continue roasting until a thermometer inserted in the thickest part of the meat registers 145°F, another 20 to 30 minutes. Allow the meat to rest for 10 minutes before untying and slicing.

1 boneless turkey breast
(2½ pounds)

1 bunch of fresh rosemary,
about 8 large sprigs

8 to 12 oil-packed anchovies

2 large garlic cloves, finely chopped

Finely grated zest of 1 lime

1 teaspoon kosher salt

1 teaspoon freshly ground
black pepper

2 tablespoons extra-virgin olive oil

TOTAL TIME: 1¼ HOURS + AT LEAST
30 MINUTES MARINATING
SERVES 6

PORK SCALLOPINI

with Sage, Black Pepper, and Apples

You can use thin slices of any meat to make these dead simple scallopini—veal, turkey, chicken—but pork will give you the deepest flavor and the most tender texture. With most scallopini recipes, the meat is cooked first, then the pan sauce is built around its flavorsome drippings. But here, because the apples take longer to cook than the pork, I sauté them first with black pepper, cinnamon sugar, and apple cider vinegar. Once they're caramelized and velvety, I remove them from the pan and very quickly sear the pork in those tangy sweet juices, along with anchovies, sage, and garlic, to bring out the savory character of the meat. It's a dish for autumn or winter that's both sophisticated and homey, and very wonderful to eat.

6 pork cutlets (4 ounces each), pounded to ⅛-inch thickness

Kosher salt and freshly ground black pepper

3 tablespoons unsalted butter

2 large apples, preferably a tart and crisp variety such as Granny Smith or Rome, cored and cut into thick wedges

Large pinch of sugar

Large pinch of ground cinnamon

1 tablespoon cider vinegar

3 tablespoons extra-virgin olive oil

6 garlic cloves, smashed and peeled

4 small oil-packed anchovy fillets (optional)

16 fresh sage leaves

TOTAL TIME: 45 MINUTES
SERVES 4

1. Season the pork all over with salt and pepper to taste.

2. In a large skillet set over medium-high heat, melt the butter. Add the apples, sugar, cinnamon, and ¾ teaspoon black pepper. Cook, stirring occasionally, until the apples are tender, 5 to 7 minutes. Then add the vinegar and cook for 1 minute more. Transfer the apples to a plate.

3. Return the skillet to the heat and add 1½ tablespoons of the olive oil. Stir in 3 garlic cloves, 2 anchovies, and 8 sage leaves; cook for 15 seconds. Add 3 pork cutlets to the skillet and cook until they are well browned, 1 to 2 minutes per side. Add a few spoonfuls of water to the skillet to help scrape up any browned bits from the bottom. Transfer the cutlets and juices to warmed serving plates. Repeat with the remaining oil, garlic, anchovies, sage, and pork. Top the cutlets with the apples and pan sauce, and serve.

BRAISED TURKEY LEGS

with Cranberries, Soy Sauce, Star Anise, and Sweet Potatoes

This recipe for turkey parts is focused on the legs, which have a rustic kind of appeal. The meat is braised with star anise–scented cranberries and served with roasted sweet potatoes. Add an arugula or spinach salad and you've got a hearty, Sunday-type supper that's both unexpected and utterly familiar. This dish also works brilliantly for a small Thanksgiving gathering, especially when everyone at the table prefers dark meat.

1. Prepare the cranberry mixture: In a small saucepan, combine ⅓ cup water with the soy sauce, the ½ cup honey, and the sherry, scallions, the 2 whole star anise pods (reserve the anise pieces for later), ginger, and garlic. Simmer over low heat for 10 minutes. Strain into a small bowl, discarding the solids, and then whisk in the oil. Pour ¼ cup of the marinade into another small bowl, add the cranberries and the remaining 1 tablespoon honey, and toss well. Reserve the remaining strained marinade and the cranberry mixture.

2. Make the drumsticks: Season drumsticks with the 1½ teaspoons salt and 1 teaspoon pepper, and place them in a large bowl. Coat with the strained marinade. Cover and refrigerate for at least 4 hours and up to overnight (in which case, also refrigerate the cranberry mixture).

3. Heat the oven to 450°F.

4. Line a rimmed baking sheet with foil and arrange the drumsticks on top. Scatter the reserved star anise pieces over the drumsticks (some will fall on the baking sheet, and that's fine). Roast for 30 minutes.

5. Meanwhile, **make the sweet potatoes:** toss with the coconut oil and a large pinch each of salt and pepper. Spread them out on a rimmed baking sheet and scatter the thyme sprigs on top. After the drumsticks have been roasting for 15 minutes, put the potatoes in the oven as well.

6. Turn the drumsticks over and reduce the oven temperature to 350°F. Turn the potatoes over as well. Pour the cranberry mixture over the drumsticks, and continue roasting until the cranberries are glazed and tender, and an instant-read thermometer inserted in the meat reads 165°F, 20 to 35 minutes. Remove the potatoes when they're caramelized and tender.

7. Drizzle everything with a little of the sauce from the baking sheet before serving.

FOR THE CRANBERRY MIXTURE

⅔ cup soy sauce

½ cup plus 1 tablespoon honey

¼ cup dry sherry

4 scallions (white and green parts), chopped

4 whole star anise pods (they look like flowers), 2 of them broken into halves

1 tablespoon grated peeled fresh ginger

1 garlic clove, grated on a Microplane or minced

3 tablespoons peanut or safflower oil

½ cup coarsely chopped fresh or frozen cranberries, thawed

FOR THE TURKEY AND SWEET POTATOES

4 turkey drumsticks (about 6 pounds total), patted dry

1½ teaspoons kosher salt, plus more as needed

1 teaspoon freshly ground black pepper, plus more as needed

1½ pounds sweet potatoes, peeled and cut into 1-inch chunks

2 tablespoons coconut or safflower oil

4 sprigs fresh thyme

TOTAL TIME: 1½ HOURS + AT LEAST 4 HOURS MARINATING

SERVES 6 TO 8

THE GRIND

CHORIZO PORK BURGERS

with Grilled Honey Onions and Manchego

Combining fresh chorizo sausage (squeezed out of its casings) with plain ground pork makes for a spicy, brawny burger. You can serve these plain, but I like to caramelize sliced onions on the grill and pile them on top. Their sweet-and-sour notes go really nicely with the pork. And a few slices of Manchego cheese add a pleasing salty creaminess that keeps with the Spanish theme here, though any sheep's milk cheese will work. One thing to note: because the burgers are made from raw pork, don't serve them rare; the fat content of the sausage and pork will ensure that your burger will stay nice and juicy even when cooked to medium. And be sure not to use cured chorizo, the salami-like kind you can slice and eat without cooking. The leathery texture won't work in a burger unless you pass it through a meat grinder.

If you can't find fresh chorizo, you can substitute spicy Italian sausages. Just increase the smoked paprika by one teaspoon. You can form the burger patties the day before grilling; wrap them well and keep them in the fridge until you're ready to light the grill.

1. Heat a grill or broiler to high.

2. In a large bowl, combine the pork, chorizo, salt, paprika, cumin, and garlic, mixing just to combine. Form into 6 to 8 patties, taking care to keep the mixture loose and not pack it tightly (which makes for a tough burger, as does overmixing; always use a light touch with ground meat).

3. In a small bowl, mix together the olive oil, sherry vinegar, and honey. Brush this over both sides of the onion slices and sprinkle them with salt. Grill or broil the onions until they are golden brown on both sides, about 2 minutes per side. Transfer the onions to a plate.

4. Grill or broil the burgers on both sides until they are cooked to medium. Since this is raw pork, the meat should be cooked until pink on the inside but not red rare (140°F will give you medium to medium-rare meat). This can take anywhere from 3 to 6 minutes per side, depending on how thick you formed your patties and how hot your fire is, so watch them carefully.

5. When the burgers are almost cooked through, top them with the cheese and let the cheese melt while the patties finish cooking. You can also toast the buns at this point if you like.

6. Serve the burgers in the buns, spread with your condiments of choice and the onions and pickles, if using, on top.

1 pound ground pork

1 pound fresh (uncured) chorizo, squeezed out of its casings

½ teaspoon kosher salt, plus more as needed

½ teaspoon smoked paprika (hot or sweet) to taste

½ teaspoon ground cumin

1 garlic clove, grated on a Microplane or minced

1½ tablespoons extra-virgin olive oil

1 tablespoon sherry vinegar

2 teaspoons honey

1 large Spanish onion, sliced

6 ounces Manchego cheese, thinly sliced

Hamburger buns, for serving

Mayonnaise, mustard, and/or ketchup, for serving (optional)

Sliced pickles, for serving (optional)

TOTAL TIME: 20 MINUTES
SERVES 6 TO 8

MARMALADE MEATBALLS
with Cider Vinegar Glaze

A little sweet from the orange marmalade, a little savory from the ginger, garlic, and scallions, these tender, comforting meatballs are easy to throw together and universally beloved once you do. Kids will devour them, picky adults will go nuts for them, and even your most sophisticated foodie friends will find these irresistible, even if they are ever so slightly reminiscent of something you'd find at a 1950 supper buffet—in the best, homiest possible way.

Even if you're not an anchovy fan, don't be put off by the ones I use here. You can't really taste them, but they do add a pleasing spike of umami funkiness to the beef and marmalade. Serve these meatballs with buttery polenta (page 277) or mashed potatoes to make the most of their comforting nature. And note that you can substitute ground pork, turkey, or dark-meat chicken for the beef.

1 pound ground beef, not too lean (80/20 chuck works well)

½ cup panko bread crumbs

4 oil-packed anchovy fillets, minced (optional)

2 scallions (white and green parts), chopped

1 egg, beaten

1 teaspoon kosher salt

1 garlic clove, grated on a Microplane or minced

1 teaspoon grated fresh ginger

¼ teaspoon freshly ground black pepper

⅛ teaspoon ground allspice

⅓ cup orange marmalade (chopped if thick-cut)

1 tablespoon cider vinegar

1 tablespoon soy sauce

¼ teaspoon red chile flakes

Fresh chives, for garnish (optional)

TOTAL TIME: 20 MINUTES
SERVES 3 OR 4

1. Set an oven rack at least 4 inches from the heat source, and heat the broiler.

2. In a large bowl, combine the beef, panko, anchovies, scallions, egg, salt, garlic, ginger, pepper, and allspice, and mix gently but thoroughly.

3. Form the mixture into 1¼-inch balls. At this point you can cover and refrigerate them overnight before cooking.

4. Arrange meatballs an inch apart on a rimmed baking sheet.

Broil until meatballs are golden all over and cooked through, 5 to 7 minutes.

5. Meanwhile, in a small saucepan, combine the marmalade, vinegar, soy sauce, and chile flakes, and bring to a simmer.

6. When the meatballs are cooked through, brush them with the marmalade glaze and return them to the broiler. Broil until the glaze is bubbling, 1 to 2 minutes. Serve with the chives scattered on top if desired.

GINGER PORK MEATBALLS

with Cilantro and Fish Sauce

These intense little meatballs taste like the filling of Chinese pork dumplings: bright with ginger, cilantro, and lime. And if you serve them over rice noodles slicked with a few drops of sesame oil, you'll get a similar textural experience, too—the slippery noodles taking the place of dumpling skins surrounding the pungent meat. But the meatballs are also great over Coconut Rice (page 381). The Smashed Sichuan Cucumber Salad (page 379) is a perfect side, adding some Asian-inflected crispness to this dish; but plain sliced radishes are nice, too.

Ground turkey, preferably dark meat, works really well here if you don't want to use pork.

1. **Prepare the meatballs:** In a large bowl, gently combine the pork, cilantro, scallions, chile, ginger, garlic, lime zest and juice, soy sauce, fish sauce, and salt. Roll the mixture into 1-inch balls. (At this point you can wrap the meatballs well and refrigerate overnight before cooking.)

2. Heat the broiler. Set the rack at least 4 inches from the heat source. Arrange the meatballs in a single layer, not touching, on one or two rimmed baking sheets.

3. Broil the meatballs, turning them occasionally, until they are golden all over and just cooked through, 8 to 10 minutes.

4. Meanwhile **prepare the dipping sauce:** In a small bowl, whisk together the vinegar, soy sauce, Sriracha, sesame oil, and brown sugar.

5. Serve the meatballs with the sauce alongside for dipping.

FOR THE MEATBALLS
1 pound ground pork

⅓ cup finely chopped fresh cilantro leaves

¼ cup finely chopped scallions (white and green parts)

1 serrano chile, seeded and chopped

1 tablespoon finely chopped peeled fresh ginger

3 garlic cloves, grated on a Microplane or minced

Finely grated zest of 1 lime

2 teaspoons fresh lime juice

2 teaspoons soy sauce

1 teaspoon Asian fish sauce

½ teaspoon kosher salt

FOR THE DIPPING SAUCE
3 tablespoons rice vinegar

2 tablespoons soy sauce

1 tablespoon Sriracha or other hot sauce

2 teaspoons toasted sesame oil

1 teaspoon light brown sugar

TOTAL TIME: 30 MINUTES
SERVES 3 OR 4

CUMIN-CHICKEN MEATBALLS *with Green Chile Sauce*

FOR THE MEATBALLS

FOR THE MEATBALLS

1 slice white sandwich bread
(or use ⅓ cup fluffy pulled-out
center of any bread, such as a
baguette or a country loaf)

2 tablespoons milk, preferably whole

¾ teaspoon cumin seeds

¼ teaspoon red chile flakes

¼ teaspoon ground cumin

1 pound ground chicken

1 large egg, lightly beaten

2 garlic cloves, grated on a
Microplane or minced

Finely grated zest of 1 lemon

2 teaspoons Worcestershire sauce

1¼ teaspoons kosher salt, plus
more for sprinkling

½ teaspoon freshly ground black
pepper

Extra-virgin olive oil, for drizzling

FOR THE SAUCE

2 to 3 jalapeños, seeded

¼ cup fresh parsley leaves

¼ cup fresh cilantro or basil leaves

2 garlic cloves, grated on a
Microplane or minced

¼ teaspoon kosher salt, plus
more to taste

2 tablespoons extra-virgin olive oil

1 teaspoon lemon juice, plus more
to taste

TOTAL TIME: 25 MINUTES

SERVES 3 OR 4

These relatively mild, cumin-flecked chicken meatballs are a gentle foil to the vibrant, fiery green chile sauce served with them. Chile pepper avoiders (i.e., my small child Dahlia) will happily eat the meatballs plain, while heat seekers (i.e., the adults, such as my husband and me) can slather them in sauce. If you love garlicky, spicy, herbal flavors, keep this sauce recipe handy. It's excellent on pretty much everything, from roast chicken and fish to grilled steaks, to burgers, to plain rice, and will keep for a week in the refrigerator. It's also nice cooled down with a drizzle of plain yogurt, which makes it appealingly creamy, too.

You can use either white- or dark-meat chicken to make the meatballs; the white meat will be milder, the dark meat more tender. Or substitute ground pork or turkey.

1. Make the meatballs: Combine the bread and milk in a large bowl, and set it aside for the bread to soak while you toast the cumin seeds.

2. In a small, dry skillet over medium heat, toast the cumin seeds until fragrant, about 2 minutes. Add the chile flakes and toast 30 seconds longer. Stir in the ground cumin and set aside.

3. To the bowl containing the bread and milk, add the chicken, egg, garlic, lemon zest, Worcestershire, salt, pepper, and toasted spices. Mix until just combined, and form into 1-inch meatballs. (At this point you can wrap the meatballs well and refrigerate overnight before cooking.)

4. Heat the broiler. Set the rack at least 4 inches from the heat source.

5. Arrange the meatballs in a single layer, not touching, on one or two rimmed baking sheets. Drizzle them with olive oil and broil, checking often and shaking the baking sheet occasionally to help them brown all over, 4 to 7 minutes.

6. While the meatballs are cooking, **make the sauce:** In a blender, combine the jalapeños, parsley, cilantro, garlic, salt, olive oil, lemon juice, and just enough water to make the mixture move in the blender (1 to 2 tablespoons). Blend until smooth, and add more salt if needed (you might need up to another ¼ teaspoon). Serve the sauce alongside the meatballs.

Kibbe-Style
LAMB MEATBALLS
with Herbed Yogurt

These Middle Eastern–inspired lamb meatballs are full of fragrant spices—allspice, cumin, and cayenne—and crunchy bulgur to give them a slightly nubby texture. Because kibbe meatballs have the grains already built in, these are an almost perfectly complete meal unto themselves, though a tomato salad on the side is refreshingly juicy in summer. Or slice up some fresh tomatoes and cucumbers and dress them with a little of the herb-flecked yogurt that goes with the meatballs. It makes the meal super easy, and the yogurt is delicious on the vegetables.

I call for fine bulgur here, which plumps up in cold water in about twenty minutes. If you've got medium bulgur on hand, soak it in boiling water instead. Serve with flatbread.

FOR THE MEATBALLS

½ cup fine bulgur wheat

1 pound ground lamb (or substitute ground beef or dark-meat turkey)

1 small onion, diced

1¼ cups chopped fresh parsley leaves

2 teaspoons ground cumin

1½ teaspoons kosher salt

¼ teaspoon cayenne pepper

⅛ teaspoon ground allspice

3 small garlic cloves, grated on a Microplane or minced

Extra-virgin olive oil, as needed

FOR THE HERBED YOGURT SAUCE

1 cup plain Greek yogurt, preferably whole-milk

½ cup coarsely chopped fresh dill leaves

2 teaspoons lemon juice

½ jalapeño, seeded

Large pinch of kosher salt

TOTAL TIME: 30 MINUTES +
20 MINUTES SOAKING TIME
SERVES 4

1. Make the meatballs: Place the bulgur in a bowl and cover it generously with cold water. Let it soak for 20 minutes; then drain well.

2. Transfer the drained bulgur to a large bowl and add the lamb, onion, ½ cup of the parsley, and the cumin, salt, cayenne, and allspice. Mix in one-third of the garlic. Form the meat mixture into 1½-inch balls. (At this point you can wrap the meatballs well and refrigerate overnight before cooking.)

3. Arrange an oven rack 6 inches from the heat source, and heat the broiler. Lightly oil a rimmed baking sheet.

4. Arrange the meatballs in a single layer, not touching each other, on the prepared baking sheet. Brush the meatballs with additional olive oil. Broil the meatballs, turning them once or twice, until they are golden and firm, 5 to 10 minutes, depending on desired doneness (I like them still a little pink on the inside).

5. While the meatballs are broiling, **make the herbed yogurt sauce:** In a blender, combine the yogurt, remaining ¾ cup parsley, and the remaining garlic with the dill, lemon juice, jalapeño, and salt. Puree until smooth. If you prefer a looser consistency, blend in 1 to 2 tablespoons of water.

6. Serve the meatballs with the yogurt sauce alongside for drizzling.

COCONUT KOFTE KEBABS

Kofte is a word used to describe kebabs made from minced meat rather than small chunks—basically they are meatballs on a stick. This makes them convenient for grilling since you can flip several of them at once instead of one by one. Skewers also ensure that the meatballs won't roll off the grill grate and into the flames (this I know from sad experience). However, if you're not grilling, there's no reason to thread these tasty lamb meatballs onto skewers at all. Just spread them out on a baking sheet and run them under the broiler.

A combination of spices makes these meatballs heady and aromatic. And using ground coconut not only lends sweetness, it also keeps these gluten-free and makes them extremely tender. If you can't find finely ground unsweetened coconut, buy unsweetened grated coconut or coconut flakes (chips) and whirl them in a food processor or blender until ground.

Serve the kofte with Coconut Rice (page 381), flatbread, or slices of crusty bread. A Citrus Salad with Olives (page 375) would also go well, offering a juicy contrast to the grilled meat.

1. If you will be broiling, lightly oil a rimmed baking sheet. If you are grilling and using wooden or bamboo skewers, soak the skewers in water for 20 minutes. Heat a grill or broiler to high.

2. In a large bowl, combine the lamb, coconut, onion, cumin, coriander, cinnamon, ginger, salt, allspice, cayenne, and lemon zest. Mix until well blended. Shape the meat into fingers that are about 3 inches long and 1½ inches wide. (At this point you can wrap the kofte well and refrigerate overnight before cooking.)

3. Arrange the kofte on skewers or lay them on the prepared baking sheet, leaving an inch between them so they brown nicely all over. Brush with coconut oil.

4. Grill or broil, turning the kebabs halfway through, until they are golden brown and cooked through, 7 to 10 minutes.

5. Meanwhile, in a small bowl, whisk together the yogurt, garlic, parsley, and salt to taste.

6. Sprinkle the cooked kebabs with salt and ground sumac if using. Serve the yogurt sauce alongside for dipping.

1¼ pounds ground lamb (or use beef or dark-meat turkey)

½ cup ground unsweetened coconut

1 onion, grated

2 teaspoons ground cumin

2 teaspoons ground coriander

1 teaspoon ground cinnamon

1 teaspoon ground ginger

1 teaspoon kosher salt, plus more as needed

½ teaspoon ground allspice

Pinch of cayenne pepper

Finely grated zest of 1 lemon

Coconut oil, as needed

½ cup plain yogurt

1 small garlic clove, grated on a Microplane or minced

1 tablespoon finely chopped fresh parsley leaves

Ground sumac, for garnish (optional)

TOTAL TIME: 25 MINUTES
SERVES 4

THAI LETTUCE WRAPS

Wrapping spicy morsels of fried pork and baby spinach with crisp lettuce leaves is definitely a more labor-intensive dinner than piling everything onto a plate. But it's also a lot more fun—and allows diners to adjust the lettuce-to-pork ratio to their taste. Serve the lettuce, herbs, vegetables, and pork separately, and let everyone combine them as they like. Small bowls of sticky or regular rice balance the heat and add to the meal. Or, if you're having a party, offer this as an hors d'oeuvre, scooping the pork into endive or the crispest, most inner leaves of a Bibb lettuce and putting it out on a platter garnished with the basil, nuts, and shallots. However you serve it, the combination of crisp-edged, chile-laden ground pork seasoned with lime and basil is addictive.

1 tablespoon soy sauce

1 tablespoon Asian fish sauce

Finely grated zest of ½ lime

1 teaspoon fresh lime juice

½ teaspoon honey

⅛ teaspoon kosher salt, plus more as needed

1 tablespoon peanut oil

3 garlic cloves, finely chopped

1 fresh Thai, serrano, or jalapeño chile, seeded and finely chopped

1 scallion (white and green parts), finely chopped, plus more for serving

1 lemongrass stalk, trimmed, outer layers removed, inner core minced (optional)

1 pound ground pork, not too lean if possible (or use ground turkey)

5 cups (5 ounces) fresh baby spinach

½ cup fresh basil leaves, torn into pieces

Chopped cashews, for serving

Thinly sliced shallots, for serving

Shredded carrots, for serving

Lime wedges, for serving

Lettuce leaves, for serving

TOTAL TIME: 25 MINUTES
SERVES 4

1. In a small bowl, whisk together the soy sauce, fish sauce, lime zest and juice, honey, and the ⅛ teaspoon salt.

2. Heat the peanut oil in a 12-inch skillet over medium-high heat. Add the garlic, chile, scallion, and lemongrass if using. Cook until fragrant, 30 seconds. Then stir in the pork and cook until it is well browned and most of the juices have evaporated, about 7 minutes. (Use a flat spatula to press down on the pork so it can get very browned and crispy on the bottom. This adds great flavor and texture.)

3. Add the soy sauce mixture and cook for 1 minute. Stir in the spinach and cook until wilted. Toss in the basil. Taste, and adjust the seasoning if needed.

4. Transfer the pork mixture to a platter, and surround it with mounds of scallion greens, cashews, shallots, and carrots. Serve lime wedges alongside for sprinkling, and lettuce leaves for wrapping.

SPICY PORK & BLACK BEAN CHILI *with Sage and White Cheddar*

We make a lot of chili in our house—it's one of my husband's all-time favorite meals. And given my predilection for experimentation, I've used just about every combination of meat and bean possible over the years. Of the myriad variations, this is one of the handful we keep coming back to, with ground pork, earthy black beans, and a hit of fresh sage. Beer adds a slightly bitter note that brings out the sweetness of the tomatoes, and the optional cheese makes it creamy and rich. If you like a medium spicy chili, opt for the poblano over the red bell pepper. Or for something hotter still, throw in a minced jalapeño or two with the onion, which I like to do when I know no children will be partaking. At any heat level, it's a homey, easy dinner, the kind of recipe you'll return to often.

As for serving, if you pair this with Skillet Brown-Butter Cornbread (page 385), you'll get a slightly sweet contrast to the heat of the chili, and then you can eat the leftover cornbread—toasted and buttered and smeared with honey—for breakfast the next morning. Or for a more classic go-with, you can't go wrong with some kind of rice—brown, regular, or Coconut Rice (page 381).

2 tablespoons extra-virgin olive oil

1 large white onion, diced

1 poblano chile or red bell pepper, diced

1 pound ground pork (or substitute turkey)

2 teaspoons kosher salt, plus more as needed

1 teaspoon freshly ground black pepper, plus more to taste

2 teaspoons dried oregano

1 tablespoon minced fresh sage

1 tablespoon chili powder, plus more as needed

2 garlic cloves, minced

1 28-ounce can diced tomatoes

3 cups cooked black beans (see pages 232 to 233), or 2 15-ounce cans, rinsed and drained

¾ cup lager beer (I tend to use Negra Modelo)

Grated white cheddar cheese or sour cream, for serving (optional)

Lime wedges, for serving

TOTAL TIME: 1 HOUR
SERVES 4 TO 6

1. Heat the olive oil in a large pot over medium-high heat. Add the onion and poblano; cook, stirring, until the vegetables have softened and are lightly browned, about 7 minutes. Add the pork and cook, breaking it up with a spoon, until it is well browned, another 7 minutes. Stir in the salt, pepper, oregano, sage, chili powder, and garlic, and cook for 1 minute.

2. Add the tomatoes and all their liquid, black beans, and beer. Stir and bring the mixture to a boil. Then reduce the heat to medium-low and simmer until the mixture is slightly thickened, 30 to 40 minutes. Taste, and add more salt and pepper if needed. Serve the chili topped with grated cheese if you like, and with lime wedges alongside.

SWEET PEPPERS & SAUSAGES *with Ricotta Salata and Fresh Oregano*

Here's a sausage sheet-pan supper featuring sweet bell peppers that practically melt in the oven's high heat. In this recipe, the sausages are roasted directly on top of the peppers, so the vegetables can absorb all the brawny, porky juices. Then both vegetables and sausages are piled onto fresh arugula leaves, some of which wilt on contact while some stay crisp and salad-like. A garnish of crumbled ricotta salata adds a milky, funky note, while a dressing made with red wine vinegar and fresh oregano is both earthy and tart next to the sweet and supple roasted peppers. Seek out a variety of different colored peppers for the prettiest dish. And if you can't find ricotta salata, substitute feta, though maybe use a little less since it's saltier. A loaf of crusty bread is all you need to round this out.

1. Heat the oven to 400°F.

2. In a bowl, toss the peppers and onion with the oil, salt, and black pepper. Spread the vegetables out in a single layer on a rimmed baking sheet, and roast until they are limp and soft but not caramelized, about 10 minutes.

3. Arrange the sausages on top of the peppers and onion, and continue roasting until the peppers are caramelized and the sausages are cooked through, 20 to 25 minutes. If the sausages and/or peppers are not browned enough at this point, you can slide the whole pan under the broiler for a minute or two. Watch it carefully so it doesn't burn.

4. Meanwhile, in a medium bowl, combine the vinegar and oregano.

5. Before serving, toss the peppers and onion with the vinegar mixture; taste, and adjust the seasonings if necessary (it might need more vinegar if your onion is very sweet). If you are using the arugula, divide it among individual serving plates, and sprinkle with a little olive oil and a few drops of red wine vinegar. Arrange the peppers, onions, and sausages over the arugula, if including. Sprinkle with the cheese, and serve.

1 red bell pepper, seeded and sliced into ¼-inch-wide strips

1 yellow bell pepper, seeded and sliced into ¼-inch-wide strips

1 small onion, peeled and sliced into ¼-inch-thick rounds

1½ tablespoons extra-virgin olive oil, plus more for sprinkling

¾ teaspoon kosher salt

Freshly ground black pepper to taste

1 pound fresh Italian sausages (sweet or hot), pricked with a fork

½ teaspoon red wine vinegar, plus more for sprinkling

1 teaspoon finely chopped fresh oregano

Fresh arugula, for serving (optional)

2 ounces ricotta salata, crumbled (about ⅓ cup)

TOTAL TIME: 45 MINUTES
SERVES 2 OR 3

SEARED SAUSAGE & RHUBARB *with Swiss Chard*

With the roster of pies, pastries, and cakes that usually feature rhubarb, it's easy to forget that the red-tinged stalks are actually vegetables, not fruit. And when not sweetened up with a ton of sugar, rhubarb's racy acidity can be a boon in savory dishes. In this unusual recipe, I've sautéed it with leafy Swiss chard, fresh ginger, currants, and a little maple syrup until everything turns thick and chutney-like, with a soft and silky texture. It makes an unexpected and delicious sauce for a pan of seared sausages, which lend a crisp and porky punch. Serve this over some kind of soft grain to absorb all the juices. I especially like polenta (page 277), but barley or quinoa would work well, too, as would mashed potatoes.

1. Heat the olive oil in a 12-inch skillet over medium-high heat. Add the sausages and cook until they are cooked through and well browned all over, about 12 minutes total. Transfer the sausages to a plate.

2. Add the onion to the skillet and cook, stirring frequently, until softened, about 5 minutes. Stir in the chard stems and continue to cook until the onion is well browned and the chard stems are almost tender, about 7 minutes. Add the rhubarb, currants, maple syrup, garam masala, salt, ginger, and bay leaf to the skillet. Cook, stirring often, until the rhubarb has fallen apart and the chard stems are tender, 7 to 10 minutes. If the bottom of the pan begins to scorch, stir in some water, a few tablespoons at a time.

3. Toss in the chard leaves and cook, stirring frequently, until they are wilted, about 5 minutes. Transfer the chard mixture to a heated serving platter and pluck out the bay leaf.

4. Return the sausages to the skillet and let them heat through, shaking the pan so they crisp a little on all sides, about 2 minutes. Serve the sausages over the rhubarb-chard mixture.

2 tablespoons extra-virgin olive oil

1 pound sweet Italian sausages, pricked with a fork

1 red onion, thinly sliced

1 bunch green, red, or rainbow Swiss chard, stems cut into ¼-inch slices, leaves torn into bite-sized pieces

8 ounces rhubarb stems, cut into ¼-inch-thick slices

2 tablespoons dried currants

2 tablespoons maple syrup

1 teaspoon garam masala

¼ teaspoon kosher salt

1 1-inch piece fresh ginger, peeled and grated

1 bay leaf

TOTAL TIME: 45 MINUTES
SERVES 4

ROASTED SAUSAGE & CAULIFLOWER

with Cumin and Turkish Pepper

Ever since I discovered the golden-edged, caramelized joys of roasted cauliflower, I've hardly prepared it any other way. Roasting condenses its juices, browns the crevices, and renders the whole thing sweet and irresistible. Whenever I serve roasted cauliflower to a group, I need to sit on my hands to avoid eating every last floret before my friends and family have had their fill.

In this recipe, the florets are roasted in the same oven as the sausages, which makes the whole dinner especially convenient to prepare since it all cooks at once. I like to serve this with a simple garlicky yogurt sauce to add a piquant creaminess to the mix. Regular (non-Greek) yogurt works best here because you want a runny texture. But if you've only got Greek yogurt in the fridge, thin it down with a bit of water or milk. A garnish of fresh herbs—parsley, dill, or mint—add color as well as their bright flavor.

1¼ pounds cauliflower, cut into florets

¼ cup extra-virgin olive oil, plus more as needed

1 teaspoon cumin seeds

½ teaspoon kosher salt, plus more as needed

¼ teaspoon freshly ground black pepper, plus more as needed

1 pound Italian sausages, pricked with a fork

⅓ cup plain yogurt, preferably non-Greek, whole milk

1 small garlic clove

Turkish or Aleppo pepper, as needed

Toasted pine nuts, for serving (see page 265; optional)

Fresh herbs such as parsley, dill or mint, for serving (optional)

TOTAL TIME: 45 MINUTES
SERVES 3 OR 4

1. Heat the oven to 425°F.

2. Spread the cauliflower florets on a large rimmed baking sheet, and toss with the olive oil, cumin seeds, salt, and pepper. Roast for 10 minutes.

3. Coat the sausages lightly with olive oil, place them on another rimmed baking sheet, and add it to the oven with the cauliflower. Roast, turning them over halfway through, until the sausages are golden and cooked through and the cauliflower is tender and caramelized, about 25 minutes.

4. While the cauliflower and sausages are cooking, prepare the yogurt sauce: Place the yogurt in a small bowl, grate the garlic clove over the yogurt, add salt and pepper to taste, and stir together.

5. Place the sausages and cauliflower on a platter or individual serving plates. Spoon the yogurt sauce on top, and sprinkle with Turkish pepper, and pine nuts and fresh herbs if using.

FISH & SEAFOOD

MISO-GLAZED SALMON
with Brown Sugar

In this minimalist salmon recipe, miso, brown sugar, ginger, and lime combine to make a bright, complex glaze that bubbles and browns under the broiler's intense heat and permeates the fish with a funky sweetness that rounds out the rich meat. Greater than the sum of its parts, and so incredibly simple that you don't need to take out your chef's knife, this will become a regular in your dinner rotation. You can use the glaze on other fish, too. It will happily season anything from mild flounder to deeply oceanic blue fish and mackerel.

Serve this with Coconut Rice (page 381) or plain white or brown rice. Or try it with a mound of steamed bok choy or spinach as a sop for the very tasty sauce.

6 tablespoons white miso

3 tablespoons mirin

3 tablespoons sake

2 tablespoons light brown sugar

1 teaspoon grated peeled fresh ginger

1 teaspoon finely grated lime zest

4 skinless salmon fillets, preferably center-cut pieces (6 to 8 ounces each)

Lime wedges, for serving

TIME: 20 MINUTES + AT LEAST
15 MINUTES MARINATING
SERVES 4

1. In a small bowl, whisk together the miso, mirin, sake, brown sugar, ginger, and lime zest. Place the salmon in a shallow dish, pour the miso mixture over it, and turn the salmon over to coat it evenly with the marinade. Cover the dish and let the salmon marinate for 15 minutes to 1 hour at room temperature or up to overnight in the fridge.

2. Heat the broiler to high, and line a rimmed baking sheet with aluminum foil.

3. Place the salmon on the prepared baking sheet, reserving the marinade. Broil for 3 to 4 minutes. Then turn the salmon over, brush it with the reserved marinade, and broil until it is cooked through to taste and golden at the edges, 3 to 4 minutes for medium rare. Serve warm, with lime wedges alongside.

ANCHOVY SALMON
with Chive Butter

It's rare to find a piece of salmon that actually tastes like fish. Farmed salmon is rich and mild, but really isn't reminiscent of the sea. Frozen wild salmon, which is what I usually seek out, has a deeper flavor, but often lacks a pronounced saline punch. Adding a few anchovies to the pan can go a long way to rectifying this. A couple of fillets will dissolve into a sauce, leaving their umami trail behind them. They'll make your salmon taste more like itself, or even a little better.

Here, I mix anchovies into softened butter along with some garlic and use the butter in two separate ways. I use half as the fat in which to sear the salmon. As the butter browns, the anchovies caramelize and the garlic sweetens. Then I stir the rest into the pan just before serving. It gets just enough contact with the hot metal to melt into a creamy sauce, but not enough to cook the garlic or anchovies, which remain raw, sharp, and pungent, contrasting with the fatty salmon.

You can use this same technique to cook any full-flavored fish—swordfish, trout, tuna, or striped bass. It will also work with boneless chicken. Just keep your eye on the protein to make sure it doesn't over- or undercook. This is good advice no matter what's on the menu.

1. Heat the oven to 400°F.

2. In a small bowl, mash together the butter, anchovies, chives, garlic, salt, and pepper.

3. Melt about half of the butter mixture in a large oven-safe skillet over high heat. Add the salmon, skin-side down, and cook for 3 minutes to brown the skin, spooning some of the pan drippings over the fish as it cooks.

4. Scatter the capers around (not over) the salmon, and transfer the skillet to the oven. Roast until the fish is just cooked through, about 5 to 8 minutes for medium rare, depending upon the thickness of the fillets—thinner ones will cook more quickly.

5. Remove the skillet from the oven, add the remaining chive butter, and let it melt. Place the salmon on individual plates and spoon the buttery pan sauce over the top. Squeeze the lemon half over the salmon, and garnish with chives. Serve.

3 tablespoons unsalted butter, at room temperature

4 oil-packed anchovy fillets, minced

1 tablespoon minced fresh chives, plus more for garnish

1 fat garlic clove (or 2 small ones), grated on a Microplane or minced

Pinch of fine sea salt

Freshly ground black pepper to taste

4 skin-on salmon fillets, preferably center-cut pieces (6 to 8 ounces each)

2 tablespoons drained capers, patted dry

½ lemon

TOTAL TIME: 25 MINUTES
SERVES 4

VIETNAMESE CARAMEL SALMON

The classic fish for this intense and sweetly aromatic recipe is catfish. In Vietnam, thick bone-in catfish steaks are simmered in a dark and highly peppery caramel for upwards of an hour, until the fish practically falls apart in its bittersweet, pungent sauce. Here, I've replaced catfish with salmon, which has a rich succulence that can stand up to the ginger, chiles, and black pepper. And by using brown sugar instead of making my own caramel, I've also hastened the process so that the whole thing is ready in less than thirty minutes. The salmon still has time to absorb all the intense flavors of the caramel, but it doesn't overcook, staying firm but tender. Serve this with some rice as a gentle foil for all the rich spiciness on the plate.

1. Set an oven rack 6 inches from the heat source (usually the second rack position, not the one closest to the heat source), and turn on the broiler.

2. Brush the salmon fillets all over with the oil and season them lightly with salt.

3. In a 12-inch oven-safe skillet set over medium-high heat, combine the brown sugar, fish sauce, soy sauce, ginger, lime zest and juice, black pepper, and 1 tablespoon of water. Bring to a simmer.

4. Place the fish, skin-side up, in the skillet. Reduce the heat to low and simmer, without moving it, until the fish is cooked through halfway, 4 to 6 minutes.

5. Spoon the pan juices over the fish and transfer the skillet to the oven. Broil until the fish is just cooked through and the skin is caramelized in spots, 2 to 5 minutes for medium rare, depending upon the thickness of the fish (thicker ones will take longer).

6. Transfer the fish to a serving plate and garnish it with scallions, jalapeños, and cilantro. Drizzle with the pan sauce, and serve.

4 skin-on salmon fillets, preferably center-cut pieces (6 to 8 ounces each)

1 tablespoon coconut or extra-virgin olive oil

Fine sea salt to taste

⅓ cup packed light brown sugar

3 tablespoons Asian fish sauce

2 tablespoons soy sauce

1 teaspoon grated peeled fresh ginger

Finely grated zest of 1 lime

Juice of ½ lime

½ teaspoon freshly ground black pepper

Sliced scallions (white and green parts), for garnish

Thinly sliced jalapeño, for garnish

Fresh cilantro leaves, for garnish

TOTAL TIME: 25 MINUTES
SERVES 4

SLOW-ROASTED TUNA
with Harissa and Olives

This dish splits the difference between confited tuna (tuna thoroughly submerged in oil and cooked at low heat) and roasted tuna (tuna drizzled with oil and cooked at high heat). Here, I cook the tuna in a moderate oven with just enough oil to coat it. The result is better than either of the cooking techniques from whence it came—with fish that's rosy centered like roasted tuna, yet with a soft exterior as in a confit, without any overcooked, chalky bits. Even better, before cooking, the tuna is coated in spicy North African harissa (a heady, cumin and coriander–laced chile paste), which gives it a complex, earthy-spice note and plenty of fiery heat.

If you don't have harissa on hand, substitute ¾ teaspoon Aleppo, Turkish, or regular red chile flakes (or to taste), ¼ teaspoon ground cumin, and a pinch of ginger, and sprinkle this all over the tuna along with the salt.

Serve the fish with plenty of its fragrant oil spooned over raw spinach or baby kale for dinner on the lighter side. Or try it with quinoa or farro (page 277) if you want to bulk it out. I often double this recipe so that there's enough tuna for dinner and plenty left over for turning into tuna-salad sandwiches the next day.

1. Heat the oven to 350°F.

2. Season the tuna chunks all over with the salt and pepper, and then rub the harissa into them. Place the tuna in an oven-safe dish that will hold the chunks snugly, such as a 9-inch loaf pan or an 8-inch cake pan (you can use a bigger dish, but then you will need more oil to cover the tuna).

3. Tuck the olives, garlic, bay leaf, and rosemary sprig around the tuna and pour in just enough olive oil to cover the fish.

4. Cover the pan with aluminum foil and bake for 12 to 20 minutes, until the fish is slightly underdone for your taste. Be careful not to cook the fish all the way through because it will continue cooking as it rests in the hot oil. So when it's just a bit too pink for you, take it out of the oven. Note that the cooking time depends not just on the heat circulation of your oven, but also on the type of material your pan is made out of. Metal pans tend to cook more quickly than glass or ceramic. So keep an eye on the fish and check it often. (Overcooked fish will be slightly chalky but still makes great tuna salad.)

5. Let the fish rest in the pan for at least 10 minutes. Then serve it warm or at room temperature, with flaky sea salt sprinkled on top and lemon wedges on the side.

1½ pounds albacore tuna, cut into 1 × 1½-inch-thick chunks

½ teaspoon fine sea salt

¼ teaspoon freshly ground black pepper

1 tablespoon harissa

2 to 3 tablespoons sliced pitted olives (black or green, as long as they are good quality)

2 garlic cloves, coarsely chopped

1 bay leaf, preferably fresh

1 large sprig fresh rosemary, or 2 to 3 sprigs fresh thyme

Extra-virgin olive oil, as needed

Flaky sea salt, for serving

Lemon wedges, for serving

TOTAL TIME: 25 MINUTES + AT LEAST 10 MINUTES COOLING
SERVES 3 OR 4

SWORDFISH

with Lemon, Chile, and Fennel

Whenever I buy thick, full-flavored fish steaks like swordfish (or tuna, mahi-mahi, or shark) I usually cut them into chunks and then cook them slowly and gently with lots of fat in the pan, effectively confiting rather than frying. I'm not looking for browning necessarily (though a little is okay), but for evenly cooked fish that stays soft and tender, without falling apart or overcooking on the surfaces. It's a much more forgiving method than using the broiler or the grill, and it gives you excellent results.

Since I can't rely on a caramelized crust to supply any flavor, I use a pan full of aromatics—fennel seeds, chile, garlic, and lemon zest—to do the job. It makes for fish that is deeply flavored and spunky, with a buttery, garlicky pan sauce that begs to be absorbed by pasta, good bread, or a bed of polenta (page 277). I love this with Green Beans with Caper Vinaigrette (page 377) or Quick-Roasted Broccoli or Cauliflower (page 382) on the side.

1 small fennel bulb, thinly sliced, fronds reserved

2 tablespoons fresh lemon juice

Kosher salt and freshly ground black pepper

1½ pounds swordfish or tuna steaks, about 1 inch thick

½ teaspoon fennel seeds

1½ tablespoons olive oil

1 tablespoon unsalted butter

2 garlic cloves, minced

Finely grated zest of ½ lemon

¼ teaspoon red chile flakes, plus more to taste

Lemon wedges, for serving

TOTAL TIME: 15 MINUTES
SERVES 4

1. In a small bowl, toss together the fennel slices, 1 tablespoon of the lemon juice, and a big pinch of salt. Set aside to marinate while you cook the fish.

2. Using a sharp knife, cut the skin off the fish, if there is skin, and then cut the fish into 1-inch cubes. Season the fish cubes generously with salt and pepper.

3. Using a mortar and pestle or the flat side of a heavy knife, lightly crush the fennel seeds to release their flavor.

4. In a 12-inch skillet, which should be large enough to hold all the fish cubes in a single layer, heat the olive oil and butter over medium heat until the butter melts. Add the fish to the pan and cook, turning the cubes and basting them with the oil and butter, for 3 minutes. (If your skillet isn't large enough, you can cook the fish in batches or use two skillets.)

5. Stir in the garlic, fennel seeds, lemon zest, and chile flakes, and continue to cook, stirring gently so as not to break up the fish cubes, until they are just cooked through, about 2 minutes. Gently stir in the remaining 1 tablespoon lemon juice. Taste, and add more salt and chile flakes if desired. Serve garnished with the marinated fennel, the reserved fennel fronds, and lemon wedges.

Roasted HAKE
with Crispy Mushrooms

Hake shows up often at the fishmonger at my local farmer's market in Brooklyn, and I love to bring it home. It's sustainable and economical (comparatively), and I adore the thick, loosely textured fillets with their clean briny flavor. You can use hake anywhere you would normally use cod, though it does cook a little more quickly.

Here, I roast it with woodsy thyme and sage to season the fish, and a bevy of different mushrooms cooked on the same baking sheet. The mushrooms curl and singe and add a meaty flavor to the hake, which absorbs all of their caramelized juices. You could think of it as a completely different take on surf and turf, no actual meat necessary. Feel free to substitute other thick fish fillets for the hake—cod, halibut, and black sea bass would all work well. Serve this with Citrus Salad with Olives (page 375) or a tomato salad in summer.

1. Heat the oven to 450°F.

2. Grate the lemon zest, and then quarter the bald lemon, seed the quarters, and set them aside.

3. Pat the hake fillets dry with paper towels. In a large bowl, combine the thyme, sage, lemon zest, ½ teaspoon of the salt, ½ teaspoon of the pepper, and the 4 teaspoons olive oil. Add the fish and turn the pieces in the mixture to coat.

4. On a large rimmed baking sheet, toss together the mushrooms, the remaining ¼ teaspoon salt, remaining ¼ teaspoon pepper, and remaining ¼ cup olive oil. Spread the mushrooms out into one layer, and roast until they are starting to turn crisp, 7 to 10 minutes.

5. Move the mushrooms to the edges of the baking sheet, leaving a large space in the center for the fish. Place the fish in the center space. Return the baking sheet to the oven and continue roasting until the fish is just opaque and flakes easily, about 10 minutes. Serve the hake and mushrooms immediately, with the lemon wedges.

1 lemon

2 boneless, skinless hake or cod fillets (12 ounces each), cut in half crosswise

2 teaspoons chopped fresh thyme leaves

1 teaspoon finely chopped fresh sage leaves

¾ teaspoon kosher salt

¾ teaspoon freshly ground black pepper

¼ cup plus 4 teaspoons extra-virgin olive oil

12 ounces mixed wild mushrooms, such as oyster and shiitake, cut into large bite-sized pieces

TOTAL TIME: 25 MINUTES
SERVES 4

BRANZINO *with Grapefruit and Rustic Olive-Caper Tapenade*

A roasted whole fish is the aquatic analogue to a roast chicken. It's easy to prepare, forgiving, and adaptable. Season it with salt, drizzle on some oil, and stuff the cavity with something tasty (or not), then stick it in the oven and let it do its thing. As long as you've sought out the freshest fish possible, you've done the hard part. Your oven will do the rest.

Fish bones and skin add intensity to a whole fish, giving it a lot more flavor than fillets. It's like the difference between roasting a whole chicken versus boneless, skinless breasts. In the case of both fish and fowl, eating around the bones can be fussy, but the increased flavor makes it worth it. Bones and skin also help keep in moisture, so you're less likely to end up with a dried-out dinner, something not uncommon with fish fillets.

In this recipe, I stuff the cavity with piney rosemary sprigs and grapefruit instead of the usual lemon to add a fruity, bittersweet character to the fish. For serving, a rustic tapenade made with coarse pieces of olives and capers adds both texture and verve. Serve this with Pan-Fried Asparagus with Lemon Zest (page 376) to make it even more elegant. And feel free to double the quantities if you're feeding a crowd.

2 whole branzino (about 1¼ pounds each), patted dry

2 tablespoons plus 2 teaspoons extra-virgin olive oil, plus more for serving

Fine sea salt and freshly ground black pepper to taste

½ grapefruit

4 sprigs fresh rosemary

½ cup pitted and coarsely chopped Kalamata olives

2 tablespoons drained and coarsely chopped capers

2 teaspoons minced fresh parsley leaves

2 tablespoons minced scallions (white and green parts)

TOTAL TIME: 30 MINUTES
SERVES 4

1. Heat the oven to 400°F. Line a rimmed baking sheet with aluminum foil.

2. Place the fish on the prepared baking sheet, drizzle the cavities and the skin with 1 tablespoon olive oil per fish. Season the fish, inside and out, with salt and pepper.

3. Slice two ¼-inch-thick rounds from the grapefruit and cut each round into 4 quarters (for a total of 8 triangles); reserve the remaining grapefruit. Stuff the grapefruit pieces and the rosemary sprigs into the fish cavities. Roast the fish until the flesh is opaque and flakes easily when pressed gently along the backbone, about 20 minutes.

4. While the fish cooks, combine the olives, capers, parsley, scallions, and remaining 2 teaspoons olive oil in a small bowl.

5. When the fish is cooked, cut the flesh away from the backbone and divide it among four individual plates. Top each portion with some of the tapenade, squeeze some grapefruit juice (from the reserved grapefruit) over it, and then add a sprinkling of olive oil.

FISH TACOS

with Red Cabbage, Jalapeño, and Lime Slaw

As much as I've always loved ordering fish tacos when I'm out, I never got into the habit of frying up my own at home. I liked the idea of it, but the deep-fried reality was always a little messier than I wanted it to be. Then my friend and longtime recipe tester Sarah Huck convinced me to give the broiler a go. A self-described fish taco "a-fish-ionado" (that Sarah just loves a pun), she promised me that broiling instead of frying was a perfectly delicious option for tacos. Essentially a vehicle for savory pickles, slaws, and condiments, the fish being fried or broiled is less important than the winning combination of flaky, chile-spiced fish wrapped in warm tortillas with crunchy cabbage slaw, garlicky lime *crema*, and velvety avocado. And that is what you get here, without any of the deep-frying mess.

You can skip the slaw and serve this with plain shredded cabbage and purchased salsa for an even quicker preparation.

1. In a small bowl, stir together the sour cream and garlic. Finely grate the zest of 1 lime into the sour cream (reserve the bald lime). Season to taste with salt. Set this lime garlic sauce aside.

2. In a large bowl, toss together the cabbage, scallions, and jalapeño. Squeeze in 2 teaspoons lime juice (from the bald lime) and the 2 tablespoons olive oil. Season with ½ teaspoon each of salt and pepper. Set this slaw aside.

3. Arrange an oven rack 4 to 6 inches from the heat source, and heat the broiler to high.

4. In a small bowl, whisk the cumin, chili powder, and remaining ¾ teaspoon salt together to combine. Place the fish on a rimmed baking sheet, and rub the spice mixture all over the fish; then coat it lightly with olive oil. Broil, turning the fish over halfway through, until it is just cooked through, 3 to 4 minutes per side.

5. To serve, flake the fish with a fork. Lightly toast the tortillas over the open flame of a burner or in a large dry skillet over high heat. Fill each tortilla with fish, slaw, and avocado slices if using. Top the filling with the lime garlic sauce and cilantro leaves. Cut the remaining lime into wedges, and serve them alongside.

½ cup sour cream or plain Greek yogurt

1 garlic clove, grated on a Microplane or minced

2 limes

1¼ teaspoons kosher salt, plus more as needed

½ small head red cabbage, thinly sliced (4 cups)

¼ cup thinly sliced scallions (white and green parts)

1 to 2 jalapeños, to taste, seeded and minced

2 tablespoons extra-virgin olive oil, plus more as needed

½ teaspoon freshly ground black pepper

1 teaspoon ground cumin

½ teaspoon chili powder

12 ounces skinless flaky white fish, such as hake or flounder

Corn tortillas, for serving

Sliced avocado, for serving (optional)

Fresh cilantro leaves, for serving

TOTAL TIME: 25 MINUTES
SERVES 4

Thai-Style SHRIMP BALLS
with Napa Cabbage

These juicy, ginger-scented shrimp balls are like the filling inside your favorite shrimp shumai, sans the wrappers. And since you don't have to enfold each one individually in dumpling dough, they come together really quickly and steam up in minutes.

If you don't have a steamer basket, it's a good thing to pick up. They are inexpensive, and the collapsible ones don't take up much space. Or, a decent hack is to crumple up four large foil balls (at least 1½ inches in diameter) and place them in the bottom of a pot with a tight-filling cover, filled with ½ inch of water. Rest a plate on top of the foil balls to keep it above the water, bring the water to a simmer, and put the food directly on the plate to steam. It's not ideal, but it works in a pinch.

Serve these shrimp balls over white rice (page 276) or rice noodles coated with a little sesame oil, which will give you a dumpling-like texture if you eat some shrimp ball and noodles in the same bite. A salad made from pea shoots and drizzled with a little of the dipping sauce, below, would round it out nicely. They also make nice hors d'oeuvres for a dinner party.

FOR THE DIPPING SAUCE

4½ tablespoons soy sauce

1½ tablespoons rice vinegar

1½ teaspoons toasted sesame oil

1½ teaspoons light or dark brown sugar

1½ tablespoons sliced scallions (green parts only)

1 pound medium shrimp, peeled and chopped into small chunks

2 tablespoons minced peeled fresh ginger

1 garlic clove, grated on a Microplane or minced

2 tablespoons minced fresh chives, plus more for serving

1 large egg white

Finely grated zest and juice of 1 lime

¼ teaspoon kosher salt

4 to 6 napa cabbage leaves, for steaming

TOTAL TIME: 25 MINUTES
SERVES 4

1. Make the dipping sauce: In a medium bowl, combine the soy sauce, rice vinegar, 1 tablespoon ginger, lime juice, sesame oil, and brown sugar, and whisk until the sugar dissolves; then add the scallions.

2. Line a baking sheet with wax or parchment paper. In a large bowl, combine the shrimp with 1 tablespoon of the ginger and the garlic, chives, egg white, lime zest, and salt. Mix well, and form the shrimp mixture into 1-inch balls. Place them in a single layer on the prepared baking sheet. Chill them up to 4 hours if not steaming immediately.

3. Lay one or two cabbage leaves over the bottom of a steamer basket to just cover the surface. Put the steamer in a pot filled with an inch of water and bring the water to a simmer. Working in batches, place the shrimp balls on the cabbage leaves, cover the pot, and steam for 3 minutes, turning them over halfway through. After each batch, transfer the shrimp balls and the cabbage leaves to a plate. Use fresh cabbage leaves for each batch.

4. Garnish the shrimp balls and cabbage with chives, and serve with the dipping sauce on the side. You can eat the cabbage or not, as you prefer.

SPICY ROASTED SHRIMP
with Eggplant and Mint

File this under: sheet-pan supper, the shrimp edition. Okay, I suppose that technically this requires two sheet pans, since I roast the eggplant separately from the crustaceans to give everything enough elbow room to sizzle and brown without steaming. The eggplant, tossed with spicy harissa, olive oil, and cumin, goes into the oven first to give it a head start, then the quicker-cooking shrimp goes in next. That way, it can all emerge at the same time, with the eggplant golden and crisp and the shrimp pink and juicy.

You may notice that I use cumin in two different ways in this recipe, both ground and the whole seeds. I find the ground spice to be earthier and rounder in flavor, while the whole seeds are more pungent. When combined, they give you a fuller, richer hit of cumin.

1. Heat the oven to 400°F.

2. In a small bowl, whisk the ⅓ cup olive oil with the harissa, ground cumin, and 1 teaspoon of the salt. Spread the eggplant chunks on a large rimmed baking sheet and toss with the harissa mixture. Roast, tossing occasionally, until lightly browned all over, about 20 minutes.

3. While the eggplant is cooking, pat the shrimp very dry with paper towels. In a bowl, toss the shrimp with the remaining 1½ tablespoons oil, cumin seeds, lemon zest, remaining ¼ teaspoon salt, and black pepper. Arrange the shrimp in a single layer on another rimmed baking sheet.

4. Raise the oven temperature to 425°F. Transfer the shrimp to the oven, and roast along with the eggplant until the shrimp are just opaque and the eggplant is golden brown and tender, about 7 to 10 minutes. If the shrimp cooks through but the eggplant needs more time, remove the shrimp from the oven and continue to roast the eggplant until browned.

5. Combine the shrimp and eggplant on a large platter or on individual serving plates. Drizzle with olive oil and lemon juice, top with mint leaves, and serve.

⅓ cup plus 1½ tablespoons extra-virgin olive oil, plus more as needed

2 tablespoons harissa

1½ teaspoons ground cumin

1¼ teaspoons kosher salt

1 large eggplant (1 pound), cut into 1½-inch chunks

12 ounces extra-large shrimp, shelled and deveined

½ teaspoon cumin seeds

½ teaspoon finely grated lemon zest

¼ teaspoon freshly ground black pepper

Lemon juice, for drizzling

Torn fresh mint leaves, for garnish

TOTAL TIME: 40 MINUTES
SERVES 2

RED COCONUT
CURRY SHRIMP

You can slather a sauce made with coconut milk and red curry paste over pretty much anything and it will be delicious. But pairing it with tender shrimp is about as good as dinner gets, combining spicy-sweet-and-creamy in every bite, plus a subtle juicy crunch from red bell pepper and daikon. It's a speedy dish, too, and will make your kitchen smell heady and fragrant, as if you've been cooking all day long. That's the beauty of a jar of red curry paste—one small spoonful in the pan goes a long way toward happiness on the plate.

2 tablespoons Thai red curry paste

1 13.5-ounce can unsweetened coconut milk

¼ cup chopped fresh basil leaves, plus more whole leaves for serving

½ cup coarsely grated or julienned daikon radish

1 tablespoon Asian fish sauce

2 tablespoons coconut sugar, or dark or light brown sugar

2 tablespoons grapeseed or peanut oil

2 garlic cloves, minced

1 small onion, halved lengthwise through the root and thinly sliced into half moons

1 red bell pepper, thinly sliced

¾ cup sliced fresh shiitake or other mushrooms (1.75 ounces)

1 pound large shrimp, shelled and deveined

Cooked white or brown rice, for serving (see page 276)

Lime wedges, for serving

TOTAL TIME: 20 MINUTES
SERVES 3 OR 4

1. In a medium pot over medium heat, whisk together the curry paste and coconut milk. Bring to a simmer and cook, whisking until the mixture is smooth, about 5 minutes. Add the basil, daikon, fish sauce, sugar, and 2 tablespoons of water; stir until the sugar has dissolved. Simmer until thickened to taste, 5 to 10 minutes.

2. While the curry sauce is simmering, heat a 12-inch skillet or wok over medium-high heat.

Once it is hot, add the oil and heat until it is shimmering. Add the garlic, onion, bell pepper, and mushrooms, and cook until the vegetables are starting to soften, about 3 minutes. Then add the shrimp and sauté until they are pink and cooked through, about 2 minutes. Pour the curry sauce into the skillet and heat it through. Serve the curry over rice, garnished with a few whole basil leaves and a squeeze of lime.

GARLICKY CALAMARI

with Basil, Chile, and Lime

Squid is one of the fastest things you can cook—faster than frying eggs, faster than cooking shrimp, faster even than heating up cold takeout from the fridge. The only downside to the speed at which it cooks is that, since it only spends a minute or two in the pan, it can be hard to get a good sear on it before it's time to move it out and onto your plate. But if you take care to get your pan screaming hot, pat your squid very dry, and don't add too many pieces to the skillet at once, you'll get a golden glow on the tentacle and rings. I use my giant 12-inch skillet to sear squid, and I can fit in about half a pound at once without crowding, so I cook this recipe in two batches. If your pan is smaller, plan on three batches just to make sure you're giving your squid rings enough personal space. If you pack them in like sardines, they will steam, not sear.

In this recipe, I sear the squid with fresh green chile and garlic, then garnish with lime juice and basil. Sometimes, I'll scatter the cooked squid over a bowl of Israeli couscous, which I started calling pasta bubbles to amuse my daughter, Dahlia, when she was a toddler, and the name stuck. Then I get to call the dish bubbles and squid, much to everyone's delight.

1. Rinse the squid under cool running water. Drain well, and then transfer the squid to a paper-towel-lined plate to dry completely.

2. Cut the squid bodies into ½-inch-thick rings and leave the tentacles whole (or halve them if large). Pat dry again with paper towels, and then transfer the squid pieces to a large bowl.

3. Place a 12-inch skillet over high heat. Let the skillet sit until it gets very hot (a good 5 minutes). Then add 1 tablespoon of the olive oil to the skillet. Sprinkle half the squid

pieces with salt, slide them into the skillet along with half of the chile, and cook without moving them for 1 minute (the pan might smoke a little, but it shouldn't be too bad). Flip the squid over and cook until just tender, 1 to 2 minutes more, adding half of the garlic for the last 20 seconds or so of cooking. Transfer the cooked squid, chile, and garlic to a plate and repeat with the remaining 1 tablespoon oil, squid, chile, and garlic.

4. Squeeze lime juice all over the squid, sprinkle with the basil, and serve with the bread.

1 pound cleaned squid

4 tablespoons extra-virgin olive oil

Kosher salt, as needed

1 jalapeño or serrano chile, thinly sliced and seeded if desired

2 garlic cloves, finely chopped

Fresh lime juice, as needed

¼ cup chopped fresh basil leaves

Crusty bread, for serving

TOTAL TIME: 20 MINUTES
SERVES 2 OR 3

SHRIMP BANH MI

This sandwich maintains all the crunchy, spicy, pickle-y goodness of a Vietnamese *banh mi*, but without having to resort to takeout to get one. Even better, instead of being filled with an array of often unidentifiable pork products (what exactly is that bologna-like cold cut anyway?), it's made from shrimp cakes seasoned with lemongrass, garlic, and ginger that you can whirl together in your food processor in minutes, then quickly pan-fry. The shrimp cakes become crisp and aromatic, with a springy texture to contrast with the juicy, quick-pickled carrots and radishes that get sandwiched alongside. You can make this as spicy or as mild as you like—just dial back or dial up the Sriracha and jalapeño to taste.

2 small carrots, peeled and shredded

½ cup thinly sliced radishes

1 jalapeño, seeded and diced, plus more thinly sliced jalapeño for serving

4 teaspoons rice vinegar

Pinch of sugar

Kosher salt to taste

2½ teaspoons Asian fish sauce

16 sprigs fresh cilantro

2 garlic cloves

2 teaspoons grated peeled fresh ginger

1 lemongrass stalk, trimmed, outer layers removed, inner core smashed and chopped

1 small fresh chile (such as Thai or serrano), halved and seeded

8 ounces shrimp, peeled and deveined

2 tablespoons toasted sesame oil

Mayonnaise, for serving

Sriracha, for serving

1 baguette, split lengthwise and crosswise, and toasted

TOTAL TIME: 25 MINUTES
SERVES 2

1. In a small bowl, toss together the carrots, radishes, jalapeño, 2 teaspoons of the rice vinegar, a pinch each of sugar and salt, and ½ teaspoon of the fish sauce. Stir to combine, and let it rest while you prepare the shrimp.

2. In a food processor, combine 8 cilantro sprigs with the garlic, ginger, lemongrass, chile, and remaining 2 teaspoons each fish sauce and rice vinegar, and process until everything is finely chopped. Add the shrimp and pulse the mixture, continually scraping down the sides of the bowl, until you have a chunky paste.

3. Heat the sesame oil in a large skillet over high heat. Add the shrimp paste, pressing it into the skillet. Cook until the paste is browned on one side, 2 to 3 minutes. Flip it over and cook until it is browned on the other side. (Don't worry if it breaks up. It can be like a hash or like a burger—both will work in the sandwich.) Sprinkle the cooked shrimp paste lightly with salt.

4. Spread mayonnaise and Sriracha to taste over the cut sides of the baguette pieces. Place the shrimp mixture on the bottom 2 pieces of baguette and top with the pickled carrots and radishes, the remaining 8 cilantro sprigs, and jalapeño slices to taste. Cover with baguette tops to form sandwiches.

SARDINE CROSTINI

with Seared Tomatoes

Anchovies are indubitably my favorite cured fish. But jarred sardines, with their mineral brawniness and soft, buttery flesh, are a close second. I love to pile them on garlic-rubbed crostini. Usually, I'll just top the fish with some slivered raw onion, a drizzle of olive oil, a few grinds of black pepper, and a squeeze of lemon. But here I trick them out a little more festively with pan-seared cherry tomatoes seasoned with sherry vinegar. The tomatoes condense and intensify in the skillet's heat, getting browned and wrinkled in some spots and sweeter overall. They make a juicy, almost chutney-like contrast to the rich fish, adding vegetables to the mix to make a more complete meal. Serve these on their own for a very light dinner or lunch, or pair them with a salad or a soup. I especially like them with Leek, Tomato & Farro Soup with Pancetta (page 319) in winter or Horta Salad with Feta and Olives (page 343) any time of the year.

2 tablespoons extra-virgin olive oil, plus more for drizzling

2 cups cherry tomatoes, halved

2 teaspoons sherry vinegar, plus more as needed

Kosher salt and freshly ground black pepper to taste

4 ½-inch-thick slices crusty bread

1 large, fat garlic clove, halved

6 ounces sardines packed in oil, any large bones removed

Thinly sliced red onion, shallots, or scallions

Chopped fresh parsley leaves or chives, for garnish

Flaky sea salt, for garnish

TOTAL TIME: 15 MINUTES
SERVES 2

1. Heat the olive oil in a large skillet over medium-high heat. Add the tomatoes and cook, without moving them, until they are slightly blistered and soft, 2 to 3 minutes. Toss in the vinegar and season with salt and pepper. Shake the skillet several times and then remove it from the heat.

2. Toast the bread and rub the slices on both sides with the garlic halves. Place the toasts on individual serving plates and drizzle with olive oil. Top with the sardines, the onions, and the tomatoes. Drizzle with additional oil, and sprinkle with parsley and sea salt.

SOFT-SHELL CRABS
with Lime Salsa Verde

Soft-shell crabs are one of those things that most people save for ordering in restaurants, when there's someone else in charge of cooking them up into irresistibly crisp and juicy morsels. But do not be deterred from making them yourself. Soft-shell crabs are one of the easiest dinners around, especially if you ask your fishmonger to clean them for you. Then all you have to do is fry them in some hot fat until they puff and redden, and serve them with some kind of piquant sauce to highlight their saline sweetness. Here, a zesty lime salsa verde with capers and parsley does the job. It's a very fast, very elegant meal that we make at least once during soft-shell season—and pine for the rest of the year.

Serve them with Pan-Fried Asparagus with Lemon (page 376), as asparagus is in season at the same time.

1. Finely chop 1 tablespoon of the capers, leaving the rest whole. Place the chopped capers in a bowl and stir in the parsley, lime zest and juice, the ¼ teaspoon salt, the garlic, and the chile flakes. Whisk in the ¼ cup olive oil. Set this salsa verde aside.

2. Heat 1 tablespoon of the remaining olive oil in a 12-inch skillet over medium-high heat. Season the crabs with salt to taste, and add 4 crabs to the skillet along with half of the reserved whole capers. Cook without moving the crabs until they are crisp and golden on the first side, 2 to 3 minutes. Then flip them over and cook on the other side, 2 to 3 minutes. Transfer the crabs to a paper-towel-lined plate and sprinkle with more salt. Repeat with the remaining oil, crabs, and capers.

3. Serve the crabs, topped with the capers, salsa verde, and lemon wedges.

2 tablespoons capers

2 cups fresh parsley leaves, finely chopped

Finely grated zest of ½ lime

2 teaspoons fresh lime juice

¼ teaspoon kosher salt, plus more as needed

1 fat garlic clove, grated on a Microplane or minced

Pinch of red chile flakes

¼ cup plus 2 tablespoons extra-virgin olive oil

8 soft-shell crabs, patted dry with paper towels

Lemon wedges, for serving

TOTAL TIME: 20 MINUTES
SERVES 4

SPICED CRAB & CORN CAKES *with Coriander Yogurt*

Good crab cakes should be all about the crabmeat and not about the binders. As necessary as the bread crumbs and eggs and the like are to help the cakes keep their shape in the pan, the more crab you can stuff in without the cakes falling apart, the better. These cakes can have minimal crumbs and eggs because the batter is augmented by sweet corn kernels, pureed to a paste. The starchiness of the corn puree helps hold the crab cakes together, and adds its own gentle, summery sweetness to the mix. Green chile, garam masala, and coriander give the cakes an Indian flavor, augmented by a gingered yogurt sauce dolloped right on top. Serve these with ice cold beer and sliced radishes or cucumbers, and more of the spicy, gingery yogurt.

1. Prepare the crab and corn cake mixture: In a food processor, coarsely puree the corn with several pulses. Transfer the corn to a large bowl. Add the crabmeat, mayonnaise, eggs, jalapeño, garam masala, cumin, coriander, and salt. Sprinkle 1 cup of the panko over the surface of the mixture and mix it in lightly. Cover the bowl with plastic wrap and refrigerate for at least 1 hour and up to 12 hours.

2. While the mixture chills, **make the yogurt sauce:** In a small dry skillet over medium heat, toast the coriander seeds until fragrant, about 2 minutes. Transfer them to a mortar and pestle, and crush lightly. In a small bowl, whisk together the yogurt, crushed coriander, ginger, cilantro, and a pinch of salt.

3. When you are ready to cook the crab cakes, scoop out ⅓-cup portions and form them into 1-inch-thick patties.

4. Heat the olive oil in a large skillet over medium-high heat. Dust both sides of the crab cakes with the remaining 1½ cups panko. Fry the crab cakes in batches (adding more oil to the skillet if needed) until the exterior is crisp and golden brown, 2 to 3 minutes per side. Serve with the yogurt sauce alongside.

FOR THE CRAB AND CORN CAKES

Kernels from 2 ears fresh corn (about 2 cups)

1 pound lump crabmeat, drained well

½ cup mayonnaise

2 large eggs, lightly beaten

1 jalapeño, seeded and finely chopped

1 tablespoon garam masala

2 teaspoons ground cumin

1 teaspoon ground coriander

½ teaspoon kosher salt

2½ cups panko bread crumbs

5 tablespoons extra-virgin olive oil or grapeseed oil, plus more as needed

FOR THE YOGURT SAUCE

1 teaspoon coriander seeds

1 cup Greek yogurt, preferably whole-milk

2 teaspoons grated peeled fresh ginger

¼ cup chopped fresh cilantro leaves

Pinch of kosher salt

TOTAL TIME: 45 MINUTES + AT LEAST
1 HOUR MARINATING
SERVES 4 TO 6 (MAKES ABOUT
16 CAKES)

WARM SQUID SALAD

with Cucumber, Mint, and Aioli

When done just right, squid is quick-cooking, deeply oceanic, wonderfully tender. And did I mention economical and sustainable, too? What squid is not is rich. Squid is as lean as proteins come. Aioli, on the other hand, is about as luscious as sauces get. So combining the two on the plate makes perfect sense so they can balance each other out. It's a stunning combination of supple squid and satiny aioli, bursting with saline and olive oil flavors.

I should warn you that with sautéed garlic in the squid pan and raw garlic in the sauce, this is a highly pungent dish for all its silky textures. You can scale back on the allium if you like, or leave it out altogether. Or take the opposite route and serve the aioli-topped squid over garlic-rubbed crostini.

1. Make the aioli: In a blender, pulse together the garlic, lemon juice, and salt. Pulse in the egg and egg yolk. With the motor running, drizzle the olive oil into the mixture in a slow, steady stream until incorporated. Scrape the aioli into a bowl, cover the bowl with plastic wrap, and refrigerate until ready to use. It will keep for at least 5 days.

2. Prepare the squid: Rinse the squid under cool running water. Drain well, and then transfer it to a paper-towel-lined plate to dry completely.

3. Cut the squid bodies into ½-inch-thick rings and leave the tentacles whole (or halve them if large). Pat dry again with paper towels, and then transfer the squid pieces to a large bowl.

4. Place a 12-inch skillet over high heat. Let the skillet sit until it gets very hot (a good 5 minutes). Then add 1 tablespoon of the olive oil to the skillet. Sprinkle half the squid pieces with salt, slide them into the skillet along with half of the chile, and cook without moving them for 1 minute. (Make sure not to crowd the skillet; if it doesn't fit the squid comfortably, cook them in smaller batches.) Flip the squid over and cook until just tender, 1 to 2 minutes more, adding half of the garlic for the last 20 seconds or so of cooking. Transfer the cooked squid, chile, and garlic to a plate, and repeat with the remaining 1 tablespoon oil, squid, chile, and garlic.

5. Squeeze lemon juice all over the squid, and toss it with the mint and cucumbers. Season with sea salt. Serve the squid with a dollop of aioli on top.

FOR THE AIOLI

2 garlic cloves, grated on a Microplane or minced

1 teaspoon fresh lemon juice

⅛ teaspoon fine sea salt

1 egg plus 1 egg yolk, beaten

¾ cup extra-virgin olive oil

FOR THE SQUID

1 pound cleaned squid

2 tablespoons extra-virgin olive oil

Kosher salt, as needed

1 jalapeño or red chile, seeded if desired and coarsely chopped

2 garlic cloves, finely chopped

Fresh lemon juice, as needed

¼ cup fresh mint leaves, torn into pieces if large

½ cup very thinly sliced Persian cucumber

Flaky sea salt, as needed

Crusty bread, for serving

TOTAL TIME: 30 MINUTES
SERVES 2 OR 3

STEAMED CLAMS

with Spring Herbs and Lime

Whenever I get my hands on a big pile of clams, the internal debate begins: do I go the linguine-with-white-clam-sauce route, or steam them up like mussels in a pot of fragrant aromatics? The linguine has a garlicky, hearty, rib-sticking appeal on its side. But steaming clams is about the easiest thing in the world, and it makes the dish more about the briny bivalves and less about the pasta. It's a lighter meal, but just as lusty.

Here, I steam the clams with fresh green herbs and plenty of lime (both juice and zest), along with the requisite garlic and butter. Unlike with mussels, you don't need to add any liquid to the pot; as they open, the clams release enough of their own juices to create a sauce. After a brief simmer, the clams emerge plump and very sweet, in a pot full of herbal, citrusy broth just waiting for the torn end of a baguette for dunking. Or a spoon works, too.

1 tablespoon extra-virgin olive oil

2 stalks of green garlic or 2 regular garlic cloves, thinly sliced

2 tablespoons chopped fresh tarragon or basil leaves

30 littleneck clams (about 2½ pounds), scrubbed

¼ cup minced fresh chives

Finely grated zest of 1 lime

Pinch of red chile flakes

2 tablespoons unsalted butter

1½ tablespoons fresh lime juice

TOTAL TIME: 20 MINUTES
SERVES 2

1. Warm the olive oil in a medium pot or a large straight-sided skillet (use one with a lid) over medium heat. Add the garlic and tarragon; cook until the garlic is slightly softened, about 2 minutes.

2. Stir in the clams and cover the pot. Cook until the clams open, 5 to 10 minutes.

3. Use a slotted spoon or tongs to divide the clams between two serving bowls, discarding any that don't open. Stir the chives, lime zest, and chile flakes into the sauce in the pot, and cook for 20 seconds. Add the butter and lime juice, whisking until the butter melts and the sauce thickens slightly. Spoon the pan juices over the clams, and serve immediately.

THAI-STYLE MUSSELS
with Coconut and Lemongrass

A Thai-style coconut and lemongrass sauce is a classic, one of those compelling combinations of flavors that is so incredibly tasty, it almost doesn't matter which protein you pour it over. Chicken, shrimp, tofu, or beef—as long as you've got sweet coconut milk spiked with chile and scented with lemongrass, and cilantro, you've got a feast in the making.

Although they may not be the first thing that springs to mind, mussels are particularly delightful with the creamy sauce—saline, plump, and meaty little bites that hold their own in the complex and spicy broth. And they're fun to eat. You can use their shells as spoons to slurp sauce and seafood all at once—not many other proteins have a utensil built in. Or use a fork to eat the mussels, then pour the fragrant, coconut-imbued liquid over white or brown rice (page 276); that way you'll be sure to catch every last drop.

1. If your mussels are farmed (and they probably are), all you need to do is rinse them under cold running water. Otherwise, if you see hairy clumps around the shell (called beards), use a sharp knife or your fingers to pull off these beards; then scrub the shells well with a vegetable brush.

2. Heat a large pot with a tight-fitting lid over medium heat. Add the oil, and when it is hot, add the shallot, garlic, lemongrass, and chile. Cook until the vegetables are soft, about 3 minutes. Add the coconut milk and the mussels.

Cover the pot and steam, stirring once or twice, until the mussels have opened, 5 to 10 minutes.

3. Remove the pot from the heat, and use a slotted spoon to transfer the mussels to wide, shallow serving bowls, leaving the liquid in the pot and discarding any mussels that have not opened.

4. Stir the lime zest and juice, fish sauce, and cilantro into the pot. Taste, and add more fish sauce and/or lime juice if needed (the fish sauce provides the salt). Ladle the pan sauce over the mussels, and serve.

2 pounds fresh mussels

2 tablespoons coconut oil
or safflower oil

1 shallot, finely chopped

2 garlic cloves, finely chopped

1 stalk lemongrass, trimmed, outer
layers removed, inner core finely
chopped

½ to 1 small fresh hot chile
(such as Thai, serrano, Scotch
bonnet, or jalapeño), seeded and
finely chopped

1 cup unsweetened coconut milk

Finely grated zest of ½ lime

1 teaspoon fresh lime juice, or to taste

½ teaspoon Asian fish sauce, or
to taste

½ cup whole fresh cilantro leaves

TOTAL TIME: 20 MINUTES
SERVES 2

EGGS

HOW TO COOK EGGS

BOILED

Place the cold eggs in a medium pot and cover with cold water. Bring to a boil. Remove from the heat, cover, and let stand 7 minutes for soft boiled, 8 to 9 minutes for hard boiled (8 minutes gives a very moist, orange yolk, 9 minutes gives you a paler, more yellow and firmer yolk). Transfer the eggs to a bowl of ice water to cool.

To peel the eggs, remove them from the ice water when just cool enough to handle (as soon as you can stand to hold them). Lightly crack the egg shell all over on the counter, or you can use a spoon. Return cracked eggs to the ice water and let rest for a few minutes to finish cooling, then peel the eggs.

Peeling Trick

If you use a pin to make a tiny hole in the bottom (the wider end) of each egg before boiling, the eggs will be easier to peel.

FRIED

This technique depends on whether you like your eggs with or without crisp, browned edges. I like the browning, so here's what I do:

Heat a heavy skillet over medium-high heat, then pour in some fat (olive oil, butter, lard, and bacon grease are all delicious). The fat should thin on contact. Let it heat up for 10 seconds, then crack in your eggs. Don't crowd the pan—leaving space between eggs increases browning. While the eggs cook, tilt the pan and use a spoon to baste the whites with some of the hot fat in the pan (add more fat if you need to). Salt and pepper the eggs, then turn off the heat. The whites should be crisp and curled and lacy at the edges and the yolks still wobbly.

For softer eggs without any brown along the whites, you need low heat, a pan with a cover, and butter, the fat of choice here. Melt the butter over low heat in a skillet, but don't let it foam. Crack in the eggs and cover the pan. Let cook, undisturbed, for 2 to 4 minutes, until the white is cooked through and the yolk is still runny.

For over-easy eggs, flip them about a minute before the whites and yolks are done to your taste, then immediately turn off the heat and let them finish cooking in the residual heat from the pan.

SCRAMBLED

Crack as many eggs as you like in a bowl and use a fork to beat them until they are just mixed (don't use a whisk or you might introduce too much air, which makes them harder to scramble). You can add a few drops of water or milk here if you like; some people think it gives you fluffier eggs. Season with salt and pepper.

Melt as much butter as you can tolerate in a heavy skillet over low heat (1 tablespoon per egg is nice, but you can get away with a lot less). Slide in the eggs. Cook gently, swirling the pan and using a heatproof rubber spatula to scramble the eggs into large curds. When the eggs are still quite runny, turn off the stove and let them finish cooking in the residual heat of the pan until done to taste.

Better to undercook them here than overcook them; you can always turn the heat back on to finish them, but once they're overcooked, you're stuck.

POACHED TRADITIONALLY

Crack each egg into a separate cup or ramekin. Bring a few inches of water to a gentle simmer in a saucepan or a deep skillet with lid. I use the saucepan when I'm just doing a couple of eggs, and the skillet when I want more room to poach four to six eggs at a time.

When the water is barely simmering, slip the eggs, one at a time, into the water. Stir the water gently to help the egg white adhere to itself, then cover the pan and turn off the heat. Let sit for 4 minutes.

If the eggs aren't done yet, cover and let them cook until they are, checking at 20-second intervals. Use a slotted spoon to scoop out the eggs one by one. Pat the bottom of the spoon dry on a clean kitchen towel as you pick up each egg. This helps eliminate excess water.

If you want a neater-looking poached egg, you can crack it into a fine-mesh strainer before sliding it into the simmering water. This gets rid of the loose and runny parts of the egg white, which slither out into ragged wisps when they hit the water. I usually don't bother.

POACHED IN THE MICROWAVE

My favorite way to poach an egg or two is in the microwave. Crack one egg into a small glass or ceramic vessel. I use a 1-cup glass measuring cup. Cover the egg with a little cold water; just a couple of tablespoons will do it. Now, this part is trial and error—you need to get to know your microwave. I set mine for 80% power and cook the egg for about 45 to 50 seconds. If it needs more time, keep microwaving for 5 seconds at a time.

When done to taste, scoop your egg out of the cup with a slotted spoon, drying the bottom of the spoon on a dish towel. Repeat with other eggs if you have more than one. Don't try to poach more than one egg at a time. They won't cook evenly and you'll end up with some overcooked parts and some undercooked parts.

FRIED EGGS *with Chiles, Tamarind Sauce, and Crispy Shallots*

A tangy Malaysian-inspired way to serve fried eggs, the sweet and sour tamarind sauce is a nice foil for the richness of the yolk. But the real jewel of the dish is the garnish of crispy fried shallots, which turn sweet and crunchy and utterly irresistible. So even if they do require a pan full of hot oil to create, don't be tempted to skip them. You can, at least, make them the day before if you like; just be sure to reserve the shallot-flavored oil so you can use it to fry the eggs. I love to serve these eggs over a bed of rice, which happily absorbs the sauce and runny yolk. But a bed of salad greens lightly dressed with sesame oil and a little lime juice is nice, too.

3 tablespoons peanut oil

6 medium shallots (10 ounces total), thinly sliced

Fine sea salt to taste

2 tablespoons tamarind paste or concentrate

2 tablespoons Asian fish sauce

2 tablespoons light brown sugar

8 large eggs

Freshly ground black pepper

1 fresh hot red chile, seeded and minced

Fresh cilantro sprigs, for garnish

Cooked white, brown, or Coconut Rice (page 381), for serving

TOTAL TIME: 25 MINUTES
SERVES 4

1. Heat the peanut oil in a 9- to 10-inch skillet over medium heat. Add the shallots and cook gently, stirring occasionally, until they are well browned, 7 to 12 minutes (they will crisp up as they cool). Remove the skillet from the heat, and use a slotted spoon to transfer the shallots to a paper-towel-lined plate, leaving the shallot-flavored oil in the skillet. Sprinkle the shallots lightly with salt.

2. Place half of the fried shallots in a small saucepan and add the tamarind, fish sauce, brown sugar, and 3 tablespoons of water. Bring to a boil and cook until the sauce has the consistency of syrup, 3 to 5 minutes.

3. Return the skillet to medium-high heat, adding more oil if needed to fry the eggs. Crack in 4 eggs and sprinkle them with salt and pepper to taste. Once the edges of the whites are set (1 to 2 minutes), cover the skillet and cook for 1 to 2 minutes more, until the yolks are just set (or instead of covering the skillet, flip the eggs for over-easy if you'd rather). Transfer the eggs to serving plates. Fry the remaining 4 eggs in the same manner, adding more oil to the skillet if needed.

4. To serve, drizzle the eggs with the tamarind sauce. Garnish with the remaining fried shallots, the minced chile, and cilantro sprigs. Serve with rice.

OLIVE OIL–FRIED EGGS

with Scallions, Sage, and Turkish Red Pepper

When it comes to fried eggs, there are some people who prefer a pristine, pillowy white, without any trace of browning or crispness. I am not one of them. When I want a cushion of soft egg white, I poach. For me the perfect fried egg has a white that curls and ruffles as soon as it makes contact with the hot fat in the pan, turning lacy and crunchy at the edges while remaining plump and soft at the yolk, which should run like hot lava at the merest touch of your fork. This recipe achieves exactly that, using olive oil as the frying medium. But what really elevates this dish are the sweet fried scallions and woodsy fried sage leaves that get caught in the white. They turn a plain breakfast staple into an unusual and very quick dinner. Serve this with toasted country bread or flatbread, and maybe a big salad if you need some vegetables. Consider this a light dinner, for nights after you've had a big lunch, when you're peckish rather than starving.

1. Heat a heavy (preferably cast-iron) 10- to 12-inch skillet over medium-high heat for about a minute; then pour in the oil. The oil should thin out on contact (but not smoke—that's too hot). Add the sage leaves and let them sizzle for about 10 seconds. Then crack the eggs into the skillet on top of the sage leaves and season them with salt and pepper to taste. As the eggs fry, baste the egg whites with some of the oil from the bottom of the skillet to encourage cooking (you can add a little more oil if you need to).

2. When the edges of the eggs are curled, crisped, and browned, and the yolks are still wobbly, remove the skillet from the heat and sprinkle the Turkish pepper and the scallions over them. Carefully slide 2 eggs onto each plate, and top with the arugula, if using, and a few drops of lemon juice. Serve.

2 tablespoons extra-virgin olive oil

4 large fresh sage leaves

4 eggs

Fine sea salt and freshly ground black pepper

Ground Turkish or Aleppo red pepper

2 scallions (white and green parts), thinly sliced

Handful of baby arugula, for serving (optional)

Lemon wedge, for serving

TOTAL TIME: 15 MINUTES
SERVES 2

SHAKSHUKA

with Golden Tomatoes and Goat Cheese

The first time I ate *shakshuka*—a dish of eggs baked in a thick and spicy tomato-pepper sauce—it was in Israel. I visited during Passover, which was slightly problematic, gastronomically speaking, because there was no falafel, no hummus, no pita in observance of the holiday. Luckily, there was plenty of *shakshuka*. This version calls for yellow tomatoes instead of the usual red. Yellow tomatoes have less acidity, which makes this *shakshuka* mellow and sweet. That said, red tomatoes make a perfectly fine and zesty substitute if that's what you have on hand. This is a great place to use up slightly overripe tomatoes, maybe those in the leaky pile on your counter when you've over-bought in heirloom season. Happens to me all the time.

¼ cup extra-virgin olive oil

1 large yellow or red bell pepper, thinly sliced

1 small onion, diced

½ teaspoon kosher salt, plus more as needed

2 large garlic cloves, finely chopped

1 teaspoon ground cumin

1 teaspoon ground turmeric

1 teaspoon sweet paprika

⅛ teaspoon cayenne pepper

2 pounds very ripe yellow tomatoes (about 4 medium), diced

¼ teaspoon freshly ground black pepper, plus more as needed

4 ounces mild goat cheese, sliced or crumbled (1 cup)

3 tablespoons chopped fresh dill leaves, plus more for garnish

6 large eggs

Fresh pita breads, for serving

Fresh chives, for serving

TOTAL TIME: 40 MINUTES
SERVES 4

1. Heat the oven to 375°F.

2. Heat the olive oil in a 10- to 12-inch oven-safe skillet over medium-high heat. Add the pepper and onion and a pinch of salt. Reduce the heat to medium and cook, stirring, until the vegetables are tender, about 10 minutes. Then stir in the garlic, cumin, turmeric, paprika, and cayenne; cook until fragrant, about 1 minute.

3. Stir in the tomatoes, ½ teaspoon salt, and ¼ teaspoon black pepper. Cook, partially covered, until the tomatoes and pepper are very soft and have formed a thick sauce, about 15 minutes; if the sauce begins to stick to the pan before the tomatoes fully break down, stir in a splash of water. Stir in the goat cheese and the 3 tablespoons dill.

4. Crack the eggs over the surface of the tomato sauce. Season the eggs with salt and pepper to taste. Transfer the skillet to the oven and bake until the eggs are just barely set, 7 to 10 minutes. Garnish with dill, and serve with pita breads alongside.

SPANISH TORTILLA
with Serrano Ham

Ham is not traditional in a Spanish tortilla, but I love the way its salty meatiness imbues the thick omelet with a brawny character. In Spain, a tortilla is often served at room temperature, so feel free to do the same. You can prepare it up to six hours ahead; keep it at room temperature until ready to serve. Serve it plain, with aioli (see page 141), or with a thick and chunky tomato sauce.

    I find this easiest to make using two skillets: a larger one for the potatoes, and a medium-sized one for the tortilla itself. The wide pan gives me room to flip the potatoes without oil splattering the stove while the smaller one results in a thicker and more appealing tortilla. However, if dirtying two skillets is just too annoying, you can make the whole thing in one oven-proof 9-inch skillet.

1¼ pounds (5 medium) Yukon Gold potatoes, peeled, halved, and thinly sliced

1 white onion, diced

1¼ teaspoons kosher salt, plus more as needed

¾ teaspoon freshly ground black pepper, plus more as needed

About 1 cup extra-virgin olive oil (see Note)

6 large eggs

4 ounces Serrano ham, diced

2 scallions (white and green parts), thinly sliced

Fresh parsley leaves, for serving

Sherry vinegar, for serving

TOTAL TIME: 1 HOUR
SERVES 4 TO 6

1. Pat the potato slices dry with paper towels. In a bowl, toss the potatoes with the onion, 1 teaspoon of the salt, and ½ teaspoon of the pepper.

2. Heat a large skillet over medium heat. Add the oil, then add the potatoes and onions. (You need enough oil to almost cover the potatoes, so adjust the amount according to your pan size.) Cook until the potatoes are just tender enough to cut with a fork, 10 to 15 minutes, adjusting the heat so the vegetables do not burn or take on too much color. Using a slotted spoon, transfer the potatoes and onions to a colander set over a bowl to cool. Reserve 3½ tablespoons oil from the skillet to use for finishing the recipe. (You can reuse the rest of the remaining oil, too; store it in the refrigerator.)

3. Heat the oven to 375°F. Heat 2 tablespoons of the reserved oil in an 8- to 9-inch nonstick oven-safe skillet over medium-low heat. In a large bowl, whisk the eggs and

season them with the remaining salt and pepper. Stir the ham and the potato mixture into the eggs. Pour the mixture into the skillet and use a spatula to flatten out the surface. Cook, using the spatula to occasionally loosen the eggs from the edges of the pan, until the top is almost set, with just a small amount of liquid remaining, about 5 minutes.

4. Transfer the skillet to the oven and cook until the top is just set, 7 to 10 minutes. Slide the tortilla onto a plate. Garnish it with the sliced scallions, parsley leaves, a drizzle of sherry vinegar, and a drizzle of the remaining reserved olive oil.

NOTE: You'll need a large amount of oil for frying the potatoes, but most of it doesn't get absorbed, so don't let the quantity scare you. Added bonus: you can reuse the onion-scented oil for any future sautéing. It will keep in the fridge for months and goes particularly well with shrimp, chicken, and salmon, turning a very simple meal into a very flavorful one.

CHILAQUILES

with Tomatillo Salsa and Baked Eggs

This version of chilaquiles is a molten, lasagna-like casserole with a Mexican bent: it's just as compelling for brunch as it is for dinner, and you can even make the salsa and assemble the whole dish the night before. If you're running short on time or can't find fresh tomatillos or just aren't in the mood to make homemade salsa, feel free to substitute 2 cups of your favorite purchased salsa (tomatillo or otherwise) for the homemade stuff. This dish is all about the intersection of runny yolk meeting nubby tortillas meeting melty cheese, so as long as you maintain those elements, you've got a little room for cheating.

1. Heat the oven to 450°F. Lay the tortillas out on a baking sheet and brush tops with oil. Sprinkle with salt and bake until crisp, 15 to 20 minutes.

2. Make the salsa: Slice one onion half into ¼-inch-thick slabs (they will look like half-moons). Spread the tomatillos, onion slabs, garlic clove, and jalapeño and poblano halves out on a large rimmed baking sheet. Transfer the baking sheet to the oven along with the tortillas and dry-roast (without oil) until the tomatillos are lightly charred and bursting, 15 to 20 minutes. Don't worry if the onions and garlic aren't tender, as long as they have a little bit of color to them.

3. Transfer the vegetables to a food processor and add 1 cup of the chopped cilantro, the lime juice, and ½ teaspoon salt. Puree until smooth; the mixture should yield about 2 cups. Taste, and add more salt and/or lime juice if needed.

4. Reduce the oven temperature to 375°F.

5. Assemble the chilaquiles: Spoon some of the salsa over the bottom of a 9-inch square baking dish or a 1½- to 2-quart shallow gratin dish. Place a layer of tortillas on top. Spoon additional salsa and a handful of the cheese over the tortillas. Repeat the layering until all these ingredients have been used, ending with salsa, then cheese (reserving ½ cup cheese for garnish). Transfer the dish to the oven and bake for 20 minutes.

6. Crack the eggs into the baking dish in a single layer, and season them lightly with salt and pepper. Return the dish to the oven and bake until the eggs are lightly set but the centers are still runny, 6 to 10 minutes. Meanwhile, dice enough of the remaining onion to make ¼ cup, and combine it with the remaining ½ cup cilantro in a small bowl.

7. Serve the chilaquiles garnished with the onion-cilantro mixture, pepitas if using, reserved cheese, and, if desired, a dollop of sour cream.

8 6-inch corn tortillas

FOR THE TOMATILLO SALSA
1 small white onion, halved lengthwise

1½ pounds tomatillos, husks removed

1 fat garlic clove

1 jalapeño, halved lengthwise and seeded

1 poblano chile, stemmed, halved lengthwise, and seeded

Oil for brushing the tortillas

Kosher salt

1½ cups coarsely chopped fresh cilantro leaves and tender stems

TO ASSEMBLE THE CHILAQUILES
10 ounces Monterey Jack, grated

6 large eggs

Freshly ground black pepper, as needed

Toasted pepitas, for garnish (optional)

Sour cream or Mexican *crema*, as needed (optional)

TOTAL TIME: 1 HOUR
SERVES 4 TO 6

EGGS POACHED

in South Indian Purgatory

Eggs cooked in a piquant tomato sauce—whether it's *shakshuka*-style with sweet peppers and onions, or Italian-style eggs in purgatory, with garlic and crushed red chile flakes—is always a satisfying and relatively stress-free meal. As long as the eggs are gently simmered in a thick, savory sauce and emerge tender-yolked and intensely flavored, the result is always going to be delicious. In this recipe, I took the basic concept and applied an Indian sensibility, seasoning the tomato sauce with a fragrant mix of garam masala, ginger, and cumin. You can make the sauce up to five days ahead and store it in the fridge if you like; just reheat it gently before adding the eggs. Although toasted bread is the usual accompaniment for egg dishes like these, you might also try this over basmati rice, dolloped with yogurt, for something a little different.

FOR THE TOMATO SAUCE

3 tablespoons extra-virgin olive oil

1 large onion, diced

2 garlic cloves, minced

2 tablespoons finely chopped fresh cilantro stems

1 tablespoon finely chopped peeled fresh ginger

1 fresh red or green hot chile (use any kind you've got), seeded and finely chopped

2½ teaspoons garam masala

1 teaspoon ground cumin

1 teaspoon sweet paprika

1 28-ounce can diced tomatoes, with their juices

½ teaspoon kosher salt

FOR THE EGGS

6 large eggs

Kosher salt and freshly ground black pepper to taste

¼ cup chopped fresh cilantro leaves

TOTAL TIME: 40 MINUTES
SERVES 4 TO 6

1. **Prepare the sauce:** Heat the olive oil in a large skillet over medium heat. Add the onion and cook, stirring occasionally, until tender, 7 to 10 minutes. Stir in the garlic, cilantro stems, ginger, and chile; cook for 2 minutes. Then stir in the garam masala, cumin, and paprika, and cook until fragrant, about 1 minute more.

2. Pour the tomatoes into the skillet, and season with the salt. Bring to a simmer and cook until the tomatoes break down and the mixture is thick and saucy, about 20 minutes (if the pan seems dry, add a tablespoon or two of water).

3. **Add the eggs:** Gently crack the eggs onto the sauce, spacing them out a bit. Season with salt and pepper to taste. Cover the skillet and cook until the eggs are opaque but the yolks are still runny, 3 to 5 minutes. Garnish with the cilantro leaves before serving.

GREEN EGGS, NO HAM

(Baked Runny Eggs with Spinach, Leeks, and Feta)

Eggs baked on a soft bed of sautéed greens and leeks is an elegant dish, the kind of thing I can imagine being served at a fancy brunch at an English country house, *Downton Abbey*–style, maybe with some smoked salmon on the side. And that was my intention when I set out to make this. But then, as I was washing and chopping and putting the flavors together in my head, I couldn't resist the urge to spice it up a bit. I ended up adding funky feta, jalapeño, and cilantro to the greens, which gives it a lot more oomph than the discreet pinch of sweet paprika I had originally planned on. Now the dish is just as elegant, but a lot more flavorful. And you can still serve it with smoked salmon on the side, maybe accompanied by thinly sliced pumpernickel bread and good butter or cream cheese. Or, for a more substantial supper, try it spooned over buttery polenta (page 277).

1. Heat the oven to 375°F.

2. Melt the butter in a 10-inch oven-safe skillet over medium-high heat. Add the leeks, jalapeños, and garlic. Cook, stirring, until the ingredients have softened, about 5 minutes. Stir in the spinach, a handful at a time, and cook until almost wilted, about 2 minutes. Then toss in the cilantro and season with the ¼ teaspoon salt. Once all the greens have wilted, stir in ¼ cup of water and 3 ounces of the feta. Stir until the cheese is almost melted.

3. Carefully crack the eggs over the surface of the greens, and season with salt to taste. Transfer the skillet to the oven and bake until the eggs are just opaque but still jiggly, 7 to 10 minutes.

4. Remove the skillet from the oven. Top with the remaining feta and chopped cilantro. Sprinkle with hot sauce to taste, and with Aleppo pepper if using.

3 tablespoons unsalted butter

2 leeks (white and light green parts), thinly sliced

2 jalapeños, seeded and chopped

2 garlic cloves, finely chopped

10 ounces (2 quarts) baby spinach

2 cups fresh cilantro leaves, coarsely chopped, plus more as needed

¼ teaspoon salt, plus more as needed

4 ounces feta cheese, crumbled

6 large eggs

Hot sauce, as needed

Ground Aleppo pepper, as needed (optional)

TOTAL TIME: 25 MINUTES
SERVES 4

JAPANESE OMELET

with Edamame Rice

Before I procreated, I hardly ever ate *tamago* at Japanese restaurants, always going for the more obscure offerings like monkfish liver and uni. But as it goes with many small children, tamago is now part of Dahlia's standing order at our local sushi place, and I have to admit that I've come to deeply appreciate the way the gentle sweetness of the airy omelet contrasts with the warm and savory rice beneath it. This recipe, while not authentic, captures some of that experience. I've streamlined the technique (classic *tamago* requires a lot of precision and skill, as anyone who has ever seen *Jiro Dreams of Sushi* might know) but kept the flavor profile the same. A hit with most kids, it also makes fine comfort food for adults, especially when served with optional beads of salmon caviar for added texture and saltiness or a squirt of Sriracha for heat.

1. In a small bowl, whisk together the eggs, sugar, soy sauce, mirin, and salt.

2. Heat the sesame oil in a small nonstick skillet over medium-low heat. Add the egg mixture and cook until the underside is just set. Swirl the pan gently so the uncooked eggs in the center move to the outer edges of the skillet.

3. When the top of the omelet is almost dry, slide it onto a plate; then flip the plate over the skillet so the omelet lands back in the skillet top-side down; cook for about 1 minute more. (If you don't want to flip the omelet, you can stick the skillet, assuming it is oven-safe, under the broiler for 20 to 30 seconds to finish cooking the top.)

4. Slide the omelet onto a plate and roll it up into a tight cylinder. Slice the cylinder into rings. Stir the edamame into the rice, and serve the omelet rings over the edamame rice, garnished with salmon roe if using, and drizzled with a little soy sauce.

3 large eggs

2 teaspoons light brown or granulated sugar

1 teaspoon soy sauce, plus more for serving

1 teaspoon mirin

Pinch of kosher salt

2 teaspoons toasted sesame oil

Cooked shelled edamame, for serving

Cooked rice (sushi rice is ideal here), for serving

Salmon roe or Sriracha, for serving (optional)

TOTAL TIME: 15 MINUTES
SERVES 1 OR 2

ASPARAGUS FRITTATA
with Ricotta and Chives

Baking a frittata in a low oven gives it a creamy, custardy texture that's a lot silkier than the usual version, more like the soft center of a quiche rather than a fluffy, airy omelet. I also find baking a frittata easier to do—it's more hands-off, which is better especially if you are making it for its more traditional meal, brunch, and have guests milling around your kitchen drinking mimosas. This one, rich with ricotta and asparagus, is perfect for any springtime meal, breakfast through dinner. But you can substitute other vegetables for the asparagus during the rest of the year. Think peppers or corn kernels in summer, radicchio in fall, Brussels sprouts in winter. Just cook the vegetables until they are thoroughly wilted before adding the egg. They don't really cook much more once they hit the oven.

2 tablespoons unsalted butter

6 ounces asparagus, trimmed and cut into ½-inch pieces (¾ cup)

1 teaspoon kosher salt, plus more as needed

8 extra-large eggs

¼ teaspoon freshly ground black pepper, plus more as needed

½ cup fresh ricotta

2 tablespoons minced fresh chives

Extra-virgin olive oil, as needed

Fresh lemon juice, as needed

Grated Parmigiano-Reggiano cheese, as needed

Flaky sea salt, as needed

TOTAL TIME: 40 MINUTES
SERVES 4 TO 6

1. Position a rack near the top of the oven, and heat the oven to 300°F.

2. In a heavy well-seasoned cast-iron or nonstick oven-safe skillet (preferably 8- or 9-inch), heat the butter over medium heat. Add the asparagus and ¼ teaspoon of the kosher salt; cook until the asparagus is tender and browned in spots, about 5 minutes.

3. While the asparagus is cooking, whisk the eggs in a large bowl; stir in the remaining ¾ teaspoon kosher salt and the ¼ teaspoon black pepper.

4. Add the egg mixture to the skillet, stirring gently to incorporate the asparagus. Spoon dollops of ricotta over the top, and sprinkle with the chives. Cook until the bottom is just set, about 2 minutes.

5. Transfer the skillet to the oven, and bake until the eggs are set around the edges but still slightly custardy in the center, 12 to 15 minutes for a 9-inch skillet, 15 to 20 minutes for an 8-inch skillet (check frequently toward the end to avoid overcooking the eggs).

6. Slide the frittata out onto a plate. Drizzle olive oil and lemon juice over it to taste. Sprinkle Parmigiano-Reggiano, flaky salt, and additional black pepper on top, and serve.

GRUYÈRE FRITTATA
with Caramelized Onions

A low-and-slow frittata, this one's custard-like texture is suffused with a wintry filling of red-wine-caramelized onions and melted Gruyère cheese. It's vaguely reminiscent of French onion soup, in a solid, eggy form. This dish goes equally well with a salad of dark, hardy greens—arugula, kale, or spinach—as it does with a side of crispy, fatty bacon. Or serve it with both.

1. Position a rack near the top of the oven, and heat the oven to 300°F.

2. In a heavy nonstick oven-safe skillet (preferably 8- or 9-inch), heat the butter over medium heat. Add the onions and cook until they are starting to turn golden at the edges, about 5 minutes. Reduce the heat to low, add the bay leaf and a large pinch of fine sea salt, and continue to cook, stirring occasionally, until the onions become nicely browned, about 15 minutes longer. Add the wine and stir until it has reduced by half, about 3 minutes. Taste, and add more salt if needed.

3. While the onions are cooking, whisk the eggs in a bowl and add the cheese, olive oil, the ½ teaspoon fine sea salt, and the pepper.

4. Remove the bay leaf from the onions and add the egg mixture to the skillet, stirring gently to incorporate the onions. Cook until the bottom is just set, about 2 minutes.

5. Transfer the skillet to the oven, and bake until the eggs are set around the edges but still slightly custardy in the center, 12 to 15 minutes for a 9-inch skillet, 15 to 20 minutes for an 8-inch skillet (check frequently toward the end to avoid overcooking the eggs). Slide the frittata out onto a plate, sprinkle it with parsley and flaky sea salt, and serve.

2 tablespoons unsalted butter

2 medium onions, sliced

1 bay leaf

½ teaspoon fine sea salt, plus more as needed

¼ cup dry red wine

8 extra-large eggs

1 cup grated Gruyère cheese

1 tablespoon extra-virgin olive oil

¼ teaspoon freshly ground black pepper

Chopped fresh parsley, for garnish

Flaky sea salt, for garnish

TOTAL TIME: 40 MINUTES
SERVES 4 TO 6

SCALLION FRITTATA CROSTINI *with Olives and Herbs*

This is an unusually wonderful way to serve frittata. Instead of being sliced into wedges, the eggy, scallion-studded cake is cut into thin ribbons, then piled onto olive oil–doused toast along with olives and fresh herbs to make crostini. Serve it on large pieces of toast—maybe cut from a boule or country-style loaf—for an entrée, or on small slices of toasted baguette as an hors d'oeuvre. You can bake the frittata a couple of hours before serving. Keep it at room temperature and slice just before piling it on the toasted bread.

In spring, try this with ramps or spring onions in place of the scallions.

1. Position a rack near the top of the oven, and heat the oven to 300°F.

2. Cut the scallions in half lengthwise; then cut each half into 3-inch lengths.

3. In a heavy, nonstick oven-safe skillet (preferably 8- or 9-inch), heat the olive oil over medium-high heat. Add the scallions and cook until they are tender and well browned in spots, 3 to 5 minutes. Season with salt to taste.

4. While the scallions cook, whisk the eggs in a large bowl; stir in the ½ teaspoon salt and black pepper to taste.

5. Add the egg mixture to the skillet, stirring gently to incorporate the scallions. Transfer the skillet to the oven and bake until the eggs are set, 5 to 8 minutes.

6. Remove the skillet from the oven and slide the frittata out onto a plate. Slice the frittata into ¼-inch-wide ribbons.

7. Rub the toasted bread slices with the garlic halves and drizzle with olive oil. Top the toasts with the frittata ribbons. Drizzle with lemon juice and additional olive oil, and then scatter the olives and herbs on top.

6 scallions (white and green parts), trimmed and left whole

2 tablespoons extra-virgin olive oil, plus more for drizzling

½ teaspoon fine sea salt, plus more as needed

4 extra-large eggs

Freshly ground black pepper to taste

4 to 6 slices crusty bread, toasted

1 garlic clove, halved

Fresh lemon juice, for serving

Pitted Kalamata olives, thinly sliced, for serving

Chopped mixed fresh herbs, such as parsley, dill, mint, and cilantro, for serving

TOTAL TIME: 25 MINUTES
SERVES 4 AS A MAIN COURSE
8 AS AN HORS D'OEUVRE

SCRAMBLED EGGS

with Roasted Green Chiles and Cheddar

We make a lot of "egg tacos" (scrambled eggs stuffed into tortillas and topped with salsa and avocado) in our house for lunch when my husband and I are both working from home. It's a super-fast meal that's packed with protein and extremely tasty. This is the (slightly) more elaborate, company-worthy dinner version, made with charred green chiles and garlic, which add a smoky flavor to the softly scrambled, cheesy eggs. You can roll the mixture up into tacos, or serve warmed tortillas alongside. Challah may seem like a rogue accompaniment to this Tex-Mex–inspired dish, but toasted slices of the braided egg bread are fantastic here—rich, buttery, and sublime against the chile spice.

1 poblano or 3 jalapeños, halved, seeded, and cut into 1-inch pieces

4 garlic cloves, smashed and peeled

1 tablespoon unsalted butter

10 large eggs

½ teaspoon fine sea salt

⅔ cup shredded cheddar cheese

Smoked paprika, either sweet or hot, to taste (optional)

Sliced tomato, for serving

Sliced avocado, for serving

Fresh cilantro leaves, for serving

TOTAL TIME: 20 MINUTES
SERVES 4 TO 6

1. Heat a large skillet over medium-high heat. Add the poblano or jalapeños and garlic, and dry-roast (without oil), stirring frequently, until they are lightly charred all over, about 5 minutes. Reduce the heat to medium, cover the skillet, and continue to cook, shaking the pan every now and then to prevent burning, until the chile and garlic are tender, about 5 minutes. Transfer the chile and garlic to a cutting board, let them cool slightly, and then coarsely chop them.

2. In a large nonstick skillet, heat the butter over medium-low heat until it has melted. In a medium bowl, beat the eggs and salt together. Pour the eggs into the skillet and cook, stirring frequently to create large curds. When the eggs start to set, add the chile, garlic, and cheese. Continue to cook until the eggs have set but are still soft. Sprinkle with smoked paprika if desired, and serve with sliced tomato, sliced avocado, and cilantro leaves.

FROGS & TOADS *in a Hole*

Breakfast sausages are the frogs, eggs are the toads, toast makes the holes. And all are layered together and baked into a cheese-laden casserole, spiked with hot sauce. It's grown-up comfort food at its best. Serve it for brunch or for a homey Sunday supper with a salad on the side.

1. Heat the oven to 350°F. Using a 2-inch cookie cutter or a knife, cut a 2-inch hole in the center of 4 slices of the bread. In a large, wide bowl, whisk together 4 eggs, the milk, the salt, and the hot sauce. Add the toast, including the cut-out pieces, to the bowl of custard and let soak 10 minutes.

2. Place a 10-inch oven-safe skillet over medium-high heat. Add the olive oil and sausage; cook, breaking the meat up with a spoon, until it starts to brown, about 3 minutes. Add the scallions and the thyme if using, and cook for 2 more minutes, reducing the heat if necessary to prevent burning. Remove the skillet from the heat.

3. Press the uncut toast slices onto the bottom of the skillet, on top of the sausages, and arrange the cut-out holes around the pieces of toast, creating an even layer in the bottom of the pan. Top with the remaining toasts and any cutouts that didn't fit in the bottom layer. Pour any remaining custard over the top. Bake for 15 minutes.

4. Crack one of the 4 remaining eggs into each hole, and sprinkle the eggs lightly with salt and pepper. Top with an even layer of the grated cheese. Return the skillet to the oven and bake until the eggs are barely set, about 15 minutes. Let cool for a few minutes, and then serve with more hot sauce if you like.

8 slices white or soft whole-wheat bread, toasted

8 large eggs

1½ cups whole milk

½ teaspoon kosher salt, plus more as needed

1 teaspoon hot sauce, plus more for serving

2 tablespoons extra-virgin olive oil

10 ounces breakfast sausage, casings removed

3 scallions (white and green parts), sliced

1 tablespoon fresh thyme leaves (optional)

Freshly ground black pepper, as needed

3 ounces Gruyère cheese, grated (¾ cup)

TOTAL TIME: 1 HOUR
SERVES 4 TO 6

SCRAMBLED EGGS

with Smoked Fish and Cream Cheese

Salty, fishy, and wonderfully creamy, this hits the same notes as my childhood brunch staple of lox-eggs-and-onions. But instead of lox, here I use smoked trout. And instead of onions, I stir chunks of mellow cream cheese into the eggs. The time-honored concept of scrambling eggs with smoked fish remains, though, and this is still excellent served with a bagel. Or, try thin slices of toasted, buttered pumpernickel bread for something a little more refined.

1. Melt the butter in a nonstick skillet over medium-low heat. In a small bowl beat the eggs with the salt; pour the eggs into the skillet. Scatter the cream cheese over the eggs and stir with a wooden spoon every 10 seconds or so until large, soft curds form, 30 seconds to 1 minute.

2. When the eggs appear almost set but are still slightly runny, remove the skillet from the heat. Fold in the trout, chives, and black pepper. Let the eggs stand until they are softly cooked, about 1 minute more. Serve topped with the salmon roe if using, and with toast on the side.

1 tablespoon unsalted butter

4 large eggs

Pinch of fine sea salt

1 ounce cream cheese, cut into small dice (about 2 tablespoons)

3 ounces smoked trout, flaked

1 tablespoon fresh chives

½ teaspoon freshly ground black pepper

Salmon or trout roe (optional)

Buttered toast or bagels, for serving

TOTAL TIME: 15 MINUTES
SERVES 2

EGG CROSTINI
with Radish and Anchovy

Fancier than your typical mayo-slathered egg salad, these open-faced sandwiches get a pungent, saline smack from anchovies and capers and a little crunch from the radish. I love to trot out this combination as an hors d'oeuvre, piling the eggs et al. onto small, thin slices of baguette. But for a light supper, late-night snack, or lunch, a crusty country loaf is a better, heartier option. In either case, it's important to use really good ingredients here since the flavor completely depends on them. Seek out farmer's market eggs, imported anchovies packed in olive oil, and good high-fat butter. Although all of this might seem overly precious, these details really matter when you're serving them practically naked. Try it and see.

4 large eggs, hard-cooked, peeled, and sliced (see page 148)

Fine sea salt

4 ½-inch-thick slices country-style bread or 8 slices baguette

2 garlic cloves, halved crosswise

Fancy salted butter, at room temperature, as needed

1 medium watermelon radish or 4 small radishes, thinly sliced

Extra-virgin olive oil, as needed

4 to 6 oil-packed anchovy fillets

4 teaspoons drained capers

Fresh lemon juice, as needed

Freshly ground black pepper to taste

Sliced scallion greens, for garnish (optional)

TOTAL TIME: 20 MINUTES
SERVES 2

1. Sprinkle the egg slices lightly with salt and set them aside.

2. Toast the bread, and rub the cut sides of the garlic over the hot toasts. Let the toasts cool for a minute or two; then slather the tops thickly with butter. You want the toast to be cool enough so that the butter doesn't melt but stays creamy. Layer the egg and radish slices over the butter, and drizzle with olive oil. Top with the anchovy fillets and capers. Sprinkle with lemon juice and season with black pepper. Drizzle with additional olive oil. Garnish with sliced scallions if using.

HERBED PARMESAN
DUTCH BABY

Golden, crunchy, and covered in a salty, *frico*-like layer of baked Parmesan, this is sort of like a giant *gougère*-style cheese puff meets Yorkshire pudding, with a crisp outer crust and a soft, cheesy, custardy interior. If you're not shy (or not serving this to a shy group), feel free to tear this apart with your hands to eat, licking the salty bits of cheese and herbs off your fingers when you're done (if this is too tactile for you, use a large spoon for serving). You can serve this for dinner with a big salad or with some kind of roasted meat, or try it for brunch in place of the usual sweet and fruity Dutch babies that people expect. Or, for something completely out of the box, this also happens to make a fantastic cocktail nosh—serve it right out of the oven, still in the pan, to your guests and let them tear off pieces. It's quite delicious with a gin martini.

1. Heat the oven to 425°F.

2. In a large bowl, whisk together the flour, salt, and pepper. In a separate bowl, whisk together the eggs and milk. Whisk the eggs into the flour mixture until just combined. Then stir in the thyme and chives.

3. Melt the butter in a 12-inch cast-iron or other oven-safe skillet over medium-high heat. Continue to cook until the butter smells nutty and turns brown, 5 to 7 minutes; then swirl the skillet so the butter coats the bottom of the pan.

4. Pour the batter into the skillet, and scatter the cheese and flaky sea salt over the top. Bake until the Dutch baby is puffed and golden, 20 to 25 minutes. Baking it a little less gives a softer interior though less rise; baking it a little more gives you more puff and a drier interior; both ways are good.

5. Serve immediately, garnished with thyme and chives, and with Sriracha and/or lemon wedges on the side if desired.

1 cup plus 2 tablespoons all-purpose flour

½ teaspoon kosher salt

½ teaspoon freshly ground black pepper

8 large eggs

¾ cup whole milk

2 tablespoons finely chopped fresh thyme leaves, plus more for garnish

2 tablespoons minced fresh chives or tarragon, plus more for garnish

6 tablespoons unsalted butter

¾ cup grated Parmesan cheese

Flaky sea salt, for garnish

Sriracha and/or lemon wedges, for serving (optional)

TOTAL TIME: 45 MINUTES
SERVES 4 TO 6

PASTA
& NOODLES

STOVETOP MAC & CHEESE

If your go-to mac and cheese comes from a box, this recipe just might change your life. Not only is it as quick to make as the boxed stuff, it's also about a thousand times tastier, and adults like it as much as kids do.

The trick here is to whisk the cheeses into the heavy cream, which instantly turns into the most velvety, luscious cheese sauce you can imagine. Don't fear the cream! Although we've been trained to think that heavy cream is a fatty devil, it's not inherently bad for you as long as you don't chug it straight from the carton (though I have been known to take tiny sips here and there). Plus, if you can find cream from 100 percent grass-fed cows, the omega-3–rich fat is actually beneficial. And, if you think about the fact that most mac and cheese recipes rely on butter-and-flour-rich béchamels, heavy cream is both lighter—it's only a couple of tablespoons per serving—and a whole lot simpler. It really does make for a delicious sauce. (Pro-cream rant over.)

I started making this for my daughter, Dahlia, as soon as she turned one, using whole-wheat pasta. Now, as much as she'd like me to buy the mac and cheese with the bunny on the box out of allegiance to small and furry creatures, she greatly prefers my version. It's a small victory over processed foods, but I'll take it.

Kosher salt, as needed

8 ounces regular or whole-wheat elbow macaroni

⅓ cup heavy cream

1¼ cups grated cheddar cheese (5 ounces)

Freshly grated nutmeg to taste

Freshly ground black pepper to taste

TOTAL TIME: 15 MINUTES
SERVES 2 OR 3

1. Bring a large pot of heavily salted water to a boil. Add the macaroni and cook until it is al dente, about 1 minute less than the package directions. Drain.

2. Return the empty pot to medium-high heat. Add the cream, and cook until it is thick, bubbling, and reduced by half, about 2 minutes. Stir in the cheese, whisking until it has melted. Then stir in the pasta and cook until well combined. Season to taste with nutmeg and pepper, add more salt if needed, and serve.

STOVETOP FUSILLI

with Spinach, Peas, and Gruyère

Similar to the basic mac and cheese on the facing page, the peas, spinach, and a touch of garam masala give this a more sophisticated flavor without much additional effort. This is the kind of thing to make after a particularly exhausting day when you're craving a comforting, vegetable-loaded, and cheesy one-pot dinner that comes together in minutes. It also makes a terrific side dish to grilled steak or roasted chicken, one that vegetarians in your group can call dinner. Feel free to play with the cheeses and seasonings here. Any firm grating cheese—cheddar, gouda, a young pecorino—can be substituted for the Gruyère, and chile powder, nutmeg, or cumin will work in place of the garam masala.

1. Bring a large pot of heavily salted water to a boil. Add the fusilli and cook until it is al dente, about 1 minute less than the package directions. If using fresh peas, stir them in 3 minutes before the pasta is done; if using frozen peas, 1 minute will suffice. Drain.

2. Return the empty pot to medium-high heat. Add the heavy cream and cook until it is thick, bubbling, and reduced by half, 2 to 3 minutes.

3. Stir in the cheese, whisking until it has melted. Then stir in the baby spinach until wilted. Add the pasta and peas to the mixture. Season with ¾ teaspoon salt, the garam masala, and black pepper to taste.

Kosher salt, as needed

1 pound regular or whole-wheat fusilli

1½ cups fresh or frozen peas

½ cup heavy cream

9 ounces Gruyère cheese, grated (2¼ cups)

10 ounces baby spinach (10 cups loosely packed), coarsely chopped

⅛ teaspoon garam masala

Freshly ground black pepper to taste

TOTAL TIME: 10 MINUTES
SERVES 6

PENNE *with Parmesan, Fresh Ricotta, and Black Pepper*

Combining black pepper, nutmeg, and crunchy Demerara sugar as a seasoning for a savory dish is a medieval technique that I picked up from reading a lot of culinary history back in graduate school, and it makes this creamy noodle dish hot, fragrant, and just a bit sweet all at once. Or, coming from another frame of reference entirely, this also reminds me of noodles with cottage cheese and cinnamon sugar, one of those Eastern European Jewish comfort-food staples of my childhood.

I particularly love the way the milky ricotta coats the pasta, while the grated lemon zest adds an aromatic high note. Make sure to finish this with a lot of freshly milled pepper. That musky hit of spice is nicely bracing against all the creaminess. Serve it with something crunchy and green on a weeknight (Quick-Roasted Broccoli or Cauliflower, page 382, would be nice), or make it an unexpected first course at a dinner party.

Kosher salt, as needed

8 ounces penne or other short-cut pasta

½ cup heavy cream

½ cup grated Parmigiano-Reggiano cheese (2 ounces)

¾ teaspoon freshly ground black pepper, plus more as needed

¾ cup fresh ricotta (6 ounces)

Finely grated zest of 1 lemon

Pinch of freshly grated nutmeg or ground cinnamon

Demerara sugar, for sprinkling (optional)

TOTAL TIME: 15 MINUTES
SERVES 2 OR 3

1. Bring a large pot of heavily salted water to a boil. Add the penne and cook until it is al dente. Drain.

2. Return the empty pot to medium-high heat. Add the heavy cream and cook until it is thick, bubbling, and reduced by half, 2 to 3 minutes.

3. Whisk in the Parmigiano-Reggiano and the ¾ teaspoon pepper. Stir in the pasta, ½ cup of the ricotta, the lemon zest, and the nutmeg. Heat until warm. Season with salt to taste.

4. Serve, topped with the remaining ¼ cup ricotta and additional black pepper. Sprinkle very lightly with Demerara if you like.

SUMMER SPAGHETTI

with Uncooked Tomato Sauce and Ricotta

If a pile of the first really gorgeous summer tomatoes makes your feet start twitching into one of those embarrassing happy dances that you sometimes accidentally do at the farmer's market (much to the consternation of your progeny), you'll understand what I mean when I say that I can't bear cooking early-season tomatoes. By late August or September, I'll reconsider. But until then, this raw tomato-sauced pasta is what I like to make. An added bonus is that a raw tomato sauce is faster and easier than even the simplest cooked one. All I do is grate the tomato flesh into a bowl, then enrich the light, sweet pureed pulp with crumbled ricotta salata for brininess, fresh ricotta for creaminess, plus a large handful of fresh soft herbs. This dish works served both warm or at room temperature, if you want to make it an hour or two ahead. If you do, don't add the herbs until just before you serve it or they'll wilt.

1. Using the coarse side of a box grater, grate the tomatoes (starting with a cut side) over a large bowl until you reach the skin; the tomato pulp will disintegrate into the bowl. Discard the skin. Stir the ¼ cup olive oil, the 1 teaspoon salt, garlic if you like, and the chile flakes into the tomato pulp, and let it stand while you cook the pasta.

2. Bring a large pot of heavily salted water to a boil. Add the spaghetti and cook until al dente, usually about 1 minute less than the package directions; drain well.

3. Toss the hot pasta with the raw tomato sauce; then mix in the ricotta salata and herbs. Spoon onto plates and serve, topped with dollops of fresh ricotta, a sprinkling of sea salt, and a drizzle of olive oil.

12 ounces very ripe, soft tomatoes, halved though their equators (2 to 3 medium)

¼ cup good-quality extra-virgin olive oil, plus more for drizzling

1 teaspoon kosher salt, plus more as needed

1 garlic clove, grated on a Microplane or minced (optional)

½ teaspoon red chile flakes, or to taste

1 pound spaghetti

5 ounces ricotta salata, crumbled

2 cups mixed soft fresh herbs, such as basil, mint, and chives, torn into pieces

Fresh ricotta, for serving

Sea salt, for serving

TOTAL TIME: 20 MINUTES
SERVES 4

CACIO E PEPE

with Asparagus and Peas

As any Italian food lover will tell you, there's no improving upon a perfect *cacio e pepe*—pasta tossed with tangy aged cheese and plenty of black pepper. But in springtime when asparagus and peas are in season, even Romans aren't above occasionally tossing them into the pan. This is a fairly rich pasta, so think light when planning the rest of the meal. A bitter green salad made with arugula or dandelion works well, with maybe some vivid, springy flavor of sorbet (lemon, rhubarb, or strawberry) for dessert.

If you can't find Pecorino Toscano, you can use a Manchego, or more of the Parmesan.

1. Bring a large pot of heavily salted water to a boil. Add the spaghetti and cook until it is just shy of al dente, about 2 minutes less than the package directions (it should be slightly underdone to your taste because you'll finish cooking it in the sauce). During the last minute of cooking, add the asparagus and peas. Drain, reserving ½ cup of the pasta cooking water.

2. In a 12-inch skillet, melt 1 tablespoon of the butter and add the pepper. Sauté until fragrant, about 1 minute. Add ¼ cup of the reserved pasta water and the remaining 1 tablespoon butter to the skillet. Stir until the butter has melted and the sauce is beginning to thicken, about 30 seconds.

3. Add the pasta, peas, asparagus, and all three cheeses, and toss until the cheese has melted and the pasta has finished cooking, about 1 minute. Add more of the reserved pasta water if the skillet seems dry. Season with coarse sea salt to taste. Serve, sprinkling each portion with more cheese and drizzling it with olive oil. Garnish with the chives.

NOTE: If you can find only thicker asparagus, slice them ¼ inch thick instead of cutting 1-inch lengths.

Kosher salt, as needed

8 ounces spaghetti or linguine

8 ounces pencil-thin asparagus, cut into 1-inch pieces (about 1 cup) (see Note)

⅔ cup English peas (thawed if frozen)

2 tablespoons unsalted butter

½ tablespoon very coarsely ground black pepper

1 ounce young pecorino, such as Pecorino Toscano, shredded (¼ cup), plus more for serving

1 ounce Pecorino Romano, shredded (¼ cup), plus more for serving

2 ounces Parmesan cheese, grated (½ cup), plus more for serving

Coarse sea salt to taste

Extra-virgin olive oil, for serving

Snipped fresh chives, preferably with blossoms, for garnish

TOTAL TIME: 20 MINUTES
SERVES 2 OR 3

FETTUCCINE

with Spicy Anchovy Bread Crumbs

There are some pasta-with-anchovies recipes in which the little brown fish fade into the background, melding seamlessly into the sauce, adding complexity without screaming their presence. Not so here, where they pretty much bask in the spotlight, with the lemony butter sauce accentuating all their fishy, salty glory, while toasted bread crumbs add a pleasant crunch. It's a super-simple dish with a big personality.

Kosher salt, as needed

8 ounces fettuccine or linguine

2 tablespoons extra-virgin olive oil

½ cup panko bread crumbs

3 tablespoons unsalted butter

6 to 10 oil-packed anchovy fillets, coarsely chopped

Finely grated zest of ½ lemon

Juice of ½ lemon, or more to taste

Chopped fresh parsley, as needed (optional)

TOTAL TIME: 20 MINUTES
SERVES 2 OR 3

1. Bring a large pot of heavily salted water to a boil. Add the pasta and cook until it is just shy of al dente (it should be slightly underdone to your taste because you'll finish cooking it in the sauce). Drain.

2. While the pasta cooks, heat the olive oil in a 10-inch skillet over medium heat. Add the panko and toast until dark golden, 5 to 7 minutes. Transfer the panko to a bowl.

3. Return the skillet to medium heat, and add the butter, anchovies, and lemon zest. Cook, breaking up the anchovies with a fork, until the mixture is well combined.

4. Add the pasta to the anchovy mixture, and toss until it finishes cooking through, about 1 minute. Remove the skillet from the heat, add the lemon juice and the bread crumbs, and toss well. Garnish with parsley if desired, and serve.

PAPPARDELLE BOLOGNESE
with Lentils and Sausages

I first envisioned this recipe without the sausage, as a warm-your-bones vegetarian pasta option for the depths of winter. And it was very good. But adding a little sausage made it great—the brawny flavor of the meat giving the lentils a deep complexity that makes them even richer and a little creamier. This said, you can make this without the meat, though don't stint on adding oil at the end to compensate for the loss of richness. Serve this with a sautéed, strongly flavored leafy green—kale, broccoli rabe, or even radicchio. And open a really nice bottle of red.

1. Heat the olive oil in a 12-inch skillet over medium heat. Add the sausage and onion, and cook until the onion has softened, 5 minutes. Stir in the carrot and celery. Cook until the onion is well browned and all the vegetables are tender, about 20 minutes. If the pan seems dry, add a bit more oil.

2. Stir in the rosemary, sage, garlic, and chile flakes. Cook until fragrant, 2 minutes. Then stir in the tomato paste and allow it to brown, 1 to 2 minutes.

3. Add the tomatoes and 1½ cups of water. Use a spoon to break up the tomatoes. Stir in the lentils, the 1½ teaspoons salt, and the ½ teaspoon pepper. Bring to a simmer, and cook gently until the lentils are tender, 40 to 60 minutes,

depending on the age of your lentils. (If the skillet begins to dry out, add more water as needed.) Cover to keep warm.

4. Bring a large pot of heavily salted water to a boil. Add the pappardelle and cook until it is al dente, usually 1 minute less than the package directions. Scoop out some of the pasta cooking water with a coffee mug, and reserve it. Drain the pasta and transfer it to a large serving bowl. Toss with the butter if desired, and then add a splash of the pasta cooking water, the lentil-sausage sauce, and the cheese. Drizzle with additional olive oil just before serving, and garnish with the parsley and more black pepper.

5 tablespoons extra-virgin olive oil, plus more as needed

8 ounces sweet Italian sausage (either pork or turkey), casings removed

1 small onion, diced

1 small carrot, diced

1 celery stalk, diced

1 tablespoon finely chopped fresh rosemary leaves

1 tablespoon finely chopped fresh sage leaves

4 garlic cloves, finely chopped

Pinch of red chile flakes

1½ tablespoons tomato paste

1 28-ounce can whole plum tomatoes, with their juices

¾ cup French green lentils (*lentilles du Puy*)

1½ teaspoons kosher salt, plus more as needed

½ teaspoon freshly ground black pepper, plus more as needed

1 pound pappardelle or other wide ribbon pasta

2 tablespoons butter (optional)

1 cup grated Parmigiano-Reggiano cheese, plus more if desired

Chopped fresh parsley or chives, for garnish

TOTAL TIME: 1¼ TO 1½ HOURS
SERVES 4 TO 6

FUSILLI *with Burst Cherry Tomatoes, Mints, and Burrata*

Adding a few tablespoons of fresh herbs to pasta is status quo. Pretty much everyone has done it. But this recipe is different. Here, I add a few *cups* of herbs to what is otherwise a fairly classic pasta with tomatoes and fresh mozzarella. The combination of mint and scallions stays crisp and distinct rather than melting into the sauce, and gives each bite a bright pungency against the al dente pasta and warm, gooey cheese (use Burrata if you can get it). It's one of my favorite summer pasta dishes. And after my guests get over the shock of all that greenery covering their pasta, they go nuts for it, too.

Kosher salt, as needed

1 pound fusilli

2 tablespoons extra-virgin olive oil, plus more for drizzling

6 garlic cloves, smashed and peeled

¼ teaspoon red chile flakes

Fine sea salt to taste

1 quart cherry or grape tomatoes, halved

3 tablespoons unsalted butter

4 ounces Parmigiano-Reggiano cheese, grated (1 cup)

8 ounces Burrata or buffalo mozzarella, torn into bite-sized chunks, for serving

3 cups fresh mint leaves (or use a combination of basil and mint), torn

6 scallions (white and green parts), thinly sliced

Flaky sea salt to taste

Freshly ground black pepper to taste

TOTAL TIME: 20 MINUTES
SERVES 4 TO 6

1. Bring a large pot of heavily salted water to a boil. Add the fusilli and cook until it is 2 minutes shy of al dente (it should be slightly underdone to your taste because you'll finish cooking it with the tomatoes). Drain the pasta, reserving ½ cup of the cooking water.

2. While the pasta is cooking, heat a 12-inch skillet over medium-high heat. Add the olive oil. Stir in the garlic, chile flakes, and a large pinch of fine sea salt. Cook until fragrant, 1 to 2 minutes. Add the tomatoes and cook until they burst, turn golden at the edges, and shrivel slightly, 5 to 8 minutes.

3. Add the pasta to the skillet and toss it with the tomatoes. If the mixture looks dry, add a little of the reserved pasta cooking water, a few tablespoons at a time. Raise the heat to high and cook until the pasta finishes cooking in the sauce. Add the butter and Parmigiano-Reggiano, and toss until they melt and coat everything.

4. Divide the pasta among warmed pasta bowls. Garnish each portion with chunks of Burrata, and top with a generous mound of fresh mint and scallions. Drizzle with olive oil, and sprinkle with flaky sea salt and lots of black pepper.

FARRO PASTA

with Zucchini, Mint, and Ricotta Salata

Most people think of farro—an ancient variety of wheat—as an excellent whole grain to toss into snappy, textured salads. And it is. But when ground to a flour, it also makes a nutty, earthy pasta that's similar to whole-wheat, but with a smoother, finer texture. Here I mix it with seared zucchini, garlic, and cherry tomatoes, and a shower of crumbled ricotta salata to make for something a little like a warm pasta salad, though creamier and juicier. Don't skimp on the lemon juice at the end; this dish really needs that spark of acid against the sweetness of the vegetables. If you can't find ricotta salata, use feta instead.

1. Bring a large pot of heavily salted water to a boil. Add the pasta and cook until it is al dente; don't overcook it, you want a little texture here. Drain.

2. While the pasta is cooking, grate the lemon zest. Then quarter the bald lemon and seed the quarters. Set the lemon zest and wedges aside.

3. Place a 12-inch skillet over medium-high heat, add the olive oil, and let it heat for 30 seconds. Then add the zucchini pieces in a single layer, and cook without touching or moving them for 5 minutes (do this in batches if necessary). Stir in the garlic and thyme sprigs, flip the zucchini over, and cook for 3 more minutes, stirring occasionally.

4. Add the tomatoes and ½ teaspoon salt to the skillet, and cook until the tomatoes start to break down, 6 to 7 minutes. Stir in the pasta, ricotta salata, and lemon zest. Season with freshly cracked black pepper, and serve garnished with a drizzle of good olive oil, plus a sprinkling of fresh thyme leaves and ricotta salata, with the lemon wedges alongside.

Kosher salt, as needed

8 ounces short farro, whole-wheat, or regular pasta, such as penne, fusilli, or rigatoni

1 lemon

2 tablespoons extra-virgin olive oil, plus some good oil for drizzling

2 small, slim zucchini (about 12 ounces total), trimmed, quartered lengthwise, and cut into 1½-inch pieces

4 garlic cloves, smashed and peeled

6 sprigs fresh thyme, plus more thyme leaves for serving

1 pint cherry or grape tomatoes, halved

2 ounces ricotta salata, crumbled, plus more for serving

Freshly cracked black pepper to taste

TOTAL TIME: 25 MINUTES
SERVES 2 OR 3

ORECCHIETTE

with Broccoli Rabe and Almonds

Broccoli rabe has a pronounced bitterness that is soothed and mellowed by starchy pasta. Usually, I add bacon or a strong pork sausage laced with fennel to the pan, both of which can hold their own next to the intensity of the rabe. But for meatless meals, sautéed sliced almonds take this dish in an entirely different direction, adding crunch and a mild sweetness. That allows the broccoli rabe to really dominate, mitigated only a little by some nicely browned caramelized onion. It's a clean, light pasta that can be either a vegetarian main dish or a wintry pasta course before a meal of simple roasted chicken or meat. Kale lovers can substitute it for the rabe; just don't use the stems.

1. Bring a large pot of heavily salted water to a boil. Drop in the broccoli rabe stems and cook for 30 seconds; then drop in the leaves and cook for another 30 seconds. Remove the stems and greens with tongs or a slotted spoon, and drain them in a colander.

2. Return the water to a boil. Add the orecchiette and cook until it is not quite al dente, about 2 minutes less than the package directions (it should be slightly underdone to your taste because you'll finish cooking it in the sauce). Drain well, reserving ½ cup of the cooking water.

3. Place a 12-inch skillet over medium heat. Add the almonds and toast, tossing them occasionally, until golden, about 5 minutes. Transfer the almonds to a small bowl.

4. Return the skillet to the stove, raise the heat to medium-high, and add 1 tablespoon of the olive oil. Add the onion and cook, tossing occasionally, until browned, about 10 minutes. Stir in the garlic and chile flakes, and cook until the garlic is lightly colored, about 1 minute. Add the remaining 3 tablespoons olive oil and the broccoli rabe; cook for 1 minute. Then stir in the pasta and ¼ cup of the reserved pasta water. Season generously with salt. Cook, tossing, until the pasta is hot and has finished cooking, about 1 minute. Make sure to scrape the browned bits from the bottom of the skillet and toss them with the pasta.

5. Serve, topped with Parmigiano-Reggiano if desired, a sprinkling of lemon juice, and a drizzle of good olive oil.

Kosher salt, as needed

1 pound broccoli rabe, trimmed, stems and leaves separated and cut into 2-inch pieces

12 ounces orecchiette

½ cup sliced almonds

4 tablespoons extra-virgin olive oil, plus good oil for drizzling

1 medium red onion, halved lengthwise and thinly sliced

2 garlic cloves, thinly sliced

¼ teaspoon red chile flakes

Grated Parmigiano-Reggiano cheese

Fresh lemon juice, as needed

TOTAL TIME: 30 MINUTES
SERVES 4

PENNE & BRUSSELS SPROUTS *with Bacon and Pecorino*

At some point during the winter, any fresh vegetable that I happen to have in my fridge will get chopped up and thrown on top of pasta. Brussels sprouts are no exception. Since Brussels sprouts and bacon make for such a winning duo, I put them together here, browning the two together in the skillet and adding some fresh green chile to really liven things up. Feel free to substitute any other hearty winter green vegetable for the sprouts. Kale, cabbage, chard, and mustard greens will all work, though you'll only get a similar browning with the cabbage.

Kosher salt, as needed

8 ounces whole-wheat or regular penne

2 tablespoons extra-virgin olive oil, plus more for drizzling

3 ounces pancetta or regular bacon, diced

1 large sprig fresh rosemary

6 garlic cloves, smashed and peeled

1 jalapeño or serrano chile, thinly sliced (or substitute a large pinch of red chile flakes)

Freshly ground black pepper to taste

8 ounces Brussels sprouts, trimmed and thinly sliced

2 teaspoons unsalted butter

Fresh lemon juice, for serving

Freshly grated pecorino cheese, for serving (optional)

TOTAL TIME: 20 MINUTES
SERVES 2 OR 3

1. Bring a large pot of heavily salted water to a boil. Add the penne and cook until it is just al dente, about 1 minute less than the package directions. Drain.

2. While the pasta is cooking, heat a 12-inch skillet over high heat and add the oil. When the oil is hot, add the pancetta and rosemary and sauté until the fat on the pancetta starts to turn translucent and very light brown, about 1 minute. Add the garlic, chile, and black pepper to taste, and sauté until the garlic and pancetta turn a rich brown, about 3 minutes.

3. Add the Brussels sprouts, a large pinch of salt, and a splash of water to the skillet, and sauté until the sprouts just start to soften, about 2 minutes. Spread the sprouts mixture out in the skillet and press it down to flatten it. Let it sear for 1 minute; then stir it up and repeat the flattening (this helps brown the sprouts). Stir in the butter and cook for another minute.

4. Add the penne and cook, tossing, until everything is well mixed. Spoon into warmed pasta bowls and top with a drizzle of olive oil, a sprinkling of lemon juice, and a little cheese if you like.

FRIED LEMON PASTA

with Chile Flakes

Have you ever eaten a whole slice of lemon, peel and all, that's been roasted or grilled or fried or otherwise turned into a brown-edged, crisp, salty-sweet chip? Because that's what happens to the lemons in this recipe, and they are killer. The key is blanching them first to get rid of the bitterness contained in the white pith. Meyer lemons, which have extremely thin skins and hardly any pith, work especially well here. If you have thick-skinned lemons, you might have to blanch them twice.

After blanching, I fry the lemons with a little sugar to encourage caramelization. The fried lemons add a lot of zip to what beyond them is a pretty traditional pasta dish. Don't overlook the celery leaves here. With their feathery texture and fresh bitter note, they make a nice contrast to the acidity of the lemon.

1. Bring a large pot of heavily salted water to a boil.

2. Finely grate the zest of 2 lemons and set the zest aside. Juice one of the bald lemons and set the juice aside. (Reserve the second bald lemon in case you want more juice.) Trim the tops and bottoms off the other 2 lemons and cut them lengthwise into quarters; remove the seeds. Slice the lemon quarters crosswise into thin triangles. Blanch the lemon pieces in the boiling water for 2 minutes; then use a slotted spoon to transfer them to a clean dish towel. Taste the lemons; if they seem bitter, repeat the blanching.

3. When the water returns to a boil, add the linguine and cook until it is just shy of al dente, about 2 minutes less than the package directions. Drain, reserving ½ cup of the pasta cooking water.

4. While the pasta is cooking, heat 1 tablespoon of the olive oil in a large skillet over high heat. Add the lemon pieces and a pinch each of salt and sugar. Cook until the lemons are browned, 3 to 5 minutes. Transfer to a plate.

5. Melt the butter with the remaining 3 tablespoons olive oil in the same skillet over medium heat. Add the chile flakes and reserved lemon zest, and cook until fragrant. Whisk in the reserved pasta cooking water.

6. Toss in the pasta, the reserved lemon juice, the cheese, 1 teaspoon salt, and black pepper to taste. Cook until the pasta is well coated with the sauce and has finished cooking, about 1 minute. Toss in the caramelized lemons, and the celery leaves and/or parsley if using. Taste, and add more lemon juice if needed. Serve, topped with a drizzle of olive oil, plus more cheese if you like, and a sprinkle of flaky sea salt.

Kosher salt, as needed

4 lemons, preferably Meyer or other thin-skinned lemons

1 pound linguine or spaghetti

4 tablespoons extra-virgin olive oil, plus more for drizzling

Pinch of sugar

3 tablespoons unsalted butter

¾ teaspoon red chile flakes, plus more to taste

⅔ cup Parmigiano-Reggiano cheese, plus more for serving (optional)

Freshly ground black pepper to taste

½ cup fresh celery leaves, coarsely chopped (optional)

⅓ cup fresh parsley leaves, coarsely chopped (optional)

Flaky sea salt, for serving

TOTAL TIME: 25 MINUTES
SERVES 4 TO 6

FUSILLI & ROASTED CAULIFLOWER *with Capers*

This dish brings out the Jack Sprat in my relationship with my husband. Daniel adores pasta. I adore roasted cauliflower. So when I make this dish, I give him most of the pasta and only a few of the soft, nutty, browned florets. Then I take most of the cauliflower and only a few pieces of the fusilli. As long as I'm careful to divide the capers and pine nuts evenly, we both end up completely and utterly thrilled. Not to say this dish isn't just as terrific if you have a more normal relationship with both your dinner and your spouse. I'm just saying it really works for us.

Feel free to substitute Brussels sprouts or broccoli for the cauliflower.

½ head cauliflower, cut into bite-sized florets (about 2½ cups)

3 tablespoons drained capers

¼ cup plus 1 tablespoon extra-virgin olive oil

¼ teaspoon kosher salt, plus more as needed

Freshly ground black pepper to taste

2 medium garlic cloves, grated on a Microplane or smashed into a paste

Finely grated zest of 1 lemon

1 tablespoon unsalted butter

3 tablespoons grated Parmigiano-Reggiano cheese (optional)

8 ounces whole-wheat fusilli pasta

⅓ cup pine nuts, toasted (see page 265)

Fresh lemon juice, as needed

TOTAL TIME: 45 MINUTES
SERVES 2

1. Heat the oven to 425°F.

2. In a bowl, toss the cauliflower and 2 tablespoons of the capers with the ¼ cup olive oil, the ¼ teaspoon salt, and black pepper to taste. Spread the mixture out in a single layer on a large rimmed baking sheet, and roast it, tossing it occasionally, until golden brown, 25 to 30 minutes.

3. Meanwhile, mince the remaining 1 tablespoon capers. Scrape the capers and garlic into a large bowl and add the lemon zest, butter, remaining 1 tablespoon olive oil, and cheese if you like.

4. Bring a large pot of heavily salted water to a boil. Cook the pasta until it is al dente; drain.

5. Add the pasta, cauliflower, and pine nuts to the bowl containing the caper mixture. Squeeze in lemon juice to taste. Season with salt and pepper, toss well, and serve.

PAPPARDELLE

with Chicken Livers and Rosemary

The hardest part about making this dish, at least for me, is finding the livers. My supermarket doesn't carry them, and I can no longer save the ones salvaged from my whole chickens in a jar in the freezer (a trick from Mom) because these days chickens usually come liver-free. However, I do try to pick some up whenever I'm at the butcher and store them in the freezer for nights when I crave pasta with rosemary-scented chicken livers. If you are a liver lover (and don't you want to be so you can let that roll off your tongue at opportune moments?), you should do the same.

Livers in hand, the dish comes together very quickly because the livers cook in minutes. A little sherry and some balsamic vinegar are all you really need to build your sauce; they add a touch of winey sharpness that accentuates the velvety texture and deep, gamy flavor of the livers.

1. Bring a large pot of heavily salted water to a boil. Add the pappardelle and cook until just al dente, usually about 1 minute less than the package directions; drain, reserving a coffee mug of the cooking water. Transfer the pasta to a large bowl, and toss with 2 tablespoons of the reserved pasta water and the butter.

2. Heat 2 tablespoons of the olive oil in a 12-inch skillet over medium-high heat. Add the shallots, rosemary, and chile flakes; cook, stirring frequently, until caramelized, about 5 minutes.

3. Raise the heat to high. Add the remaining 1 tablespoon olive oil and the chicken livers; cook, without moving them, until the undersides are browned, about 1 minute. Add the garlic and stir for 10 seconds. Add the sherry and vinegar. Give the livers a quick stir and continue cooking, scraping up any browned bits from the bottom of the skillet, until they are just cooked through but still dark pink on the inside, 1 to 2 minutes.

4. Scrape the mixture into the bowl containing the hot pasta, and add ½ teaspoon salt, the pepper, and the parsley. Toss well, adding a little more pasta cooking water if the mixture seems dry.

Kosher salt, as needed

8 ounces fresh pappardelle

2 tablespoons unsalted butter

3 tablespoons extra-virgin olive oil

½ cup thinly sliced shallots

2 teaspoons finely chopped fresh rosemary leaves

Large pinch of red chile flakes

1 pound chicken livers, membranes removed, lobes cut into 1-inch chunks

1 garlic clove, finely chopped

2 tablespoons dry sherry

2 teaspoons balsamic vinegar

½ teaspoon freshly ground black pepper

Chopped fresh parsley leaves, for serving (optional)

TOTAL TIME: 25 MINUTES
SERVES 2

PASTA CARBONARA TORTE

with Tomatoes and Sage

This recipe has all the porky, cheesy flavors of a traditional pasta carbonara, but the resemblance stops there. Instead of slippery, floppy, pancetta-fat-swabbed noodles falling onto your plate, this heretical baked version slices up neatly, like a golden brown cake filled with pockets of bacon, stretchy chunks of Gruyère, and tidbits of juicy cherry tomato. If you like, you can assemble this in advance, then refrigerate it for up to eight hours before popping it in the oven. Serve it with a tomato salad on the side if it's the heart of summer (page 372), or a citrus salad all the other times of the year when the tomatoes look sad (page 375).

Kosher salt, as needed

1 pound spaghetti

8 ounces pancetta or thick-cut bacon, diced

2 tablespoons minced fresh sage leaves

1½ cups whole milk

7 ounces Gruyère cheese, grated (1¾ cups)

7 ounces young pecorino cheese, such as Pecorino Toscano, grated (1¾ cups)

3 ounces Parmigiano-Reggiano cheese, grated (¾ cup)

½ cup cherry tomatoes, quartered

3 large eggs, lightly beaten

2½ teaspoons freshly ground black pepper

Fresh chopped chives, for garnish

TOTAL TIME: 1 HOUR
SERVES 6

1. Bring a large pot of heavily salted water to a boil. Add the spaghetti and cook until it is just shy of al dente, usually about 2 minutes less than the package directions (it should be slightly underdone to your taste because you'll finish cooking it in the oven). Drain well.

2. While the pasta is cooking, heat the oven to 425°F.

3. In a 10-inch oven-safe skillet over medium-high heat, cook the pancetta until it is crisp and golden brown, 7 to 10 minutes. Stir in the sage and cook for another minute.

4. Remove the skillet from the heat and toss in the pasta, the milk, 1½ cups of the Gruyère, 1½ cups of the pecorino, the Parmigiano-Reggiano, and the tomatoes, eggs, pepper, and 2 teaspoons salt. Scatter the remaining Gruyère and pecorino over the top. Transfer the skillet to the oven and bake until the pasta is bubbling and golden on top, about 40 minutes. Let the torte cool slightly before serving. Garnish with chopped chives.

LEMONY PASTA

with Chickpeas and Parsley

Once I discovered that I could throw some unsoaked dried chickpeas into my slow cooker in the morning and come home to cooked chickpeas in the evening, I started using them in everything, including my take on the classic Italian dish *pasta con ceci*. Of course, if you've got canned chickpeas, this is still an excellent, quick-cooking dinner with loads of protein and fiber and other good-for-you things. But even more appealing is the way the soft earthiness of the chickpeas plays off the al dente pasta, coating it like a rich sauce but without any fat. The whole dish is zipped up with some lemon, garlic, and chile. Serve this with something juicy and tangy alongside; Citrus Salad with Olives (page 375) is pretty much perfect.

Kosher salt, as needed

8 ounces regular or whole-wheat fusilli or other short, sturdy pasta

2 cups cooked chickpeas, homemade (see pages 232 to 233) or canned, rinsed and drained

¼ cup extra-virgin olive oil, plus more for drizzling

2 garlic cloves, smashed and peeled

½ onion, diced

1 tablespoon finely chopped fresh rosemary leaves

Pinch of red chile flakes, plus more as needed

1½ cups chickpea cooking liquid or water

3 cups fresh parsley leaves (from 1 large bunch)

⅔ cup grated Parmigiano-Reggiano cheese, plus more for serving

1 tablespoon unsalted butter

Finely grated zest of ½ lemon

Freshly ground black pepper to taste

TOTAL TIME: 30 MINUTES
SERVES 2

1. Bring a large pot of heavily salted water to a boil. Add the fusilli and cook until it is just shy of al dente (it should be slightly underdone to your taste because you'll finish cooking it in the sauce). Drain well.

2. While the pasta is cooking, prepare the chickpea sauce: Place the chickpeas in a large bowl and use a potato masher or a fork to lightly mash them; they should be about half-crushed.

3. Heat the oil in a 12-inch skillet over medium heat. Add the garlic cloves and fry until they are golden brown, about 2 minutes. Stir in the onion, rosemary, chile flakes, and a pinch of salt. Cook, stirring occasionally, until the onion is soft, about 10 minutes. Then stir in the chickpeas and the cooking liquid. Bring to a simmer and cook gently until most of the liquid has evaporated, about 5 minutes.

4. Stir in the pasta and the parsley, and cook until the pasta has finished cooking and is coated in the sauce, 1 to 2 minutes. Quickly toss in the cheese, butter, lemon zest, black pepper to taste, and salt if needed. Drizzle with olive oil and shower with additional cheese before serving.

SPICY PORK NOODLES
with Ginger and Baby Bok Choy

This pan-fried noodle dish can be the blueprint for many varied dinners. You can use the basic pan-frying technique and Asian flavorings (ginger, sesame oil, chile, and soy sauce), but change up the vegetable and protein as the seasons and your appetite dictate. In addition to pork and bok choy, some of my other favorite combinations include kale and diced shrimp, shredded butternut squash and ground lamb, and Brussels sprouts and ground beef. If you like this dish, it's worth seeking out the black vinegar. Although balsamic makes an okay approximation, it's a bit sweeter and winier than Chinese black vinegar, which is made from fermented rice and has a smokier, woodsier character.

1. Thinly slice the bok choy stems. Finely chop half of the ginger, and slice the remaining half into thin matchsticks.

2. Bring a large pot of heavily salted water to a boil. Add the noodles and cook according to the package instructions. Drain, run under cool water, and drain again.

3. Heat 1 tablespoon of the peanut oil in a 12-inch skillet over medium-high heat. Add the pork and cook, breaking it up with a fork, until it is golden and cooked through, about 10 minutes. Season the pork with ¼ teaspoon salt, the 1½ tablespoons soy sauce, and ½ tablespoon of the rice vinegar. Use a slotted spoon to transfer the meat to a bowl.

4. Add the remaining 1 tablespoon peanut oil to the skillet. Stir in ¼ cup of the scallions, the finely chopped ginger, and the garlic and chile. Cook until fragrant, about 1 minute. Add the bok choy stems and ¼ teaspoon salt. Cook until the bok choy is almost tender, about 2 minutes. Then toss in the bok choy leaves and return the pork to the skillet.

5. Toss in the noodles, remaining ¼ cup soy sauce, and remaining ½ tablespoon rice vinegar. Cook until just warmed through. Transfer the noodles to a large bowl and toss with the remaining ¼ cup scallions and the sesame seeds, sesame oil, and cilantro. Taste and drizzle with more sesame oil if needed. In a small bowl, combine the ginger matchsticks with just enough black vinegar to cover. Serve the ginger mixture alongside the noodles as a garnish.

12 ounces baby bok choy
(3 to 4 small heads), trimmed, dark green leaves and stems separated

1 2-inch piece fresh ginger (1 ounce), peeled

Kosher salt, as needed

About 8 ounces dried rice stick noodles (if your package is a little smaller or larger, it's fine)

2 tablespoons peanut or safflower oil

1 pound lean ground pork
(or turkey)

¼ cup plus 1½ tablespoons soy sauce

1 tablespoon rice vinegar

½ cup thinly sliced scallions (white and green parts)

3 garlic cloves, finely chopped

1 fresh Thai or habanero chile, seeded if desired, thinly sliced

2 tablespoons toasted sesame seeds

1½ teaspoons toasted sesame oil, plus more for drizzling

Fresh cilantro or basil leaves, torn, for serving

Chinese black vinegar or balsamic vinegar, for serving

TOTAL TIME: 40 MINUTES

SERVES 4

COCONUT RICE NOODLES
with Ginger and Eggplant

Make this Thai curry in summer when you can get excellent eggplant, corn, and a variety of fresh hot chiles. Don't get hung up about authenticity here. Yes, the Thai chiles, lemongrass, and *rao ram* (a Southeast Asian herb that tastes like a cross between cilantro and basil) are great to use if you can easily get them. But this dish really is about the harmony of ginger, coconut milk, curry powder, and cilantro, which makes a green herbal curry that tastes good on almost anything, but especially pliant rice noodles and soft, custardy eggplant. Filled with vegetables, this is a complete meal on its own, though it also goes really well with simply grilled fish, shrimp, or chicken.

1. Soak or cook the rice noodles according to the package instructions (these can vary widely with the type of noodle you're using). Drain well.

2. In a mini food processor or blender, combine the chiles, lemongrass if using, garlic, ginger, and curry powder. Add 1 tablespoon of the coconut oil and pulse until a coarse paste forms. Drop in the cilantro leaves and lime zest; pulse again. Set aside.

3. Heat the remaining 2 tablespoons coconut oil in a 12-inch skillet over medium-high heat. Add the eggplant and sauté until it is well browned, about 10 minutes. Transfer the eggplant to a plate.

4. Stir the onion wedges into the skillet and cook until they are tender, about 7 minutes. Stir in the reserved spice paste and cook for 1 minute. Pour in the stock and coconut milk, and bring to a simmer. Return the eggplant to the skillet, along with the tomatoes and fish sauce. Simmer until the eggplant is very tender, 7 to 10 minutes; in the last minute of cooking, stir in the corn and spinach if using. Season the sauce with lime juice to taste and with the Vietnamese coriander.

5. To serve, divide the noodles among individual bowls. Top with the sauce, and garnish with additional cilantro.

4½ ounces dried rice noodles

2 fresh Thai or other very hot chiles, seeded and chopped

2 lemongrass stalks, trimmed, outer layers removed, inner core chopped (optional)

4 garlic cloves, coarsely chopped

1 1-inch piece fresh ginger, peeled and finely chopped

½ teaspoon curry powder

3 tablespoons extra-virgin coconut oil

1 cup fresh cilantro leaves, plus more for garnish

Finely grated zest and juice of 1 lime

1½ pounds eggplant, cut into 1-inch cubes

1 small onion, halved lengthwise and sliced into thin wedges

2 cups chicken or vegetable stock

1 13.5-ounce can unsweetened coconut milk

5 ounces cherry tomatoes, halved (⅔ cup)

2 tablespoons Asian fish sauce

Kernels from 1 ear fresh corn (optional)

Large handful of fresh baby spinach (optional)

1 tablespoon finely chopped fresh *rao ram* (Vietnamese coriander) or basil leaves

TOTAL TIME: 45 MINUTES
SERVES 4

SHRIMP PAD THAI

with Sugar Snap Peas and Basil

When a dish that I adore is on the carb-dense side of the spectrum, my preferred way to lighten it up is to add more vegetables. The sweet-and-sour Thai noodle dish is one of my absolute favorites, but there's no denying the fact that in most of its incarnations, it's heavier on the thick rice noodles than any other component (in Thailand this might be a whole different story; I'm talking urban American takeout). So here I add some sugar snap peas to make it less dense with noodles. The peas add crunch and sweetness, and are easy to toss into the pan without much prep work.

8 ounces *pad Thai* rice noodles

3½ tablespoons Asian fish sauce

3 tablespoons light brown sugar

1½ tablespoons tamarind paste or concentrate

1 lime

5 tablespoons peanut oil

Kosher salt, as needed

12 ounces medium shrimp, peeled and deveined (or use large shrimp and halve them)

Freshly ground black pepper, as needed

2 large shallots, thinly sliced

2 garlic cloves, finely chopped

1 to 2 fresh Thai or other hot chiles with seeds, thinly sliced

4 ounces sugar snap peas, thinly sliced (1 cup)

2 large eggs, lightly beaten

Fresh Thai or regular basil leaves, as needed

Bean sprouts or fresh pea shoots or leaves, as needed

Roasted unsalted peanuts, chopped, for garnish

TOTAL TIME: 40 MINUTES
SERVES 2

1. Place the noodles in a large bowl of warm water and soak until pliable, 15 to 20 minutes. Drain well.

2. In a small bowl, whisk together the fish sauce, brown sugar, and tamarind paste. Grate the zest of half of the lime and reserve it; squeeze 1 tablespoon lime juice into the fish sauce mixture. Whisk in 2 tablespoons of the peanut oil. Season with salt to taste.

3. Season the shrimp with salt and pepper to taste. In a 12-inch skillet over medium-high heat, warm 1 tablespoon of the peanut oil. Add the shrimp and cook, tossing them often, until they are just barely opaque, 2 to 3 minutes. Transfer the shrimp to a plate.

4. Return the skillet to medium-high heat and add 1 tablespoon of the peanut oil. Stir in the shallots, garlic, and chiles; cook until soft, 3 to 4 minutes. Stir in the remaining 1 tablespoon peanut oil along with the noodles, snap peas, shrimp, and fish sauce mixture; toss to combine. Pour in the eggs, and toss until the noodles are coated and both eggs and noodles are cooked through, 1 to 2 minutes. Remove the skillet from the heat and toss in the basil and bean sprouts or pea shoots or leaves. Garnish with chopped peanuts before serving.

COLD SESAME NOODLES
with Celery Salad

As much as I love cold sesame noodles, their oily richness always makes me crave something fresh and crunchy to go with them. So here, I've mixed a lively scallion-laced celery salad right into the bowl. It freshens things up and adds a great textural contrast to the softness of the noodles. If you can plan ahead, it's worthwhile to source the Sichuan peppercorns. They add both a musky pepperiness and a camphor-like note. And once you get some, they will last for years in your pantry. Serve this on its own, or with pork chops or grilled meat.

FOR THE CELERY SALAD

1 teaspoon Sichuan peppercorns or regular peppercorns, coarsely crushed

2 teaspoons toasted sesame oil

4 celery stalks, thinly sliced (1½ cups)

3 tablespoons thinly sliced scallions (white and green parts)

2 tablespoons chopped fresh cilantro leaves

1½ teaspoons rice vinegar

¼ teaspoon kosher salt

FOR THE NOODLES

2 tablespoons toasted sesame oil

3 tablespoons soy sauce

2 tablespoons rice vinegar

2 tablespoons Chinese sesame paste (see Note)

1 tablespoon smooth or chunky peanut butter

2 teaspoons dark brown sugar

2 teaspoons chile garlic paste

2 garlic cloves, grated on a Microplane or minced

1 1-inch piece fresh ginger, peeled and finely grated

1 pound Chinese egg noodles or spaghetti, cooked according to the package instructions

Sesame seeds, as needed

TOTAL TIME: 15 MINUTES
SERVES 4

1. Prepare the salad: Heat the peppercorns in a dry 8-inch skillet over medium heat until fragrant. Stir in the sesame oil, and remove from the heat.

2. In a large bowl, toss together the celery, scallions, cilantro, vinegar, salt, and peppercorn sesame oil.

3. Prepare the noodles: In a large bowl, whisk together the sesame oil, soy sauce, vinegar, sesame paste, peanut butter, brown sugar, chile garlic paste, garlic, and ginger. Toss in the noodles and the sesame seeds.

4. Serve cold, topped with the celery salad.

NOTE: Chinese sesame paste has a richer, deeper, more toasted flavor than tahini (Middle Eastern sesame paste). But tahini works well here as long as you increase the toasted sesame oil quotient. If you're substituting, use tahini instead of the Chinese paste, and increase the sesame oil in step 3 to 2½ tablespoons.

VIETNAMESE RICE NOODLES *with Daikon Radishes and Cucumbers*

This cooling, salad-like rice noodle dish is all about contrasting textures and bright flavors. In the texture department, you've got slippery noodles against crisp radishes, juicy cucumbers, and crunchy toasted peanuts. And the brightness comes from plenty of lime juice and fresh ginger, which do wonders to wake up the peanut butter and coconut–based sauce. This is a great dish to make ahead for a potluck or a picnic, or just if you're organized enough in the morning to get dinner ready for that night. For maximum crunch, though, don't garnish with the peanuts until just before serving so that they don't get soggy. Leftover noodles make excellent lunchbox fare.

1. In a large bowl, whisk together the peanut butter, coconut milk, ¼ cup soy sauce, garlic, ginger, chile oil, fish sauce, and lime juice; set aside.

2. In a dry 12-inch skillet, heat the peanuts until they are just warm and the oils are beginning to release, 1 to 2 minutes. Transfer the nuts to a cutting board and allow them to cool completely; then coarsely chop them and set them aside for the garnish.

3. In the same skillet, heat the peanut oil over medium heat. Add the sesame oil, daikon, and cucumbers; cook until the vegetables are just beginning to soften, about 2 minutes. Add the remaining 1 tablespoon soy sauce and toss to coat; then add the rice noodles and cook until heated through. Add the noodles to the bowl containing the peanut sauce, and toss until well coated. Serve garnished with the chopped toasted peanuts and the cilantro.

½ cup smooth peanut butter

½ cup unsweetened coconut milk

¼ cup plus 1 tablespoon soy sauce

2 garlic cloves, grated on a Microplane or minced

1 tablespoon minced peeled fresh ginger

1 tablespoon chile oil

1 tablespoon Asian fish sauce

Juice of 2 limes

⅓ cup dry-roasted peanuts

1 tablespoon peanut oil

1 teaspoon toasted sesame oil

4 daikon radishes, halved lengthwise and cut into ⅛-inch-thick slices (about 4 cups)

8 Persian or 4 large cucumbers, halved lengthwise and cut into ⅛-inch-thick slices (about 4 cups)

4 ounces vermicelli rice noodles, cooked according to the package instructions, cooled

Fresh cilantro leaves, for garnish

TOTAL TIME: 30 MINUTES
SERVES 4 TO 6

TOFU
(& A TOUCH OF SEITAN)

STIR-FRIED TOFU

with Summer Squash, Basil, and Coconut

The key to browning tofu in a stir-fry is to avoid moving it around too much: let it sit until it forms a caramelized crust on one side, then give it a toss in the pan. The same technique works for summer squash, which can get soggy and fall apart if you keep agitating it. So it's no surprise that the two go together terrifically well in this summery stir-fry. I've also added coconut flakes for sweetness, and plenty of lime juice and basil leaves for a fresh and lively bite.

1. In a bowl, whisk together the soy sauce, 1 tablespoon of the sesame oil, and the ginger. Using a Microplane, grate in 1 garlic clove. Place the tofu on a small rimmed baking sheet or other wide, shallow vessel (a baking dish, a gratin dish, a pie plate, but preferably not a deep bowl in which the marinade will pool at the bottom and not cover the tofu). Pour the marinade over the tofu and toss very gently. Let it rest while you prepare the rest of the dish.

2. In a dry 12-inch skillet over medium heat, toast the coconut flakes until golden, 2 to 3 minutes. Transfer the coconut to a bowl and wipe out the skillet if necessary.

3. Return the skillet to the stovetop and raise the heat to high. Add 2 tablespoons of the sesame oil. Stir in the onion and cook until softened, about 7 minutes. Stir in the squash and ½ teaspoon each of salt and pepper. Thinly slice the remaining 3 garlic cloves and add them to the skillet. Cook, stirring

only occasionally, until the squash is nicely browned, 5 to 10 minutes. Pour any marinade surrounding the tofu into the skillet and let it bubble for a few seconds. Then pour the squash mixture into a large bowl.

4. Drizzle the remaining 1 tablespoon sesame oil into the skillet and let it heat for a good 1 to 2 minutes; it should be blazing hot. Pat the tofu dry with paper towels. Add the tofu to the skillet and cook without moving it until the undersides are golden brown. The pan may smoke, but fear not, it means the skillet was hot enough. (Turn on your fan and open your windows.)

5. Flip the tofu pieces over and repeat on the other side. Transfer the tofu to the bowl containing the squash.

6. Toss the mixture well with the basil, lime juice, and additional salt if needed. Garnish with the toasted coconut, and serve.

2 tablespoons soy sauce

4 tablespoons toasted sesame oil

1 tablespoon finely grated peeled fresh ginger

4 garlic cloves

1 package (14 to 16 ounces) firm tofu, drained, patted dry, and cut into 1-inch cubes

1 cup unsweetened coconut flakes

1 medium white onion, halved lengthwise and cut into thin half-moons

3 small to medium yellow squash or zucchini, halved lengthwise and cut into thin half-moons

½ teaspoon fine sea salt, plus more if needed

½ teaspoon freshly ground black pepper

1 cup fresh Thai and/or regular basil leaves, torn

Fresh lime juice, as needed

TOTAL TIME: 35 MINUTES
SERVES 2 OR 3

SWEET & SOUR TOFU
with Corn

You rarely see corn and tomatoes combined with tofu in a stir-fry, but there's really no reason for that other than tradition. Turns out, they work wonderfully well here, adding a juicy sweetness that softens the chiles and lime juice in the pan. You can make this dish as mellow or as fiery as you want with the variety and quantity of chiles. Jalapeños in general are milder than serranos; small Thai bird chiles can make you dizzy with heat—which can be good or bad depending on your chile-tolerance. Or for a dish that's perfectly mild, you can skip the chiles altogether. It's got enough going on that you won't even miss them.

4 large garlic cloves, grated on a Microplane or minced

2 small jalapeño or serrano chiles, or 1 Thai bird chile, seeds and veins removed if you want to reduce the heat, thinly sliced

1½ tablespoons soy sauce

1½ teaspoons grated peeled fresh ginger

1½ tablespoons fresh lime juice, plus more to taste

1½ teaspoons toasted sesame oil, plus more if needed

1½ teaspoons Asian fish sauce

1 teaspoon honey

2 tablespoons peanut or grapeseed oil, plus more if needed

1 package (14 to 16 ounces) extra-firm tofu, drained, patted dry, and cut into 1-inch cubes

Fine sea salt, for sprinkling

2 cups fresh corn kernels (cut from 2 to 3 ears), or frozen corn (do not thaw)

3 scallions (white and green parts), thinly sliced

1 cup cherry tomatoes, halved

Toasted sesame seeds, for serving (see Note)

Fresh cilantro or basil, for serving

TOTAL TIME: 20 MINUTES
SERVES 2 OR 3

1. In a small bowl, combine the garlic, chiles, soy sauce, ginger, lime juice, sesame oil, fish sauce, and honey.

2. Heat a 12-inch skillet over high heat until it is very hot, about 5 minutes. Add the peanut oil and let it heat for 30 seconds; then carefully add the tofu. Don't touch the tofu for 2 to 3 minutes to let it sear until golden brown. Then toss and stir-fry for another 2 to 3 minutes. The pan may smoke, but fear not, it means the skillet was hot enough. (Turn on your fan and open your windows.) Transfer the tofu to a plate and sprinkle it with fine sea salt to taste.

3. Add the corn, scallions, and tomatoes to the skillet, along with a few more drops of peanut oil if needed. Stir-fry the vegetables until they start to soften, 1 to 2 minutes. Stir in the soy sauce mixture and cook for 1 minute to bring the flavors together. Return the tofu to the skillet and spoon the sauce over it.

4. Sprinkle sesame seeds all over the tofu and vegetables, and serve with cilantro.

NOTE: To toast sesame seeds, heat a dry skillet over medium heat for 1 minute. Add the seeds and stir until you can smell them, 1 to 2 minutes. Immediately pour them onto a plate to cool. You may not actually see the seeds turn golden until after they come off the heat, so use your nose here rather than just your eyes.

STIR-FRIED TOFU
with Spring Vegetables

Pea season is so fleeting that I try to take advantage of the whole plant—the leafy shoots and the sweet green peas themselves. Here, I stir-fry them both with tofu, seasoning everything pretty gently, with just a splash of soy sauce, some nutty rice wine (or dry sherry), and a little fresh ginger, all in the service of letting the vegetables really shine. When you can't get fresh peas and pea shoots, you can use frozen peas (or frozen edamame for that matter) and baby spinach instead. It turns the dish into more of an all-seasons kind of thing, which is also nice.

I like to serve this by itself for a light dinner, but a side of rice or rice noodles adds heft for those who need it.

1 tablespoon Shaoxing rice wine or dry sherry (or dry white wine in a pinch)

2 teaspoons soy sauce, plus more as needed

2 tablespoons peanut oil

1 package (14 to 16 ounces) extra-firm tofu, drained, patted dry, and cut into 1-inch cubes

Fine sea salt to taste

1 cup shelled fresh peas (from about 14 ounces pea pods)

1 tablespoon finely chopped fresh ginger

1 large garlic clove, finely chopped

4 ounces fresh pea shoots (about 4 cups)

1 tablespoon fresh lime juice, plus more to taste

½ teaspoon toasted sesame oil, plus more to taste

Chopped fresh chives to taste

TOTAL TIME: 20 MINUTES
SERVES 2 OR 3

1. In a small bowl, stir together the rice wine and 2 teaspoons soy sauce.

2. Heat a 12-inch skillet or wok over high heat until it is very hot (a drop of water hitting the pan should evaporate immediately). Add 1 tablespoon of the peanut oil. Stir in the tofu and sprinkle with salt to taste. Cook without moving the tofu cubes until the undersides are crisp and golden brown, about 2 minutes. The pan may smoke, but fear not, it means the skillet was hot enough. (Turn on your fan and open your windows.)

3. Stir in the remaining 1 tablespoon peanut oil and the peas. Cook until the peas are almost tender, about 2 minutes. Add the ginger and garlic, and stir for 1 minute. Then stir in the rice wine mixture and the pea shoots. Once the pea shoots have wilted and the sauce is absorbed, remove the skillet from the heat.

4. Stir in the lime juice, sesame oil to taste, additional soy sauce to taste, and the chives.

ROASTED TOFU
with Broccoli Rabe and Garlic

Roasting broccoli rabe at a high heat makes it crisp-leafed and tender-stemmed, and it's extremely easy to prepare this way. In this recipe I match it up with Asian fish sauce–laced tofu, which lends a saline, funky element that can stand up to the sharp bite of the rabe. It's a gutsy, assertively flavored dish in the best possible way.

This said, if you're in the mood for something a little milder, substitute diminutive broccolini, or tender broccoli cut into ½-inch florets, for the rabe. The dish will be sweeter and mellower, without the strident bitterness of the rabe (which I happen to adore though I know not everyone else is with me here).

You can serve this with any kind of rice (page 276), but I suggest going with brown rice. Its pronounced earthy flavor will stand up to the intensity of this dish better than meeker white rice. Along those same lines but maybe less intuitively, farro (page 277) would work well, too.

1. Heat the oven to 450°F. Lightly oil a rimmed baking sheet.

2. Slice the tofu crosswise into ¾-inch-thick slabs. Pat the slabs very dry with paper towels, and arrange them in a single layer on the prepared baking sheet.

3. In a small bowl, whisk half of the garlic with the fish sauce, lemon juice, and ¼ cup of the olive oil. Sprinkle both sides of the tofu slabs with salt to taste, and brush them with half of the fish sauce mixture. Transfer the baking sheet to the oven and roast the tofu for 20 minutes.

4. While the tofu is roasting, prepare the broccoli rabe: Using the flat side of a knife blade or a mortar and pestle, lightly crush the coriander seeds, if using, to break them up a bit (you don't need to grind them).

5. In a large bowl, toss the remaining garlic and the crushed coriander seeds with the broccoli rabe, the ½ teaspoon salt, the chile flakes if using, and the remaining ¼ cup olive oil. Spread the broccoli rabe in a single layer on a baking sheet.

6. Flip the tofu over and brush the tops with the remaining fish sauce mixture. Return the baking sheet to the oven and continue to roast the tofu until the undersides are golden brown, 5 to 10 minutes. At the same time, put the broccoli rabe in the oven and roast it, tossing it once or twice, until it is tender and golden around the edges, 10 to 13 minutes.

7. Toss the warm broccoli rabe with the lemon zest and drizzle with olive oil. Serve it mounded on top of the tofu.

2 packages (14 to 16 ounces each) extra-firm tofu, drained and patted dry

4 garlic cloves, grated with a Microplane or minced

4 teaspoons Asian fish sauce

4 teaspoons fresh lemon juice

½ cup extra-virgin olive oil, plus more for drizzling

½ teaspoon kosher salt, plus more as needed

1 teaspoon coriander seeds (optional)

1½ pounds trimmed broccoli rabe (from about 2 medium bunches)

2 pinches red chile flakes (optional)

Finely grated zest of ½ lemon

TOTAL TIME: 45 MINUTES
SERVES 4 TO 6

MAPLE-ROASTED TOFU
with Winter Squash

Winter squash gets sweeter and more intense the longer you roast it, especially if you glaze it in some kind of syrupy liquid. Here the squash is basted with a ginger-infused maple syrup until it becomes sweet and very tender—almost like squash candy. Warning: if you start nibbling on pieces of roasted squash snatched from the baking pan, you might not be able to stop. Any squash that you haven't devoured by yourself then gets served with slabs of firm tofu that are brushed with a maple, chile, and soy sauce marinade and roasted. Combined on the plate, they make for a vibrant dish, both spicy *and* sweet, perfect for a cold evening. Serve this as a meatless main dish with rice at a dinner party or at your Thanksgiving table, where it can accompany the turkey or replace it altogether.

If your squash options run deep, you can use other varieties in place of the butternut. Added bonus: sliced acorn, delicata, and dumpling squash don't require peeling; the peels are not only edible, they also look really pretty for serving.

1. Heat the oven to 425°F.

2. Slice the tofu into 1-inch-thick slabs. Pat them very dry with paper towels and arrange them in a single layer on a rimmed baking sheet. Cover the tofu slabs with more paper towels and let them sit while you make the sauce.

3. Combine the maple syrup, ginger, and chile powder in a small saucepan, and simmer until the syrup thickens and reduces by a third, about 3 minutes. Stir in the olive oil.

4. Place the squash on a rimmed baking sheet and toss it with a generous pinch each of salt and pepper, the sage, and half of the maple syrup mixture. Spread the squash cubes out into an even layer, place the baking sheet in the oven, and roast, tossing the squash occasionally, until golden brown, about 45 minutes.

5. Once the squash is in the oven, add the soy sauce and sherry vinegar to the remaining maple syrup mixture. Remove the paper towels from under and over the tofu, and sprinkle the top of the tofu slabs with salt. Brush half of the soy-maple mixture over the tofu. Add the baking sheet of tofu to the oven and roast it for 20 minutes. Then turn the pieces over, brush the tops with the remaining soy-maple mixture, and cook for 15 to 20 minutes longer.

6. Toss the squash with the cilantro. Transfer it to a plate and top it with the tofu. Garnish with sliced scallions and drizzle with more sherry vinegar.

1 package (14 to 16 ounces) extra-firm tofu, drained and patted dry

¼ cup maple syrup

2 teaspoons grated peeled fresh ginger

¼ teaspoon good chile powder such as ancho or New Mexico

3 tablespoons extra-virgin olive oil

2¼ pounds butternut squash, peeled, trimmed, seeded, and cut into 1-inch cubes (6 cups)

Fine sea salt, as needed

Freshly ground black pepper, as needed

1 tablespoon chopped fresh sage leaves

2 teaspoons soy sauce

½ teaspoon sherry vinegar, plus more for drizzling

½ cup fresh cilantro leaves or chopped fresh basil leaves

Sliced scallions (white and green parts), for garnish

TOTAL TIME: 1 HOUR
SERVES 4

POMEGRANATE ROASTED
TOFU *with Eggplant and Toasted Cumin*

Roasting is probably my favorite cooking technique for preparing eggplant. I love how the center softens to an almost custard-like texture while the outer surfaces turn as brown and crisp as potato chips. You can roast cubes of eggplant and thick slabs of tofu at the same time, which makes this dish convenient once you've got everything tucked away in the oven. The eggplant, seasoned with cumin, becomes the more savory element, while the pomegranate molasses–glazed tofu is a sweet, tangy, and soft counterpart. Serve this with Coconut Rice (page 381) to play up the sweetness, or over soba noodles tossed with a little sesame oil and a finely grated garlic clove for something more savory.

If you don't have pomegranate molasses handy, substitute a tablespoon of honey that is cut, to taste, with balsamic vinegar. It will give a similar sweet-tartness, though without the same fruitiness. And look for Japanese eggplant. They tend to have fewer seeds than other varieties and are particularly well-suited here—though any eggplant variety will work.

2 packages (14 to 16 ounces each) extra-firm tofu, drained and patted dry

4 teaspoons soy sauce

1 tablespoon plus 2 teaspoons pomegranate molasses

¼ cup plus ⅓ cup extra-virgin olive oil

Fine sea salt, as needed

3 pounds eggplant (preferably Japanese), trimmed and cut into 1-inch cubes

Freshly ground black pepper, as needed

2 teaspoons cumin seeds

Lots of fresh chopped dill, cilantro, and/or mint leaves, for serving (use what you've got)

Lemon wedges, for serving

TOTAL TIME: 1 HOUR
SERVES 4

1. Heat the oven to 425°F.

2. Slice the tofu crosswise into 1-inch-thick slabs. Pat them very dry with paper towels and arrange them in a single layer on a rimmed baking sheet. In a small bowl, whisk together the soy sauce, the 2 teaspoons pomegranate molasses, and the ¼ cup olive oil. Sprinkle the tops of the tofu with salt, and brush with half of the soy mixture.

3. Spread the eggplant cubes on a separate rimmed baking sheet. Toss them with the remaining ⅓ cup olive oil and season with salt and pepper to taste; spread the eggplant out into one layer.

4. Transfer the tofu and eggplant to the oven. Cook the eggplant, tossing the pieces once or twice, until golden brown, 35 to 45 minutes; during the last 10 minutes of cooking, toss the eggplant with the cumin seeds. Cook the tofu for 20 minutes; then turn the pieces over, brush the tops with the remaining soy mixture, and cook for another 15 to 20 minutes.

5. Toss the eggplant with the remaining 1 tablespoon pomegranate molasses and the herbs. Transfer it to a plate and top with the tofu. Serve with lemon wedges alongside for squeezing over everything.

MAPO TOFU

with Mushrooms and Pork

The hardest thing about making a reasonably authentic mapo tofu is sourcing the Sichuan ingredients that make the soft, stew-like, and very spicy braised tofu and pork come alive. You'll need Sichuan peppercorns, which have a mouth-numbing, camphor bite, and fermented black bean garlic sauce, both available at Asian markets and online. Once you've got them, this dish comes together very quickly, and, if you love funky, meaty, fiery flavors as much as I do, it will certainly become a staple in your weeknight lineup.

If you can't get Sichuan peppercorns, you can use black peppercorns instead; the dish won't be quite as complex, but it's still absolutely worth making. If you can't find black bean garlic sauce, you can substitute fermented (also called salted) black beans; just chop them fine and add them with the pork.

Serve this with either white or brown rice to catch every bite of the good, spicy sauce.

1. In a dry 10-inch skillet over medium heat, toast the peppercorns until they are aromatic, about 1 minute. Transfer the peppercorns to a mortar and pestle and crush them (or use the flat side of a heavy knife blade, pressing down).

2. Return the skillet to medium-high heat, and add the peanut oil. Stir in the pork and mushrooms. Cook, stir-frying, until most of the liquid has evaporated and both meat and mushrooms are well browned, 5 to 10 minutes.

3. Stir in the garlic, ginger, and chile flakes; cook for 1 minute. Stir in the rice wine, black bean paste, soy sauce, and ⅔ cup of water. Then gently stir in the tofu cubes and the cornstarch slurry. Cook until the mixture is heated through and has thickened slightly, 1 to 2 minutes. Garnish with sliced scallions and a sprinkling of sesame oil before serving.

1½ teaspoons Sichuan peppercorns

3 tablespoons peanut, grapeseed, or safflower oil

4 ounces ground pork (or use turkey)

4 ounces fresh shiitake mushroom caps, coarsely chopped (1½ cups)

2 garlic cloves, grated on a Microplane or minced

1 1-inch piece fresh ginger, peeled and finely chopped

Pinch of red chile flakes

2 tablespoons Shaoxing rice wine or dry sherry

1 to 2 tablespoons black bean garlic sauce, to taste

1 tablespoon soy sauce

1 package (14 to 16 ounces) firm tofu, drained and cut into ¾-inch cubes

1 teaspoon cornstarch dissolved in 1 tablespoon water

Sliced scallions (white and green parts), for serving

Toasted sesame oil, for serving

TOTAL TIME: 20 MINUTES
SERVES 4

CRISPY TOFU

with Ginger and Spicy Greens

This is of the deep-fry first, toss-with-sauce later models of cooking, which makes it complexly flavored and doubly decadent. The tofu is coated with cornstarch before frying, helping it become especially crispy and golden before it gets saturated with a glossy brown sauce pungent with ginger, shallots, and a heady dose of black pepper. The pan sauce also contains two ingredients that may seem surprising: molasses and butter. But they add sweetness and roundness to the mix, and help mitigate the sting of the fresh hot chiles. As a final touch, baby bok choy (or Swiss chard) adds a green vegetable factor, lightening up everything.

This is a pretty complete one-pan meal, though because it doesn't stint on the chiles, you might want rice or Coconut Rice (page 381) on the side to put out any palate fires.

1. Heat ¼ inch of grapeseed oil in a 12-inch skillet over medium-high heat. In a bowl, toss the tofu with the cornstarch until well coated. Fry the tofu in the hot oil until it is browned and crisped, about 5 minutes. Transfer the tofu to a paper-towel-lined plate to drain. Sprinkle with salt to taste.

2. Pour off the oil from the skillet and return the skillet to medium heat. Add the butter, and when it has melted, add the shallots, garlic, ginger, and chiles. Cook, stirring frequently, until soft, about 10 minutes.

3. While the shallots are cooking, whisk the soy sauce, molasses, and black pepper together in a small bowl.

4. Stir the soy sauce mixture into the skillet, along with the sliced bok choy stems and the scallions. Cook until the stems are almost tender, 2 to 3 minutes. Add the bok choy leaves and stir until they are just wilted. Then stir in the tofu, and serve hot.

Grapeseed or safflower oil, as needed

1 package (14 to 16 ounces) firm tofu, drained, patted dry, and cut into 1-inch cubes

¼ cup cornstarch

Fine sea salt to taste

3 tablespoons unsalted butter

6 small shallots, thinly sliced

6 garlic cloves, grated on a Microplane or minced

1½ tablespoons finely chopped peeled fresh ginger

1 green serrano chile, seeded and thinly sliced

1 fresh hot red chile, seeded and thinly sliced

3 tablespoons soy sauce

2 tablespoons molasses

2 teaspoons freshly ground black pepper

1 pound bok choy or Swiss chard, stems and leaves separated and thinly sliced

8 small scallions (white and green parts), cut into 1¼-inch lengths

TOTAL TIME: 35 MINUTES
SERVES 2 OR 3

TOFU SPAETZLE
and Gruyère Gratin

One of the coolest by-products of learning about shredding tofu (page 225) was discovering that the light and fluffy strands have a very similar texture to spaetzle—small eggy dumplings popular in Germany and Austria. But while spaetzle-making is a somewhat involved endeavor, grating tofu is a snap. Tofu also provides a lot more protein than the tiny dumplings. And, added bonus, if you use gluten-free panko, this dish is gluten-free.

You can substitute any kind of semi-firm melting cheese for the Gruyère, including fontina, gouda, smoked mozzarella (regular mozzarella is too bland here), or cheddar. But with its pronounced nutty flavor, Gruyère is my personal favorite here.

Cheesy, gooey, with bits of sweet caramelized onion, this is one of the coziest of casseroles out there.

5 tablespoons unsalted butter

2 large onions, halved and thinly sliced

4 sprigs fresh thyme

2 packages (14 to 16 ounces each) extra-firm tofu, drained and patted dry

8 ounces Gruyère cheese, grated (2 cups)

1 teaspoon freshly ground black pepper

¼ teaspoon freshly grated nutmeg

½ teaspoon kosher salt

½ cup panko bread crumbs

TOTAL TIME: 1½ HOURS
SERVES 4 TO 6

1. Place a 12-inch skillet or heavy-bottomed pot over medium-high heat. Stir in 3 tablespoons of the butter, the onions, and the thyme sprigs. Cook, tossing frequently, until the onions are completely limp and deeply caramelized, 40 to 55 minutes. Keep an eye on the onions as they cook and adjust the heat as needed so they don't burn.

2. Line a baking sheet with a clean kitchen towel. Using the large holes on a box grater, coarsely shred the tofu. Then spread it out on the prepared baking sheet, and lay another kitchen towel on top to absorb excess moisture.

3. Heat the oven to 375°F.

4. In a large bowl, toss together the shredded tofu, caramelized onions, 1¼ cups of the cheese, and the pepper, nutmeg, and salt. Place the mixture in a shallow gratin dish or an 8 × 12-inch baking dish. Top with the bread crumbs and the remaining ¾ cup cheese. Dot with the remaining 2 tablespoons butter. Bake until the cheese has melted and the casserole is golden, 25 to 35 minutes.

RED CURRY & COCONUT TOFU *with Cherry Tomatoes and Green Beans*

For a long time, I was resistant to the idea of jarred Thai curry paste. It seemed too much like cheating. After all, I'm not the kind of person given to spooning jarred gravy over my Thanksgiving turkey or jarred tomato sauce over my pasta. Cooking these things from scratch is my livelihood. So why would jarred curry paste be any different?

Then, a curry-loving friend explained that curry paste is not a prepared sauce. It's a *condiment*, like Sriracha or mustard or mango chutney. It's meant to be an element of a sauce, not to *be* the sauce.

This was all the encouragement I needed.

Since then, Thai curry paste has earned a permanent place between the preserved lemons and the miso, and I use a tablespoonful whenever I want to add toasty, spicy, earthy notes to stir-fries, soups, stews, and sauces.

In this recipe, I keep things pretty streamlined, sautéing a base of aromatics—onion, ginger, garlic, chiles, and cilantro stems—then building a pan sauce from there with the coconut milk and curry paste before adding the tofu and vegetables. It's a very adaptable curry. You can substitute cubes of chicken breast or shrimp for the tofu, and other vegetables for the ones I've listed below (sugar snap or snow peas are great stand-ins for the green beans, by the way). Just adjust the cooking times if need be.

1. Season the tofu cubes lightly with sea salt.

2. Heat the coconut oil in a 10- or 12-inch skillet over medium-high heat. Add the ginger, shallots, garlic, chile, and cilantro stems, and sauté until tender, about 5 minutes. Add the mushrooms and cook until they are golden brown and tender, about 5 minutes. Season with the ½ teaspoon sea salt. Stir in the curry paste and cook for 2 minutes. Pour in the coconut milk, scraping up any curry paste with a wooden spoon. Add the fish sauce, lime zest, and lime juice. Add the tofu cubes and the green beans. Simmer, stirring frequently, until the sauce thickens slightly and the green beans are tender, 7 to 10 minutes. Taste, and add more salt and/or fish sauce if needed.

3. Serve with a scattering of basil on top.

1 package (14 to 16 ounces) extra-firm tofu, drained, patted dry, and cut into 1-inch cubes

½ teaspoon fine sea salt, plus more for seasoning

1 tablespoon coconut, peanut, or safflower oil

1 1-inch piece fresh ginger, peeled and minced

2 shallots or 1 small onion, minced

2 garlic cloves, minced

1 fresh Thai or 2 serrano chiles, seeded and thinly sliced

2 tablespoons chopped fresh cilantro stems

4 ounces shiitake mushroom caps, sliced (about 1½ cups)

3 tablespoons prepared Thai red curry paste

1 cup unsweetened coconut milk

2 teaspoons Asian fish sauce, plus more as needed

Grated zest and juice of 1 lime

1 cup cut green beans, in 1-inch lengths

Fresh basil or cilantro leaves, torn, for garnish

TOTAL TIME: 25 MINUTES
SERVES 4

CHILE & GINGER–FRIED TOFU SALAD *with Kale*

In this spicy salad, cubes of fried tofu act like tender-bellied croutons amid the leaves of baby kale, only with much more protein and spunk than the usual toasted bread. You'll need to marinate the tofu for at least an hour before cooking, so plan ahead. And if you don't feel like frying, you can broil the tofu. Skip the cornstarch and run the tofu under the broiler for two to three minutes per side, until golden brown. It won't be as crispy, but the flavor is still good and spicy. And it's a lot less messy.

Serve this with rice noodles tossed with a little sesame oil, or with a sliced baguette. And something to note: this might be the only tofu recipe in the book that's actually not great served with rice, which can be hard to eat with the salad greens here.

1. Arrange the tofu on a plate or baking sheet. In a blender, combine the soy sauce, chile sauce, chile halves, cilantro, garlic, and ginger; puree until smooth.

2. Using a pastry brush, coat the tofu on both sides with two-thirds of the chile mixture (reserve the rest for serving). Cover with plastic wrap and refrigerate for at least 1 hour and up to 6 hours.

3. Fill a 12-inch skillet with ½ inch of peanut oil and heat it over medium-high heat. Dip the slabs of tofu in the cornstarch, coating both sides, and tap off the excess.

4. Working in batches, add the tofu to the hot oil and cook, turning it over once, until it is golden brown, 1 to 2 minutes per side. Transfer the tofu to a paper-towel-lined plate to drain off the excess oil.

5. In a large bowl, toss the kale with the olive oil and fine sea salt to taste. Add the tofu and toss. Some of the kale will wilt, which is what you want. Serve hot, topped with sliced scallions and cilantro leaves, and with the reserved chile marinade alongside for drizzling.

1 package (14 to 16 ounces) firm tofu, drained, patted dry, and cut into 8 pieces

⅓ cup soy sauce

¼ cup hot chile sauce, such as Sriracha or *sambel olek* chile sauce

1 serrano chile, halved, seeded if desired

⅓ cup chopped fresh cilantro leaves

6 garlic cloves, coarsely chopped

1 tablespoon coarsely chopped peeled fresh ginger

Peanut oil, for frying

½ cup cornstarch

5 ounces baby kale or spinach

2 tablespoons extra-virgin olive oil

Fine sea salt to taste

Sliced scallions (white and green parts), for garnish

TOTAL TIME: 30 MINUTES + AT LEAST
1 HOUR MARINATING
SERVES 4

SEARED TOFU

with Bacon, Shiitakes, and Chives

Chunks of crispy bacon tucked in among mushrooms and scallions make this a rich and filling tofu dish with a porky, brawny personality. It's a nice change from some of the more vegetable-heavy tofu recipes in this book, with the bacon adding both a chewy-crunchy texture and its inimitable meaty flavor to the golden cushions of tofu. That said, if you'd rather go meatless, nix the bacon and double the mushrooms. You can add a pinch or two of sweet or hot smoked paprika to make up for the lacking smoky note.

I really like this dish served with rice (page 276) and the Winter Vegetable Salad with Kale, Cabbage, and Thai Lime Dressing (page 369) to make a full and harmonious meal.

2 tablespoons peanut or safflower oil

1 package (14 to 16 ounces) extra-firm tofu, drained, patted dry, and sliced crosswise into ¾-inch-thick slabs

Fine sea salt to taste

4 ounces fresh shiitake mushrooms caps, thinly sliced (about 1½ cups)

3 ounces thick-cut bacon or pancetta, cut into ¼-inch pieces

2 scallions: white and light green parts thinly sliced; dark green parts sliced and reserved for garnish

¼ cup chicken or vegetable stock

2½ teaspoons soy sauce

2 teaspoons mirin

Rice vinegar to taste

Thinly sliced fresh chives, for garnish

TOTAL TIME: 20 MINUTES
SERVES 2

1. Heat a 12-inch skillet over high heat until it is very hot, about 5 minutes. Add the peanut oil and let it heat for 30 seconds. Then carefully add the tofu. Don't touch the tofu for 2 to 3 minutes to let it sear until golden brown. Flip the tofu over and sear for another 2 to 3 minutes. The pan may smoke, but fear not, it means the skillet was hot enough. (Turn on your fan and open your windows.) Transfer the tofu to a plate and sprinkle it with salt to taste.

2. Add the mushrooms, bacon, and white and light green parts of the scallions to the skillet. Cook, tossing occasionally, until the mushrooms are softened and light golden and the bacon is crisp, 3 to 4 minutes.

3. Stir the stock, soy sauce, and mirin into the mushroom mixture. Cook until the sauce reduces and thickens slightly, about 1 minute.

4. If the tofu is no longer hot, push the vegetables in the skillet to one side, add the tofu, and cook until it is heated through. Transfer the hot tofu to serving plates and top it with the mushroom mixture and the pan sauce. Sprinkle with vinegar to taste, and garnish with chives and the dark green scallion slices.

THAI-STYLE SHREDDED
TOFU *with Brussels Sprouts*

I thought I'd run the gamut of tofu techniques.

I've stir-fried it, simmered it into stews and soups, pureed it into mousses and dressings. I'd baked it, grilled it, sautéed it, kebabed it, ground it up into chili, even eaten it raw, doused in a soy vinaigrette.

But until very recently, I'd never shredded it, only because the thought hadn't occurred to me.

I got the idea from Heidi Swanson, who writes the *101 Cookbooks* blog. She sautés the shredded tofu in olive oil with pumpkin seeds, pea greens, and a little buttermilk, which sounds like a nearly instant and delightful summer meal.

For this recipe, I took the basic premise and swerved it in a more autumnal direction, with sliced Brussels sprouts for sweetness and some chile, garlic, and ginger to give it a bite. And in the same way that Heidi uses pumpkin seeds for a textural contrast, I also tossed in peanuts for crunch.

One of the most liberating things about stir-frying shredded tofu—as opposed to tofu cubes or wedges—is that you're not trying to brown it. The aim is for a fluffy, downy mound that's deeply flavored, but soft. Think of scrambled eggs or egg noodles in terms of texture. The idea is to heat up the tofu and integrate it with the sauce, but it won't be in the pan long enough for you to worry about it sticking.

You can vary this basic recipe with other vegetables if you like, such as substituting sliced kale leaves (not baby kale) or napa cabbage for the Brussels sprouts. It's a quick-cooking recipe that's highly adaptable.

1. Using the large holes on a box grater, coarsely shred the tofu. Spread the shredded tofu on a clean kitchen towel to absorb the excess liquid.

2. Halve the Brussels sprouts lengthwise through the root ends and thinly slice them.

3. In a small bowl, whisk together the lime zest and juice, brown sugar, fish sauce, and soy sauce.

4. Heat the peanut oil in a large skillet over medium-high heat. Add the Brussels sprouts, chile, and garlic. Sauté until the sprouts are tender, 3 to 5 minutes. Stir in the tofu and cook to heat it through, about 2 minutes. Stir in the sauce and the ¼ teaspoon salt; cook for 1 minute. Remove the skillet from the heat and toss in the peanuts, scallions, and basil. Taste, and adjust the seasoning if needed before serving.

1 package (14 to 16 ounces) extra-firm tofu, drained and patted dry

8 ounces Brussels sprouts, trimmed (about 4 cups)

Finely grated zest and juice of 1 lime

1½ tablespoons light brown sugar

1½ tablespoons Asian fish sauce

1 teaspoon soy sauce

2 tablespoons peanut oil

½ to 1 fresh red chile, seeded and thinly sliced

2 large garlic cloves, grated on a Microplane or minced

¼ teaspoon fine sea salt, plus more if needed

½ cup chopped peanuts

¼ cup thinly sliced scallions (white and green parts) or shallots

Torn fresh basil leaves to taste

TOTAL TIME: 20 MINUTES
SERVES 4

SHREDDED TOFU

with Spicy Ground Chicken and Edamame

These fluffy pieces of shredded tofu are like soft, tiny dumplings and cook up in no time at all. Here, ground chicken gives them a meaty depth and a caramelized flavor while edamame adds texture and a vegetable to the mix.

If you want to make this vegetarian, leave out the meat, and instead sauté 4 ounces of chopped fresh shiitake or cremini mushrooms with the scallions and ginger. Make sure to get the shiitakes nice and golden; you need the extra flavor that caramelization provides.

Serve this by itself, with the Smashed Sichuan Cucumber Salad on page 379, or with a simple salad of baby spinach dressed with a little sesame oil, salt, and lime juice.

1. Heat the sesame oil in a 10-inch skillet over medium-high heat. Add the scallions, ginger, and garlic. Cook, stirring occasionally, until softened and golden at the edges, about 5 minutes. Stir in the chicken and cook until it is well browned all over, about 5 minutes.

2. While the chicken cooks, coarsely shred the tofu on the large holes of a box grater.

3. Stir the tofu, edamame, soy sauce, and salt into the chicken. Cook until warmed through, about 3 minutes. Remove the skillet from the heat and season the mixture with the lime juice and Sriracha. Toss in the herbs and extra scallions, and serve immediately.

¼ cup toasted sesame oil

¼ cup thinly sliced scallions (white and green parts), plus more for serving

1 1-inch piece fresh ginger, peeled and finely chopped

1 large garlic clove, minced

4 ounces ground chicken (or use turkey or pork)

1 package (14 to 16 ounces) extra-firm tofu, drained and patted dry

½ cup shelled edamame, thawed if frozen

1½ tablespoons soy sauce, plus more as needed

¼ teaspoon fine sea salt, or to taste

1 tablespoon fresh lime juice

1 teaspoon Sriracha

½ cup coarsely chopped fresh cilantro and/or mint leaves

TOTAL TIME: 20 MINUTES
SERVES 4

SEITAN ENCHILADAS

with Cheese and Pickled Jalapeños

Seitan is protein-packed wheat gluten with a pleasingly chewy, meaty texture and not much flavor. It fades into the background in this robust casserole, becoming anonymously and texturally chicken-like as it blends with the tangy tomato-jalapeño sauce, gooey cheese, and sweet bite of the raisins. Despite any raised eyebrows you might get for serving seitan to the uninitiated, this really is a crowd-pleasing vegetarian enchilada dish and a potential gateway to the realm of seitan love, where I happily reside.

This said, if seitan is off the menu for any reason (maybe you avoid gluten), feel free to substitute strips of extra-firm or baked tofu or tempeh. Or, if you eat meat, cooked leftover chicken is also an option.

You can assemble the enchiladas up to four hours in advance. Keep them covered in aluminum foil and refrigerated until ready to bake. Then add a few minutes to the cooking time.

2 tablespoons extra-virgin olive oil

1 medium red onion, diced

2 garlic gloves, minced

1 tablespoon chopped fresh oregano leaves

1 tablespoon chopped fresh basil leaves

1 teaspoon ancho chile powder

1 28-ounce can chopped tomatoes, with their juices

½ cup pickled jalapeños, with their liquid

Kosher salt to taste

Freshly ground black pepper to taste

3 cups seitan strips (about 2 pounds)

1 cup black or golden raisins

12 6-inch corn tortillas

1¾ cups sour cream

2 cups shredded cheddar cheese

Sliced scallions (white and green parts), for garnish

Fresh cilantro leaves, for garnish

TOTAL TIME: 45 MINUTES
SERVES 4 TO 6

1. Heat the oven to 375°F.

2. Heat a 12-inch skillet over medium heat. Then add the olive oil and let it heat up until it shimmers. Add the onion and garlic, and sauté until they are fragrant, about 3 minutes. Stir in the oregano, basil, and chile powder. Add the chopped tomatoes and 2 tablespoons of the liquid from the jalapeños. Simmer the enchilada sauce until it begins to thicken, about 6 minutes. Season with salt and pepper to taste.

3. In a bowl, combine the seitan, jalapeños, raisins, and 2 cups of the sauce.

4. Spread ½ cup of the remaining enchilada sauce over the bottom of a 9 × 13-inch baking dish.

5. Heat a small dry skillet over medium heat. Heat 1 tortilla in the skillet until it is just softened, about 10 seconds per side. Place the warm tortilla on a work surface, and spread 1 tablespoon of the sour cream in a strip down the center. Top with ¼ cup of the seitan filling, sprinkle with grated cheese, and roll the tortilla up. Place the enchilada, seam side down, on top of the sauce in the baking dish. Repeat, making 11 more enchiladas. Spoon the remaining sauce over the enchiladas, and sprinkle more cheese on top. Cover the dish with aluminum foil.

6. Bake until the enchiladas are heated through, 15 to 20 minutes. Uncover the baking dish, and top the enchiladas with dollops of the remaining sour cream. Garnish with sliced scallions and cilantro leaves, and serve.

BEANS, LEGUMES & VEGETABLE DINNERS

USING BEANS, BOTH CANNED AND DRIED

Freshly cooked dried beans are always going to be better—firmer and more richly flavored—than anything you can get from a can. But there are times when the convenience factor of the canned stuff makes them the only choice for getting dinner on the table in a timely fashion. My general rule of thumb is pretty simple: use dried beans when you have the time to cook them properly, and use canned beans when you don't. No matter which kind you use, here are some tips for getting the most out of them.

TIPS FOR DRIED BEANS

• Check for a date on the package because even though they're dried, fresher beans are still better. Dried beans will last for up to 2 years, but they're best cooked within a year of harvest. If you're buying bulk beans, it can be hard to know exactly how old the beans are. Definitely avoid any that are starting to visibly deteriorate and break down (at that point they are either ancient or have been poorly stored). But even perfectly fine *looking* beans can be stale and you won't be able to tell by sight. Buying dried beans at a store with a big turnover is usually a fairly safe bet, and you can always try asking.

• Dried beans are not cleaned before packaging, so always rinse them before cooking, and check for tiny pebbles and bits of twigs and leaves.

• If your beans don't cook through, it might be because there was an acidic ingredient in the cooking water (lemon or tomato, for example). Or perhaps your water is hard (i.e. mineral rich), or your beans were old and stale. But it's not because of adding salt. It's a myth that adding salt to bean cooking water slows down or prevents the beans from cooking through, and I always cook my beans in salted water. It seasons them more thoroughly and evenly. If you've had problems with your beans not cooking through in the past, try cooking your beans in bottled water next time and see if that helps.

SOAKING DRIED BEANS

You don't *need* to soak beans, but it does help them cook faster and more evenly (and the process can make them more digestible by leaching out the enzymes that cause intestinal gas). And, if you do add salt to the soaking water—in other words, make a brine—your beans will cook faster because the salt helps break down the bean skins.

This said, if you don't soak your beans, they will cook through given enough time and liquid for simmering.

To soak beans, cover them with water by two inches, add 1 tablespoon fine sea salt per pound of beans, and let them soak for at least 4 hours or up to 12 hours. Drain and rinse before cooking.

You can also quick soak your beans. You don't necessarily save any time here because if you just cooked them for an extra hour instead of letting them soak in hot water for an hour, they would probably end up cooking through in the same amount of time. But quick soaking does leach out the enzymes that cause intestinal gas if that's a concern. **To quick soak beans**, put the beans in a pot on the stove. Cover them with water by two inches, add salt if you like, and bring to a boil. Turn off the heat and let them soak for an hour. Drain and rinse

HOW TO COOK ANY DRIED BEANS

These methods will work for any kind of dried bean. Bear in mind that un-soaked beans take longer to cook than soaked beans; the times given below are for soaked beans. For most bean varieties, 1 cup of dried beans yields 3 cups cooked.

To cook your beans on the stove, cover your beans by at least 2 inches of water, add 1 teaspoon of fine sea salt for every pound of beans, and simmer over low heat. Stir the beans gently and occasionally, never letting them hit a strong boil (this can burst their skins and make them mushy or unevenly cooked). Smaller beans such as lentils, split peas, adzuki, and navy beans will be done in 30 to 60 minutes (with the exception of red lentils, which take only 15 to 20 minutes). Larger beans such as kidney, cannellini, and chickpeas can take 1½ to 3 hours.

To cook your beans in a pressure cooker, put the beans, water, salt, and a little oil (to keep the vent from clogging) into the pot, making sure not to fill it more than halfway. Cook at high pressure for 5 to 10 minutes for small beans such as lentils, black-eyed peas, and split peas, and up to 40 minutes for larger beans such as kidney beans and chickpeas.

To cook your beans in a slow cooker, cover your beans with water by 2 inches, add salt, and cook on low for usually 4 to 6 hours, or high for usually 2 to 4 hours. If you're cooking kidney beans, you need to boil them on the stove for 10 minutes before adding to the slow cooker. This helps destroy a gut-irritating toxin that those beans in particular contain.

To test for doneness, scoop up a couple of beans and blow on them. The skin should curl and wrinkle. Then taste the beans. They are done when they're tender and cooked through to the center (but not mushy). At this point, add more salt if needed while the beans are still hot, then let them cool in the cooking liquid. If not using immediately, store cooked, cooled beans in their cooking liquid in the refrigerator for up to 1 week or in the freezer for up to 2 months.

TIPS FOR CANNED BEANS

• Always rinse and drain canned beans before using. The liquid in the can is not delicious.

• Unsalted canned beans are very bland, so unless you're on a low-sodium diet, it's best to choose beans cooked with sea salt.

• Since canned beans tend to be softer in texture than their freshly cooked counterparts, they're best used in dips, soups, and stews rather than salads, where you generally want a firmer bean.

HOW TO USE CANNED BEANS

Canned beans are great in a pinch. If you are making hot soup or chili, add them during the last 15 to 30 minutes of cooking. Just give the beans time to absorb and meld with the other flavors in the pot. If you're adding canned beans to a salad, add them after all the other ingredients have been tossed together, then very gently toss in the beans to coat them with dressing. This helps maintain their texture; excessive tossing can turn them into bean mush.

Store leftover canned beans in a sealed container in the fridge for up to 5 days or so, or in the freezer for up to 3 months.

ONE-POT MUJADARA
with Crispy Leeks and Spinach

Mujadara is the essence of comfort food, a humble dish of lentils and rice topped with fried onions. Made from pantry staples, it's the Middle Eastern analogue of Italy's pasta with garlic and oil, the kind of thing to make when there's nothing in the house for dinner, with a spectacular end result. In *mujadara*'s case, you'll get aromatic lentils and rice spiced with allspice, cumin, and cinnamon. The browned onions, burnished and crackling, are arguably the best part, adding sweetness and texture to the mix.

Classic *mujadara* recipes call for cooking the onion, rice, and lentils separately, them combining them for serving. Here, I streamline the process and cook everything in stages in the same pot.

And perhaps even more untraditionally, right at the end, I also add some baby spinach to the mix, letting it wilt in the steam wafting up from lentils and rice. It adds welcome color and enough vegetables to make this a one-pot meal.

1 cup brown or green (*lentilles du Puy*) lentils

¼ cup extra-virgin olive oil

2 leeks (white and light green parts only), halved lengthwise and thinly sliced

2¼ teaspoons kosher salt

2 garlic cloves, minced

¾ cup long-grain rice

1½ teaspoons ground cumin

½ teaspoon ground allspice

¼ teaspoon cayenne pepper

1 bay leaf

1 2-inch-long cinnamon stick

4 cups fresh baby spinach (or baby kale if you like)

Hot sauce, for serving (optional)

TOTAL TIME: 40 MINUTES
SERVES 6

1. Place the lentils in a large bowl and add enough warm tap water to cover them by 1 inch. Let the lentils soak while you cook the leeks.

2. Heat the olive oil in a Dutch oven or other large pot over high heat. Add the leeks and cook, stirring occasionally, until they are dark brown at their edges, 5 to 10 minutes. A few black strands are okay and better than having undercooked, blond leeks, which won't be as crispy. Leaving half of the leeks in the pot, transfer the remainder of the leeks to a plate, sprinkle them with ¼ teaspoon of the salt, and set them aside for the garnish.

3. Stir the garlic into the remaining leeks in the pot, and cook until fragrant, about 15 seconds. Stir in the rice and sauté for 2 minutes. Stir in the cumin, allspice, and cayenne; sauté for 30 seconds.

4. Drain the lentils and add them to the pot. Add 4¼ cups of water, the remaining 2 teaspoons salt, the bay leaf, and the cinnamon stick. Bring to a simmer. Cover and cook over low heat for 15 minutes.

5. Spread the spinach over the lentil mixture, re-cover the pot, and cook until the rice and lentils are tender and the spinach has wilted, 5 minutes. Remove the pot from the heat and let it stand, covered, for 5 minutes. Serve, topped with the reserved crispy leeks and sprinkled with hot sauce if you like.

SWEET POTATO DHAL
with Coconut

As you can probably tell from the three dhal recipes in this chapter, I've fallen in love with making dhals. I've always adored eating the simmered legumes (usually split peas or lentils) in Indian restaurants, but for whatever reason, I only started cooking them myself relatively recently. What makes dhals so attractive is how easy they are for such a deep and complexly flavored payoff. Most of the character comes from a spiced oil or butter mixture, called a *tarka*, that gets mixed in after the legumes have finished cooking.

In this version, I add grated sweet potatoes to yellow split peas as they cook. The sweet potato adds a velvety texture and sweetness to the mix. As a topping, I drizzle on shallots and mustard seeds cooked in coconut oil, plus toasted coconut flakes and a dollop of thick coconut cream. The dhal is definitely a bit decadent with a lot going on, but it isn't all that complicated to make. Serve this with something plain on the side—Quick-Roasted Broccoli or Cauliflower (page 382) and some rice or flatbread would round it out nicely.

1. In a medium pot, bring 6 cups of water to a simmer. Add the drained split peas, grated sweet potatoes, turmeric, and salt. Simmer until the peas have fallen apart and the potatoes are tender, about 1 hour, adding more water as needed to keep the mixture from drying out. By the end it should be thick and stew-like (or you can add more water to taste if you like a thinner dhal).

2. While the dhal is cooking, place a small, dry skillet over medium-high heat, add the coconut flakes, and toast until they are lightly colored, 2 to 5 minutes. Transfer the coconut to a bowl.

3. Return the skillet to medium-high heat and add the coconut oil. Once it is hot, add the shallots and cook, stirring frequently, until they are tender and golden brown (reduce the heat if they begin to burn), about 10 minutes. Stir in the ginger, mustard seeds, cumin seeds, and cayenne; cook for 1 minute, and remove from the heat.

4. Stir the shallot mixture into the dhal. Taste, and adjust the seasoning if necessary. In a small bowl, whisk the coconut cream a few times to loosen it. Spoon some coconut cream onto each serving of dhal. Garnish with the toasted coconut and fresh cilantro.

2 cups yellow split peas, preferably soaked for at least 1 to 4 hours and drained (see pages 232 to 233)

2 medium sweet potatoes, peeled and coarsely grated

1 teaspoon ground turmeric

2 teaspoons kosher salt, plus more if needed

½ cup unsweetened coconut flakes

¼ cup coconut oil

1 cup sliced shallots (from 4 to 5 shallots)

2 teaspoons grated fresh ginger

2 teaspoons brown or black mustard seeds

2 teaspoons cumin seeds

⅛ teaspoon cayenne pepper, plus more if needed

1 5.4-ounce can unsweetened coconut cream, or ¾ cup plain whole-milk yogurt or unsweetened coconut yogurt

Fresh cilantro leaves, for garnish

TOTAL TIME: 1¼ HOURS
SERVES 4 TO 6

RED LENTIL DHAL

with Spiced Brown Butter and Yogurt

Red lentils are one of the quickest-cooking legumes, collapsing into softness in half an hour or less. This makes them convenient to have on hand for throwing together weeknight dinners in a flash. Here, I simmer them with ginger and chile, then gild them with a spice-infused brown butter studded with shallots. This recipe is both hotter (in the chile-and-ginger sense) and richer than the other dhals, and is the fastest of the three to make.

I like it over brown basmati rice, but any rice will do.

2 cups red lentils

1½ teaspoons kosher salt

1 teaspoon ground turmeric

1 2-inch piece plus 1 1½-inch piece fresh ginger, peeled

4 green cardamom pods, lightly bruised with the flat side of a knife or mortar and pestle

1 dried red chile, or ¼ teaspoon red chile flakes

4 tablespoons (½ stick) unsalted butter

2¼ teaspoons cumin seeds

3 large shallots, thinly sliced

2 jalapeños, seeded and coarsely chopped

3 garlic cloves, finely chopped

¾ teaspoon garam masala

Fresh cilantro leaves, for garnish (optional)

Plain Greek yogurt, preferably whole-milk, for serving

Flaky sea salt to taste

TOTAL TIME: 45 MINUTES
SERVES 4

1. In a medium pot, combine the lentils, salt, turmeric, 2-inch piece of ginger, cardamom, chile, and 6 cups of water. Bring to a boil over medium-high heat. Then reduce the heat and simmer, stirring occasionally, until the lentils are soft and the mixture has thickened, about 30 minutes.

2. Meanwhile, finely chop the remaining 1½-inch piece of ginger. In a large skillet, melt the butter over medium heat. Cook until the foam subsides and the butter turns a deep nut brown, about 5 minutes. You'll know the butter is nearly browned when the furious bubbling in the pan grows quiet; this is a sign that the moisture is being evaporated, after which the fat turns from golden to brown quite quickly. So use your ears as well as your eyes here (and your nose; you'll be able to smell the nuttiness).

3. Add the cumin seeds to the brown butter and cook for 30 seconds. Add the shallots and jalapeños, and cook, stirring occasionally, until the shallots are caramelized and well browned, 7 to 10 minutes. Stir in the chopped ginger, garlic, and garam masala; cook for 30 seconds.

4. Thin down the dhal with a little water if it seems too thick (do this to taste). Spoon the dhal into bowls, discarding the chunk of ginger, the cardamom pods, and the whole dried chile. Top with the brown butter mixture, cilantro leaves if using, and a dollop of yogurt. Sprinkle with flaky sea salt.

TOMATO DHAL
with Mango Pickle

Tomatoes make this dhal extremely bright and savory, a quality that is played up by the mango pickle stirred in at the end. Do not confuse mango pickle with mango chutney. The pickle is, well, pickle-y, with a vinegar tartness and a stinging slap of chile, while the chutney is soft, sweet, and gently spiced. For this assertive dhal, you want the pickle's tang and heat. You can substitute another Indian pickle. If mango isn't available, try lime, lemon, carrot, or garlic. And in a pinch, if none of these are available, some preserved lemon will offer a similar kind of salty-fermented flavor to round out the spiced lentils and tomatoes. Serve this over white basmati rice for a cooling, neutral contrast to all the intensity of the dhal.

1½ cups red lentils

1 teaspoon kosher salt

2 tablespoons unsalted butter

1 teaspoon cumin seeds

1 teaspoon coriander seeds

1 large white onion, thinly sliced

1 ½-inch piece fresh ginger, peeled and grated

4 garlic cloves, grated on a Microplane or minced

2 tablespoons finely chopped fresh cilantro stems (leaves saved for garnish)

½ teaspoon freshly ground black pepper

½ teaspoon ground turmeric

½ teaspoon good chile powder such as ancho or New Mexico

Large pinch of ground cloves

1 28-ounce can diced tomatoes, with their juices

1 to 2 tablespoons chopped mango pickle (or other Indian pickle such as lime or lemon), to taste

Greek yogurt, for serving

TOTAL TIME: 45 MINUTES
SERVES 4

1. In a medium pot, combine the lentils, 3½ cups of water, and the salt. Bring to a simmer over medium heat; then reduce the heat to medium-low and simmer until the lentils are completely cooked through, 15 to 20 minutes. At this point, all or most of the liquid will be absorbed.

2. Meanwhile, melt the butter in a large pot over medium-high heat. Add the cumin and coriander seeds, and toast until fragrant, about 1 minute. Add the onion and cook, tossing occasionally, until it is dark golden brown and tender, about 10 minutes.

3. Add the ginger, garlic, cilantro stems, black pepper, turmeric, chile powder, and cloves. Pour in the tomatoes and their juices. Simmer, uncovered, until the tomatoes are broken down and the mixture is thick and sauce-y, 15 to 20 minutes. If it starts to dry out before it's done, add a little more water as you go.

4. Stir the lentils into the tomato mixture and cook for 5 minutes to meld the flavors. Then stir in the mango pickle.

5. To serve, spoon the dhal over bowls of rice. Top it with yogurt and the reserved cilantro leaves.

TOMATO-BRAISED WHITE BEANS *with Chorizo*

Chorizo gives this hearty and rich white bean stew a complex, cured pork-and-paprika flavor that adds a lot of depth to the dish. Make sure to buy dried Spanish-style chorizo rather than the fresh, raw kind. If you can't find it, you can substitute salami and a teaspoon of smoked sweet paprika, which will approximate the flavors.

I like this with the mildly sweet Skillet Brown-Butter Cornbread (page 385) on the side, if you're in the mood to bake. Otherwise, any crusty bread will work.

1. Heat the olive oil in a large pot over medium-high heat. Add the chorizo and cook until the slices are browned, about 3 minutes. Using a slotted spoon, transfer the sausage to a paper-towel-lined plate.

2. Add the tomato paste, cumin, and paprika to the pot. Cook, stirring, until the mixture is caramelized and dark gold, about 2 minutes. Then add the carrots, celery, onion, and garlic; cook, stirring, until the vegetables have softened, about 5 minutes. Stir in the beans, tomatoes, 2 cups of water, the ½ teaspoon salt, the thyme and rosemary sprigs, and the bay leaf. Bring the mixture to a boil over high heat. Return the sausages to the pot, reduce the heat to low, and simmer gently until the tomatoes break down and the mixture thickens, 25 to 30 minutes. Discard the bay leaf and herb sprigs.

3. Add the spinach, stirring until it has wilted, and then add the 1 teaspoon vinegar and the ½ teaspoon black pepper. Taste, and adjust the seasoning if necessary. Ladle the mixture into warmed bowls, and drizzle additional vinegar and olive oil over each serving.

2 tablespoons extra-virgin olive oil, plus more for drizzling

8 ounces dried (cured) chorizo, thinly sliced

1 tablespoon tomato paste

½ teaspoon ground cumin

¼ teaspoon hot smoked paprika

2 medium carrots, finely diced

2 celery stalks, finely diced

1 onion, chopped

2 garlic cloves, finely chopped

3 cups cooked white beans, homemade (see pages 232 to 233) or canned, rinsed and drained

1 cup canned diced tomatoes and their juices

½ teaspoon fine sea salt, plus more to taste

2 sprigs fresh thyme

2 large sprigs fresh rosemary

1 bay leaf

5 ounces (about 5 cups) baby spinach

1 teaspoon sherry vinegar, plus more as needed

½ teaspoon freshly ground black pepper, plus more if needed

TOTAL TIME: 45 MINUTES
SERVES 6

Warm WHITE BEAN SALAD
with Arugula Pesto and Preserved Lemon

White beans dressed with pesto is a classic for a reason; the garlicky herb paste gives a huge flavor lift to the soft and earthy beans. In this salad, arugula does double duty, acting both as an herb in the pesto in place of the usual basil, and as a salad green on top of which the pesto-coated beans are mounded. Warming the beans before tossing them with the pesto is an important step because warm beans absorb flavors more effectively than cold beans. But after you mix in the pesto, you can serve the beans at room temperature if you want to make this salad ahead. The pesto-coated beans will keep well for up to four hours; spoon them on top of the fresh arugula just before serving.

If you don't have the preserved lemon for the pesto, substitute grated lemon zest and some extra salt. You won't get that same deep, funky tang, but at least the acidity and salt balance will remain intact.

6 to 8 cups arugula

⅓ cup sliced almonds

¼ cup grated Parmigiano-Reggiano cheese

2½ tablespoons chopped preserved lemon

1 garlic clove, chopped

¼ teaspoon kosher salt, plus more to taste

⅓ cup extra-virgin olive oil, plus more to taste

3 cups cooked white beans, homemade (see pages 232 to 233) or canned, rinsed and drained

Fresh lemon juice to taste

Freshly ground black pepper to taste

2 to 3 tablespoons thinly shaved shallots or red onion (optional)

TOTAL TIME: 20 MINUTES
SERVES 4

1. In a food processor or blender, combine 2 packed cups of the arugula with the almonds, cheese, preserved lemon, garlic, and the ¼ teaspoon salt. Process or blend until everything is finely chopped. With the motor running, blend in the ⅓ cup olive oil.

2. Warm the beans in the microwave for about 1 minute, or in a small pot on the stovetop for about 2 to 3 minutes. The beans should be warm to the touch but not hot.

3. In a medium bowl, toss the arugula pesto with the warm beans, and adjust the seasoning to taste.

4. In a large bowl, toss the remaining arugula with lemon juice, a drizzle of olive oil, and salt and pepper to taste. (If you're unsure, add the seasonings a little at a time, tasting as you go, until you like it. Be generous with the black pepper.) Arrange the arugula salad on a large platter, and spoon the beans on top. Sprinkle the shaved shallots over the beans, and serve.

CURRIED LENTILS

with Poached Eggs and Garlicky Yogurt

Curried lentils are the first place my mind goes when I ponder cooking the tiny legumes. I think that of all possible seasonings, the pungently fragrant combination of garlic, ginger, cumin, and other curry spices—really brings out the earthy and nutty qualities in lentils. Here I've added poached eggs for the rich, runny yolk factor, and tangy cool yogurt for creaminess.

I especially love this served with garlic-rubbed crostini and Pan-Fried Asparagus (page 376), both of which are perfect for dunking in the broken yolks. Or try it over Coconut Rice (page 381) to add a subtly sweet element.

1. Heat the olive oil in a medium pot over medium heat. Add the shallots and a pinch of salt, and cook until softened, about 5 minutes.

2. While the shallots are cooking, finely chop 4 of the garlic cloves.

3. Add the chopped garlic, ginger, garam masala, turmeric, and cumin to the shallots; cook for 1 minute. Then stir in the lentils. Add 4½ cups of water, the dried chile, and 1 teaspoon of the salt. Bring to a boil, reduce the heat to medium-low, and simmer, uncovered, until the lentils are tender, 30 to 60 minutes (depending on the freshness of the lentils). If the lentils seem dry at any point, add more water, ½ cup at a time, to maintain a stew-like consistency. Taste, and add more salt if needed. Cover to keep the lentils warm.

4. Prepare the yogurt sauce: Place the yogurt in a small bowl. Grate in the remaining garlic clove, and season with salt and pepper to taste.

5. Poach the eggs: Fill a wide pot with salted water and bring it to a simmer. Crack 1 egg into a cup. Gently slip the egg into the simmering water in one fluid motion. Repeat with the remaining eggs. (If they don't all fit comfortably in the pot, poach them in 2 batches.) Reduce the heat to a simmer, and cook the eggs without disturbing them until the yolks are semi-firm, 2 to 3 minutes. Use a slotted spoon to transfer the eggs to a paper-towel-lined plate to drain. (See page 149 for egg-poaching tips.)

6. To serve, spoon the lentils into individual warmed bowls. Carefully place 1 or 2 eggs on top of each serving. Season the eggs with salt and pepper. Top each bowl with a dollop of the yogurt sauce, a drizzle of olive oil, a few cilantro leaves, and chile flakes to taste.

2 tablespoons extra-virgin olive oil, plus more for drizzling

½ cup diced shallots (2 to 3 shallots)

Fine sea salt and freshly ground black pepper, as needed

5 garlic cloves

2 tablespoons grated peeled fresh ginger

1 tablespoon garam masala

1½ teaspoons ground turmeric

1½ teaspoons ground cumin

12 ounces (about 1½ cups) brown lentils

1 dried *chile de árbol* or other dried whole chile (or ¼ teaspoon red chile flakes)

⅓ cup plain yogurt, preferably whole milk (mixed with a little milk to thin it down if using Greek yogurt)

4 to 8 eggs

Fresh cilantro leaves, for serving

Red chile flakes, for serving

TOTAL TIME: 1 TO 1½ HOURS
SERVES 4

Smashed WHITE BEAN TOASTS
with Roasted Asparagus and Sumac

Although you can always substitute canned beans for home cooked, there are some recipes where it's worth the effort to simmer up a pot of beans from scratch. My rule of thumb is that when the beans in question are served without much else—that is, when their inherent beany flavor is the main draw of the dish—you should take the time to cook them yourself. Home cooked have so much more flavor than canned beans, and you also get the pot liquor, which is as good as chicken broth, without any extra effort. And you can freeze it, too.

Because there's not a lot for the beans to hide behind in this crostini recipe, if you have the time, do make them yourself: you'll get a much deeper, richer puree from home-cooked white beans than from canned. In either case, the beans are mashed into a thick-textured paste, then slathered on garlicky crostini and topped with roasted asparagus. Asparagus takes kindly to gentle pairings, particularly starchy ones that tame the grassiness of the stalks. Here, the soft bean mash and crunchy pieces of toast do just that. A sprinkling of sumac adds a fruity acidity and a jolt of color, but if you don't have any on hand, use sweet paprika instead.

1. Heat the oven to 425°F.

2. Place the asparagus on a rimmed baking sheet and toss it with 2 tablespoons of the oil, ¼ teaspoon salt, and pepper to taste. Roast until tender, 10 to 12 minutes.

3. Meanwhile, put the beans and bean cooking liquid in a bowl. Using a Microplane, grate in 1 garlic clove (or finely mince it and add it to the bowl). Stir in the remaining ¼ cup of olive oil, the lemon zest and juice, the remaining ¼ teaspoon salt, and the chives. Mash the beans coarsely with a fork; season with pepper and more salt and lemon juice if needed.

4. Toast the bread in batches in a toaster or under the broiler. Halve the remaining garlic clove and rub the cut sides all over the warm toasts. Drizzle the toasts with a little olive oil, and top them with the beans and asparagus. Drizzle with additional olive oil, and sprinkle with sumac if desired. Serve at once.

1 pound asparagus, trimmed

6 tablespoons extra-virgin olive oil, plus more as needed

½ teaspoon fine sea salt, plus more as needed

Freshly ground black pepper, as needed

3 cups cooked white beans, homemade (see pages 232 to 233) or canned, rinsed and drained

2 tablespoons bean cooking liquid (if you've cooked your beans from scratch) or water

2 garlic cloves

Finely grated zest and juice of ½ lemon, plus more juice as needed

2 tablespoons minced fresh chives

6 to 8 large slices country-style bread

Ground sumac, for garnish (optional)

TOTAL TIME: 20 MINUTES
SERVES 4 TO 6

BLACK BEAN & ROASTED POBLANO QUESADILLAS

Here's a universal truth: everyone loves a quesadilla. That might be a slight exaggeration, but as crowd-pleasing dishes go, quesadillas are right up there with pizza, cheesy casseroles, and pancakes as home runs.

This version is a little more involved (but not much) than the usual cheese-filled tortillas, calling for highly seasoned black beans, smoked mozzarella, and roasted poblano chiles. (You can make the bean mixture up to five days ahead; warm it up in the microwave or in a pot on the stove before assembling the quesadillas.) But it's also a lot more sophisticated and interesting, and makes for an unexpected Mexican-inspired meal that is in no way authentic.

I also like to trot these out as a party hors d'oeuvre, cutting them in thin wedges and serving with guacamole, pea-studded (page 356) or otherwise, or lime *crema* (page 249) on the side for dipping. Or, treat them like a fancy side dish and serve them next to a simple grilled steak, maybe one marinated with cilantro, honey, and lime (page 67).

4 poblano chiles

2 tablespoons extra-virgin olive oil, plus more as needed

1 onion, sliced

1 teaspoon kosher salt, plus more if needed

2 tablespoons tomato paste

4 garlic cloves, minced

2 teaspoons chili powder

3 cups cooked black beans, homemade (see pages 232 to 233) or canned, rinsed and drained

8 large or 16 small flour or corn tortillas

1 pound smoked mozzarella, shredded

½ cup fresh cilantro leaves

Lime wedges, as needed

Avocado slices, for serving (optional)

TOTAL TIME: 35 MINUTES
SERVES 4 TO 6

1. Roast the poblanos over an open flame on a gas burner or under the broiler, turning them regularly until they are blackened all over, about 8 minutes. Place the roasted poblanos in a large bowl, cover it with a plate, and let them steam until they have softened, about 15 minutes. Using paper towels, rub off the poblano skins, remove the stems and seeds, and slice the chiles into narrow strips.

2. While the peppers are steaming, heat a 12-inch skillet over medium heat, then add 2 tablespoons olive oil. Add the onion and ½ teaspoon of the salt; cook until the onion is nicely browned at the edges, 8 to 10 minutes. Add the tomato paste, garlic, and chili powder, and cook until fragrant, 1 to 2 minutes. Then add the beans, 1 cup of water, and the remaining ½ teaspoon salt, and mash with a potato masher or the back of a large fork until about half of the beans are mashed and the liquid has been absorbed, about 7 minutes.

3. Arrange a rack as far from the heat source as possible, and heat the broiler.

4. To assemble the quesadillas, brush one side of half of the tortillas with olive oil, and flip them over onto a baking sheet, oiled-side down. Spread ⅔ cup of the bean mixture evenly over each tortilla, and then layer it with poblano strips, shredded cheese, cilantro leaves, and a squeeze of lime juice. Top with the remaining tortillas, and brush the tops with olive oil. Broil until the quesadillas are nicely browned, 3 to 5 minutes. Serve with lime wedges and avocado slices if you like.

BLACK BEAN SKILLET DINNER *with Quick-Pickled Red Onion and Lime* Crema

This is my version of vegetarian chili, which I simmer in a shallow skillet instead of a deep pot so that it comes together quickly enough for any given weeknight (wider pan = quicker evaporation = dinner on the table faster). I like to serve this with quick-pickled onions—red onions soaked in lime juice, salt, and sugar—to add a tangy bite to the beans, contrasting with their starchy softness. There's also a lime *crema* in this recipe, which may feel like one step too many on a weeknight, in which case you can absolutely skip it. Or substitute a dollop of yogurt straight from the container to add a little creaminess. But do make the pickles; they're worth the extra three minutes it takes to throw them together.

If you can't get cubanelle peppers (also called Italian frying peppers), substitute green bell pepper.

Serve this with some kind of tomato salad in summer (page 372) or a citrus salad in winter (page 375). Warm corn or flour tortillas are also nice alongside.

1. **Make the *crema*:** In a small bowl, combine the lime zest, garlic, and sour cream. Season with the pinch of salt.

2. **Make the pickled onion:** In another small bowl, combine the lime juice, red onion, sugar, and salt. Let the mixture stand while you prepare the beans.

3. **Cook the beans:** Heat the olive oil in a large skillet over medium-high heat. Add the onion, cubanelle peppers, and jalapeño. Cook, stirring frequently, until the vegetables are softened and browned at the edges, 10 to 12 minutes. Stir in the garlic, oregano, and chili powder, and sauté until the mixture smells garlicky, 1 to 2 minutes. Then stir in the black beans, tomatoes and juices, ⅔ cup of water, and the salt. Reduce the heat to medium and simmer until the mixture has thickened, about 20 minutes. Taste, and add more salt if needed.

4. To serve, spoon the beans into individual warmed bowls. Top them with diced avocado, dollops of the *crema*, pickled onions, and cilantro.

FOR THE *CREMA*
Finely grated zest of 1 lime

1 garlic clove, grated on a Microplane or minced

1 cup sour cream or Greek yogurt

Pinch of kosher salt

FOR THE PICKLED ONION
Juice of 1 lime

1 small red onion, very thinly sliced

1 teaspoon sugar

¼ teaspoon kosher salt

FOR THE BEANS
1½ tablespoons extra-virgin olive oil

1 small yellow onion, diced

3 medium cubanelle peppers, seeded and diced (about 1 cup)

1 small jalapeño, seeded and finely chopped

1 garlic clove, grated on a Microplane or minced

2 teaspoons dried oregano

1 teaspoon chili powder

3 cups cooked black beans, homemade (see pages 232 to 233) or canned, rinsed and drained

1 15-ounce can diced tomatoes, with their juices

1 teaspoon kosher salt, plus more if needed

Diced avocado

Fresh cilantro leaves

TIME: 40 MINUTES
SERVES 4

OLIVE OIL–BRAISED CHICKPEAS

and Swiss Chard with Cumin

A can of chickpeas in the pantry means a satisfying dinner on the table, no matter what else you've got in the fridge, even if the answer is not much. Simmer the chickpeas with olive oil, chile flakes, and a hint of garlic, and you've got a filling stew that belies its meager beginnings. While I've made that bare-bones braise on many cold nights, when there are leafy greens in the house, I add them. They make for a more complex meal that's prettier and a bit lighter, too. And I love the way they wilt into the broth, giving it an almost herbal flavor. In this recipe, I use chard, but feel free to substitute spinach, kale, or mustard greens, which have a sharper bite. Simmered with the chickpeas and olive oil, along with cumin for an earthy spiciness and shallots for sweetness, you'll get a warming one-pot meal that's somewhere between a soup and a stew.

If you want to cook your own chickpeas for this (and that will make this even better), save the chickpea cooking liquid to use in place of the stock.

5 garlic cloves

½ cup extra-virgin olive oil, plus more for serving

2 bunches Swiss chard, stems removed and cut into 1-inch pieces, leaves torn into bite-size pieces

2 teaspoons cumin seeds

¾ teaspoon fine sea salt, plus more if needed

Large pinch of red chile flakes

2 shallots, thinly sliced

4 cups cooked chickpeas, homemade (see pages 232 to 233) or canned, rinsed and drained

1 cup chicken or vegetable stock or water

4 to 6 slices country-style bread

Fresh lemon juice, for serving

Sweet smoked paprika, for serving

TOTAL TIME: 35 MINUTES
SERVES 4 TO 6

1. Thinly slice 4 of the garlic cloves. Cut the remaining clove in half and set the halves aside.

2. Heat the ½ cup olive oil in a medium pot over medium-high heat. Add the sliced garlic and cook until the edges are pale gold, about 3 minutes. Add the chard stems, cumin seeds, salt, and chile flakes. Cook until the stems are beginning to soften, about 5 minutes.

3. Add the shallots and cook for 3 minutes. Then stir in the chickpeas, chard leaves, and stock. Cover the pot and reduce the heat to medium-low. Simmer until the chard is meltingly tender, 10 to 15 minutes.

4. Using an immersion blender, partially puree the mixture until it is thick and stew-like but still chunky. Taste, and add more salt if needed. (If you don't have an immersion blender, you can transfer half of the mixture to a regular blender or food processor, puree it, then return it to the pot.)

5. Toast the slices of bread in a toaster or under the broiler, and rub them on both sides with the reserved cut garlic. Place a piece of toast in the bottom of each bowl, and ladle the stew on top. Drizzle with olive oil and lemon juice. Sprinkle with smoked paprika, and serve.

CURRIED CHICKPEAS

with Eggplant

When I first made this dish, I fried the eggplant slices instead of broiling them. My thinking was that since I was cooking a meatless main course, frying the eggplant would make the dish richer and a little more substantial. And it did, making a colossal mess along the way. And it took me forever to fry 2 pounds of baby eggplant in batches in one skillet. But the combination of the golden eggplant braised with chickpeas, tomatoes, and garam masala until soft and velvety was such a hit, I knew I'd have to try the dish again using the broiler, where I'd make less mess and save time. Yes, the fried version was slightly better. But the broiled version was so much easier that it won out.

Serve this over rice or with flatbread as a meatless main course, or as a side to grilled meats or fish.

2 pounds baby or small Italian eggplant, sliced into ¼-inch-thick rounds

3 tablespoons extra-virgin olive oil, plus more as needed

Fine sea salt, as needed

1 large white onion, halved lengthwise through the root and very thinly sliced

3 garlic cloves, minced

1 fresh hot green chile, such as a jalapeño or serrano chile, seeded and minced

1½ teaspoons garam masala

½ teaspoon sweet paprika

¼ teaspoon freshly ground black pepper

⅛ teaspoon cayenne pepper

1 pound ripe tomatoes, chopped (about 2 cups)

1½ cups cooked chickpeas, homemade (see pages 232 to 233) or canned, rinsed and drained

Fresh lemon or lime juice to taste

½ cup fresh mint leaves, torn

3 scallions (white and green parts), thinly sliced

Plain Greek yogurt, for serving (optional)

TOTAL TIME: 1 HOUR
SERVES 4

1. Arrange an oven rack 6 inches from the heat source, and heat the broiler.

2. Lay the eggplant slices out in one layer on two or three baking sheets, and brush both sides of the slices with olive oil. Season the eggplant slices all over with fine sea salt. One pan at a time, broil the eggplant until the tops are browned, 3 to 5 minutes; then flip the slices over and continue to cook until well browned and soft, another 3 to 5 minutes. Set the cooked eggplant aside.

3. Heat a 12-inch skillet over high heat. Add the olive oil and heat until it is shimmering. Add the onion slices and cook until they are limp and browned in spots, about 7 minutes. Add the garlic and chile, and cook until fragrant, 1 to 2 minutes longer. Stir in the garam masala, paprika, black pepper, and cayenne; cook for 1 minute, and then add the tomatoes, chickpeas, and 2 tablespoons of water.

4. Partially cover the skillet and simmer until the tomatoes start to break down, 10 to 15 minutes. Add the eggplant to the skillet and cook until the sauce thickens, about 5 minutes. Taste, and add a little more fine sea salt if needed and a sprinkling of lemon juice to taste.

5. Serve the eggplant topped with the mint and scallions, and with dollops of yogurt if you like.

BRAISED PINTO BEANS

with Bacon and Winter Vegetables

Pinto beans braised with bacon is a cowboy classic, with the smokiness of the pork suffusing flavor into the beans. Here, I've added lots of vegetables—parsnip, celery root, and baby greens—to turn it into a one-pot meal. It's homey, rustic, and completely satisfying on a freezing winter evening. Serve with the Skillet Brown-Butter Cornbread (page 385) or Rye & Cheddar Biscuits (page 380) for a cozy meal.

1. If you plan to cook the beans in the oven (see step 4), heat the oven to 325°F.

2. In a large Dutch oven over medium-high heat, cook the bacon until crisp, about 5 minutes. Transfer the strips to a paper-towel-lined plate to drain. Then crumble the bacon.

3. Add a drizzle of olive oil to the Dutch oven if it seems dry. Stir in the onion and cook until the slices are dark brown and caramelized around the edges, 7 to 10 minutes. Add the parsnip, celery root, 2 teaspoons of the sage, 2 teaspoons of the rosemary, and the garlic; cook until fragrant, 1 to 2 minutes.

4. Stir in the beans, bay leaf, 6 cups of water, and salt. Bring to a boil and cover the pot. Either put the pot in the preheated oven or reduce the heat under the Dutch oven to medium-low. Simmer or bake until the beans are tender, 1½ to 3 hours (soaked beans will cook more quickly than unsoaked ones). Add more water if the beans start to look dry before they are soft.

5. Stir in the greens, crumbled bacon, remaining 1 teaspoon sage, and remaining 1 teaspoon rosemary. Taste and season with additional salt if needed. Stir in hot sauce to taste.

4 to 5 ounces sliced bacon

Extra-virgin olive oil, as needed

1 large onion, halved and thinly sliced

1 large parsnip or 2 medium carrots, diced (1 cup)

½ cup diced celery root or celery stalk

1 tablespoon finely chopped fresh sage leaves

1 tablespoon finely chopped fresh rosemary leaves

2 garlic cloves, finely chopped

1 pound dried pinto beans, preferably soaked and rinsed (see page 232)

1 bay leaf

1½ teaspoons fine sea salt, plus more if needed

5 ounces (5 cups) baby greens, such as kale, mustard greens, or spinach

Hot sauce, chile-spiked vinegar, or apple cider vinegar, for serving

TOTAL TIME: 2 TO 3½ HOURS
SERVES 6

ASPARAGUS CARBONARA

Imagine pasta carbonara, but with asparagus instead of noodles. That's what this dish is. It has that same irresistible pancetta-, cheese-, and egg-rich sauce, just much, much lighter with stalks of bright green asparagus as the center of the plate. This can be a meal on its own when you accompany it with some crusty bread for mopping up the sauce and maybe some good cheese on the side (something with personality, a runny-centered washed-rind cheese would be nice). You could also serve it as a first course at a dinner party, or a fancy side dish for a simple roast fish or chicken. If you can't find pancetta, bacon works, too, and will give this a smoky flavor, which changes the dish a bit, but in a delightful way.

1 pound asparagus, ends trimmed

4 ounces pancetta, cubed

2 large egg yolks, lightly beaten

½ tablespoon unsalted butter

3 tablespoons freshly grated Parmigiano-Reggiano cheese

Fine sea salt, as needed

¼ teaspoon freshly ground black pepper

TOTAL TIME: 15 MINUTES
SERVES 2

1. If the asparagus are thicker than ½ inch, slice the spears in half lengthwise (if using thin ones, you can skip this step). Next, slice crosswise into 2-inch pieces.

2. Heat a large skillet over medium-high heat, add the pancetta, and cook until crisp, 3 to 5 minutes.

4. Leaving just enough fat to coat the skillet and cling to the pancetta, pour off the remaining fat if there is any. Add the asparagus and 2 tablespoons of water, and cook until the asparagus is just tender, 2 to 4 minutes.

5. Immediately toss the egg yolks and butter into the skillet. Cook, tossing, until the butter has melted. Toss in the cheese, a large pinch of salt, and ¼ teaspoon pepper, and serve immediately, adding more salt if needed.

EGGPLANT GRATIN

with Tomato and Goat Cheese

Sometimes when I want to impress, I call this layered baked vegetable dish a *tian* instead of a gratin. I think it lends the dish an air of chic mystery and makes me imagine that I'm serving it out of a cute little farmhouse in southern France with vegetables I've just harvested from the garden. Pastoral fantasy aside, no matter what designation you choose (and casserole also works), this is a rustic, summery baked vegetable dish filled with enough tangy goat cheese to melt and ooze between the slices of eggplant and tomatoes, making the vegetables collapse into one another in a harmonious and appealing way.

Serve this with a simple green salad (page 371), preferably made with baby lettuces you've just harvested from next to your eggplant and tomato vines. Or, you know, the very best greens you can find at the supermarket.

1. Heat the oven to 400°F.

2. In a large bowl, combine the eggplant, tomatoes, lemon zest, thyme leaves, garlic, 1 teaspoon salt, pepper to taste, and the ¼ cup olive oil. Toss together.

3. Arrange the vegetables in layers in a gratin dish, dropping in pieces of the goat cheese as you go. Make sure to end with a layer of the vegetables; you want the goat cheese to be underneath, not on top. Drizzle the remaining 2 tablespoons olive oil over the vegetables. Sprinkle with the panko, drizzle generously with additional olive oil, and season with salt and pepper to taste.

4. Transfer the dish to the oven and bake until the gratin is tender and golden brown, about 45 minutes.

1¼ pounds eggplant, sliced into thin rounds

1 pound tomatoes, sliced into thin rounds

Finely grated zest of ½ lemon

1 teaspoon chopped fresh thyme leaves

1 garlic clove, grated on a Microplane or minced

1 teaspoon kosher salt, plus more to taste

Freshly ground black pepper to taste

¼ cup plus 2 tablespoons extra-virgin olive oil, plus more for drizzling

4 ounces soft goat cheese, cut into small pieces

⅓ cup panko or other bread crumbs

TOTAL TIME: 1 HOUR
SERVES 4

ROASTED EGGPLANT
and Corn with Ricotta and Mint

It may seem counterintuitive to crank up your oven in the middle of summer during eggplant and corn season. But this luscious dish makes your hotter kitchen absolutely worth it. At least the vegetables cook fairly quickly; you can have it all in and out of the oven in twenty-five minutes or less by roasting everything all at once. You start with the eggplant, letting the cubes get crisp at the edges and soft in the centers. Then you add the sweet corn kernels, which soften and plump while the eggplant browns. Slivered red chile adds a touch of heat, and a topping of creamy ricotta and torn mint leaves is decadent, bright, and fresh.

Dairy avoiders, take note: another excellent option here is to skip the ricotta and top the eggplant and corn with fried eggs. Runny yolk will do no harm.

1. Heat the oven to 450°F.

2. On one or two rimmed baking sheets, toss the eggplant chunks and chile slices with the ¼ cup olive oil and the ½ teaspoon fine sea salt; then spread the mixture out into one layer. The eggplant pieces can touch, but they shouldn't overlap.

3. Roast until the eggplant is golden on the bottom, about 10 minutes; then flip the pieces over with a spatula and roast for 5 minutes more. Sprinkle the corn all over the eggplant, and continue roasting until the eggplant is well browned and very tender and the corn is cooked, 5 to 10 minutes.

4. Scoop the eggplant and corn into a large and preferably shallow bowl (the shallower your bowl, the more surface area you will have for the ricotta, and it's the ricotta that makes this extra-delicious). Add the garlic, black pepper, some mint leaves, and more olive oil and salt to taste, tossing gently to combine. Dollop with the fresh ricotta, and scatter more mint on top, along with raw chile slices if you like. Sprinkle with flaky sea salt and grind on more black pepper. Serve hot or warm.

2¼ pounds eggplant, trimmed and cut into 1- to 1½-inch chunks

1 to 2 small fresh red chiles, halved, seeded, and thinly sliced, plus more sliced chile for garnish (optional)

¼ cup extra-virgin olive oil, plus more as needed

½ teaspoon fine sea salt, plus more to taste

Kernels from 2 ears fresh corn (about 2 cups)

1 garlic clove, grated on a Microplane or minced

Freshly ground black pepper to taste

Fresh mint or basil leaves, torn

Fresh ricotta (the best you can find), for serving

Flaky sea salt to taste

TOTAL TIME: 35 MINUTES
SERVES 4

SCALLOPED POTATO SKILLET GRATIN

with Gruyère, Leeks, and Black Pepper

Whenever it's served, a scalloped potato gratin is usually the best thing on the table. With tender potatoes suffused with cream and herbs, and a burnished lid of melted, buttery cheese, there are few things more delicious. That's why I think you should make potato gratin the centerpiece of your meal, rather than as a side dish to a juicy steak or a roast chicken. Or, if you really want both meat and potatoes, why not mix things up and make the steak *the side dish* to the gratin?

2 tablespoons unsalted butter, plus more for greasing the pan

3 large leeks (white and light green parts), halved lengthwise and thinly sliced

1 teaspoon kosher salt, plus more to taste

¾ teaspoon freshly ground black pepper, plus more to taste

2 tablespoons chopped fresh sage leaves

2½ pounds Yukon Gold potatoes, peeled

1¼ cups crème fraîche

½ cup whole milk

2 fat garlic cloves, finely chopped

2 bay leaves

4 large eggs, lightly beaten

¼ teaspoon freshly grated nutmeg

1¼ cups grated Gruyère cheese (5 ounces)

TOTAL TIME: 1½ HOURS
SERVES 6

1. Heat the oven to 350°F.

2. Melt the 2 tablespoons butter in a 12-inch oven-safe skillet over medium heat. Add the leeks, ¼ teaspoon each salt and pepper, and the sage leaves. Cook, stirring, until the leeks are tender and golden, 7 to 10 minutes. Remove the leeks from the skillet and set them aside.

3. Using a mandoline or a sharp knife, slice the potatoes into ⅛-inch-thick rounds. In a large bowl, toss the potatoes with the remaining ¾ teaspoon salt and ½ teaspoon pepper.

4. Add the crème fraîche, milk, garlic, and bay leaves to the skillet, scraping up the browned bits of leeks. Simmer gently for 5 minutes; then remove the skillet from the heat and discard the bay leaves.

5. In a large heatproof bowl, lightly beat together the eggs and nutmeg. Slowly pour the hot crème fraîche mixture into the eggs, whisking constantly while pouring, and set the mixture aside.

6. Wipe out the skillet, and grease it with butter. In the skillet, carefully layer half of the potatoes, seasoning the layer lightly with salt and pepper. Then scatter half of the leeks on top. Pour half of the egg mixture over the leeks. Arrange the remaining potatoes over that, season the layer with salt and pepper, and then scatter the remaining leeks over the potatoes. Follow with the remaining egg mixture, and then sprinkle the Gruyère over the top.

7. Cover the skillet with aluminum foil and transfer it to the oven. Bake for 40 minutes; then uncover it and bake until the cheese is bubbling and golden, another 20 to 25 minutes. Let the gratin cool slightly before serving.

POLE BEAN SALAD

with Tomatoes, Almonds, and Pepitas

This is the kind of thing I'll whip up on a summer weeknight when I want to make vegetables the focus of the meal (which is happening more and more in our house). The nuts and seeds give the dish some heft, crunch, and protein, and I also usually serve it with salami or prosciutto, or maybe a nice milky Burrata if I can get one, along with some good bread. It makes a simple but incredibly satisfying meal because of the diversity of textures and the richness of the avocado. It also works as a side dish to a simple grilled steak or piece of fish.

1. In a large pot, bring generously salted water to a boil over high heat. Add the beans and cook until they are al dente, 2 to 3 minutes. Drain, and immediately rinse them under cold running water to stop the cooking. Then pat the beans dry with a clean kitchen towel and place them in a large bowl.

2. In a medium skillet, heat the oil over medium-low heat. Add the almonds and pepitas and cook until the almonds are starting to turn golden, 1 to 2 minutes. Remove the skillet from the heat, add the tomato and garlic, and stir until the tomato is warmed through.

3. Add the tomato mixture to the beans, season with fine sea salt to taste, and toss to combine. Top with the herbs and avocado slices, and serve.

1 pound wax beans, green beans, or a combination, trimmed and cut into 1-inch pieces

2 tablespoons coconut oil or olive oil

¼ cup sliced almonds

¼ cup pepitas (raw pumpkin seeds)

1 medium-sized ripe tomato, diced

1 garlic clove, grated on a Microplane or minced

Fine sea salt to taste

½ cup mixed fresh herbs, such as cilantro, mint, and basil

1 ripe avocado, pitted, peeled, and sliced

TOTAL TIME: 20 MINUTES
SERVES 2 TO 4

ROASTED CARROTS

with Walnuts, Feta, and Dill

More than the other recipes in this chapter, these sweet roasted carrots really walk the line between main course and side dish. And they do make a fantastic accompaniment to just about anything—roasted or stewed meats, bean dishes, even tofu stir-fries. But the flavors of caramelized carrot mixed with toasted walnuts, salty feta, and plenty of feathery dill are so compelling that they truly deserve to be the focal point of a meal, maybe arranged over a deep platter of something flavorful and starchy—quinoa (page 277), polenta (page 277), or white beans (page 232).

If you can get a mix of carrots in different colors—orange, white, and burgundy—they'll make for an especially stunning presentation.

1 pound medium carrots, halved lengthwise

1 tablespoon extra-virgin olive oil, plus more for serving

½ teaspoon kosher salt

½ teaspoon freshly ground black pepper

¼ cup coarsely chopped walnuts

2 ounces feta cheese, crumbled (½ cup)

1 tablespoon chopped fresh dill or mint leaves

Pomegranate molasses or balsamic vinegar, for serving

TOTAL TIME: 45 MINUTES
SERVES 2 TO 4

1. Heat the oven to 425°F.

2. Toss the carrots with the olive oil, salt, and pepper. Arrange them on a rimmed baking sheet. Roast, tossing after 20 minutes, until the carrots are golden and almost tender, about 35 minutes. Add the walnuts to the baking sheet and continue cooking until the walnuts are golden and fragrant, about 7 minutes.

3. Arrange the carrots on serving plates. Sprinkle the nuts and crumble the feta over the top. Finish with the dill and a good drizzle each of olive oil and pomegranate molasses.

CURRIED OKRA

and Tomatoes with Browned Onions and Lime

Okra is one of those divisive ingredients up there with squid, broccoli rabe, and scrapple. You either love it or you don't, and I'm not here to try to convince you otherwise. But if you count yourself among the okra fans of the world (I'm there with you), this is an excellent way to enjoy the plump green pods, which are stewed with sweet browned onions, juicy tomatoes, and curry spices. This is best made in summer when you can get fresh okra and ripe tomatoes. But if you're craving okra in the middle of winter, frozen okra and canned diced tomatoes work pretty well here, too. Serve this over white or brown rice (page 276), quinoa (page 277), or farro (page 277) or with Skillet Brown-Butter Cornbread (page 385) on the side.

2 tablespoons extra-virgin olive oil

1 onion, sliced into thin half-moons

2 garlic cloves, grated on a Microplane or minced

1 teaspoon grated peeled fresh ginger

2 teaspoons curry powder

1 teaspoon ground cumin

1 pound okra, trimmed and sliced into ½-inch-thick rounds

1½ pounds ripe tomatoes, diced small

½ teaspoon fine sea salt, plus more as needed

Finely grated zest and juice of 1 lime

Plain yogurt, preferably whole-milk, for serving

TOTAL TIME: 25 MINUTES
SERVES 4

1. Place a 12-inch skillet over medium-high heat. Add the olive oil and heat until it is shimmering. Add the onion and cook, tossing occasionally, until dark golden brown and tender, about 10 minutes. Stir in the garlic, ginger, curry powder, and cumin; cook for 1 minute.

2. Stir in the okra, tomatoes, ½ teaspoon salt, and ¼ cup of water. Reduce the heat to medium and simmer, partially covered, until the okra is tender and the sauce is thick, about 10 minutes.

3. Stir in the lime zest and some of the lime juice to taste. Taste, and adjust the seasoning if necessary. Serve topped with dollops of yogurt.

GREEN & WAX BEANS

with Olives, Tomatoes, and Mozzarella

This is another dish where vegetables (in this case, green and wax beans) are tossed with a heady pan sauce that might usually go on pasta. Here, the intense saline combination of olives and anchovies, plus sweet tomatoes, mellow mozzarella, and plenty of toasted garlic, would work just as well over penne. But the beans add their own delicate sweetness and soft texture to the mix. If you can't get both green and wax beans, use either one here. Serve this with a side of farro (page 277) or a crusty loaf for a little added texture.

1. Bring a large pot or kettle of water to a boil (I use an electric kettle). Put the beans in a colander in the sink and pour the boiling water over them. (This blanches them quickly and easily without requiring an ice bath.)

2. Place a 10- to 12-inch skillet over medium-high heat. Add the olive oil and heat it until it is shimmering. Add the garlic, and the anchovies if using, and sauté until the garlic turns golden brown around the edges, 1 to 2 minutes. Add the olives, the ½ teaspoon coarse salt, and the chile flakes, and sauté for another minute. Then add the blanched beans and the cherry tomatoes. Cook until the beans are crisp-tender and

the tomatoes are starting to break down, about 5 minutes. Remove the skillet from the heat.

3. Toss the bocconcini and the 1 teaspoon vinegar into the beans in the skillet, stir well, and taste for seasoning, adding more salt and/or vinegar if needed. Spoon everything onto a serving platter and garnish with the basil, cracked black pepper, and toasted pine nuts if using.

NOTE: To toast pine nuts, heat the nuts in a small saucepan or skillet set over medium heat, shaking the pan occasionally to ensure even toasting. Toast the nuts until they are golden and fragrant, watching carefully to ensure they do not burn, 2 to 3 minutes.

1 pound fresh green beans, trimmed

1 pound fresh wax beans, trimmed

2 tablespoons extra-virgin olive oil

4 garlic cloves, smashed and peeled

4 to 6 oil-packed anchovy fillets (optional)

⅓ cup sliced pitted Kalamata or other good olives

½ teaspoon coarse kosher salt, plus more as needed

Large pinch of red chile flakes

1 cup halved cherry tomatoes

8 ounces bocconcini, or fresh mozzarella cut into cubes

1 teaspoon red wine vinegar or balsamic vinegar (red wine is sharper, balsamic is sweeter), plus more if needed

Torn fresh basil leaves, for garnish

Freshly cracked black pepper to taste

½ cup pine nuts, toasted, for garnish (optional; see Note)

TOTAL TIME: 20 MINUTES
SERVES 4 TO 6

FRIED HALLOUMI
with Spicy Brussels Sprouts

When I was a young and eager food journalist, I once asked a world-famous chef what the most delicious thing he ever ate was, expecting a flowery discourse about multicourse, foie gras–and-caviar-studded meals.

What he said was: fried cheese.

I had to agree. There really are few things more pleasing than fried cheese, melty and gooey on the inside and browned on the surface, be it mozzarella sticks, Greek *saganaki*, or the part of the cheddar than oozes out of the grilled cheese and onto the skillet, singeing at the edges.

In this dish, I fry cubes of halloumi, a salty-firm Greek cheese, and toss them with roasted Brussels sprouts, seasoning everything with lemon juice, cumin seeds, and Turkish red chile. It's an easy, homey one-pot meal that you can spoon into a deep bowl and eat on the sofa on a chilly evening.

If you can't find halloumi, you can use other frying or grilling cheeses such as *queso para la parrilla* from Central and South America, Italian provolone, or Greek *kefalotyri*. You need something that will hold its shape enough to soften and brown when fried, but that won't totally melt.

1 pound Brussels sprouts, trimmed and halved through the stem

4 tablespoons extra-virgin olive oil, plus more for serving

½ teaspoon kosher salt

Freshly ground black pepper to taste

1 teaspoon cumin seeds

8 ounces halloumi cheese, cut into 1-inch cubes

1 tablespoon fresh lemon juice, plus more for serving

Large pinch of Turkish red pepper or Aleppo pepper, plus more for serving

TOTAL TIME: 25 MINUTES
SERVES 4

1. Heat the oven to 450°F.

2. In a large bowl, toss the Brussels sprouts with 1½ tablespoons of the olive oil, the salt, and black pepper to taste. Spread the sprouts out on a rimmed baking sheet and roast, tossing them occasionally, until they are crispy and dark gold, 15 to 20 minutes.

3. Meanwhile, heat a 10- to 12-inch skillet over medium-high heat. Add the cumin seeds to the dry skillet and toast until fragrant, 1 to 2 minutes. Pour the seeds into a large bowl to stop the cooking.

4. Add 1½ tablespoons of the olive oil to the hot skillet and let it heat until it is shimmering. Add the halloumi cubes and fry, turning them occasionally, until they are golden on all sides, about 5 minutes. Transfer the halloumi to the bowl containing the toasted cumin seeds.

5. Add the Brussels sprouts to the halloumi. Add the lemon juice, remaining 1 tablespoon olive oil, and Turkish red pepper to taste. Transfer the mixture to a serving platter and top it with additional lemon juice, olive oil, and Turkish red pepper before serving.

Winter VEGETABLE HASH
with Jalapeños and Fried Eggs

My friend and neighbor Daniel Bernstein came up with this stellar and very clever recipe. I never would have thought to fry broccoli, shiitakes, and Brussels sprouts into a hash-like cake, but it turns out to be a terrific idea. The bottom of the cake crisps and browns, especially where the mushrooms hit the pan, and everything turns very savory and deeply flavored. Because there are no potatoes, this is lighter than other hashes, but the chopped broccoli helps bind the other vegetables so the whole thing holds its shape. With fried eggs and slivered chiles on top and a splash of Chinese black vinegar, it's one of the tastiest and sprightliest hashes out there. Serve it for a meatless dinner or an elegant brunch.

If you can't get Chinese black vinegar, you can substitute balsamic. The two don't taste at all alike (the black vinegar is less tart, smokier, and more savory than the fruity and syrupy balsamic). But the balsamic adds the needed acid and is pleasing here in an entirely different and sweeter way.

2 tablespoons extra-virgin olive oil, plus more as needed

1 leek (white and light green parts), halved lengthwise and thinly sliced

1 cup Brussels sprouts (about 3½ ounces), trimmed and halved through the stem

1 cup chopped broccoli (about 3 ounces)

1 cup sliced fresh shiitake mushroom caps (about 2½ ounces)

Kosher salt and freshly ground black pepper to taste

4 to 6 large eggs

1 to 2 tablespoons Chinese black vinegar or balsamic vinegar, or to taste

Flaky sea salt to taste

2 jalapeños, sliced, seeds removed if desired

Fresh cilantro leaves, for garnish

TOTAL TIME: 20 MINUTES
SERVES 4 TO 6

1. Heat 1 tablespoon of the olive oil in a large skillet over medium heat. Add the leeks and sauté until they are beginning to soften, about 4 minutes.

2. Stir in the Brussels sprouts, broccoli, and another tablespoon of oil if the pan looks dry, and cook, stirring occasionally, until the vegetables are beginning to brown at the edges, about 7 minutes. Add the mushrooms, salt, and pepper; let the mixture cook for 2 to 3 minutes, pressing down with a spatula to form a browned cake.

3. In a separate skillet, heat 1 tablespoon of the olive oil. When the oil is hot, fry the eggs until the whites are set and the yolks are still runny (you can flip them if you want them over-easy).

4. Sprinkle the vinegar over the vegetables and transfer them to individual plates. Top the vegetable hash with the fried eggs, flaky sea salt, jalapeño slices, and cilantro leaves. Serve immediately.

ZUCCHINI-CORNMEAL CAKES *with Mint Chutney and Yogurt*

Fried cornmeal cakes, whether Latin American *arepas*, Southern hoecakes, or Rhode Island johnny cakes, all have the same enticing crunch, the result of cornmeal meeting hot oil and turning lacy, brittle-crisp, and ever so slightly sweet. In this iteration, the cornmeal is mixed with shredded zucchini and eggs and fried into soft and mild pancakes with golden brown edges. You can offer them plain for a gently appealing meal, maybe topped with fried eggs and bacon for brunch or a cozy supper. But I like to take a more assertive route and slather them with a bracing, herbal mint-and-chile chutney to contrast with all the sweetness. It transforms them into zesty, fiery little morsels that taste especially good dunked into yogurt to cool them down.

1. In a large colander, toss the grated zucchini with ½ teaspoon of the salt. Let it sit in the sink (or in a bowl) for 10 minutes to drain.

2. **Make the zucchini-cornmeal cakes:** In a large bowl, combine the cornmeal, flour, baking powder, baking soda, cumin, and remaining ½ teaspoon salt; mix to combine.

3. In a separate bowl, whisk the eggs with the melted butter. Then add the egg mixture to the cornmeal mixture, whisking to make a thick batter. Squeeze as much of the remaining moisture out of the salted zucchini as possible, and then add the zucchini, scallions, and garlic to the batter; fold everything together gently.

4. In a large skillet over medium heat, add just enough olive oil to coat the bottom of the skillet.

When the oil is hot, drop as many 2-tablespoon-sized balls of the zucchini batter into the skillet as you can to form a single layer, without the balls touching. Flatten each one with the back of a metal spoon. Fry until they are deep golden brown, 3 to 4 minutes per side. Transfer the zucchini cakes to a paper-towel-lined plate to drain, sprinkling them with salt to taste while they're still hot. Repeat with remaining batter.

5. **Make the mint chutney:** In a blender, combine the mint, cilantro, jalapeño, garlic, lime juice, shallot, salt, and 2 tablespoons of water. Blend until smooth, adding more water, a tablespoon at a time, if needed.

6. Serve the zucchini cakes with the mint chutney and the yogurt alongside.

FOR THE ZUCCHINI-CORNMEAL CAKES

2 medium zucchini, grated (about 3 cups)

1 teaspoon kosher salt, plus more as needed

½ cup cornmeal

½ cup all-purpose flour

1 teaspoon baking powder

½ teaspoon baking soda

¼ teaspoon ground cumin

2 large eggs

3 tablespoons unsalted butter, melted

3 large scallions (white and green parts), minced

1 small garlic clove, grated on a Microplane or minced

Extra-virgin olive oil, for frying

FOR THE MINT CHUTNEY

2 cups fresh mint leaves and tender stems

2 cups fresh cilantro sprigs

½ to 1 jalapeño

2 garlic cloves, grated on a Microplane or minced

2 tablespoons fresh lime juice

1 shallot, coarsely chopped

¼ teaspoon kosher salt

Plain yogurt, for serving

TOTAL TIME: 45 MINUTES
SERVES 4 TO 6 (MAKES ABOUT 16 FRITTERS)

FRESH CORN CAKES

with Tomatoes and Fried Sage

These delicate little corn cakes work well either on their own as a light summery meal, or as a fantastic starter to a more elaborate feast. They have a deep and especially sweet corn character that comes from pureeing kernels into the batter, which releases both their flavor and their starch, helping the pancakes come together. For a topping, cubes of fresh tomatoes fried in butter are juicy and rich. I've also skipped the tomatoes and sage and topped these with a little salmon roe, crème fraiche, and some fresh chives for garnish. It's a bit more festive and just as pretty.

1 cup corn kernels (from about 2 ears of fresh corn, or use frozen, thawed)

1 large egg, beaten

1 cup buttermilk, plus more as needed

¾ cup cornmeal

¼ cup all-purpose flour

1 tablespoon sugar

1 teaspoon baking powder

1 teaspoon kosher salt, plus more as needed

6 tablespoons unsalted butter, melted

Extra-virgin olive oil, for frying

FOR THE TOMATO TOPPING
1 tablespoon whole small fresh sage leaves

3 garlic cloves, smashed and peeled

1 pound tomatoes (about 2 large), roughly diced into ¼-inch pieces

Freshly ground black pepper

Coarse salt, for sprinkling

Whole-milk Greek yogurt or crème fraîche, for serving (optional)

TOTAL TIME: 40 MINUTES
SERVES 4 (MAKES 12 CAKES)

1. In a food processor or blender, grind the corn kernels to a rough puree, then add the egg and buttermilk, and pulse to mix. Add the cornmeal, flour, sugar, baking powder, and salt, and pulse until just mixed to make a thick batter. Stir in 4 tablespoons melted butter. Set aside for 5 minutes. Thin with a little more buttermilk if necessary. The mixture should be thick but still pourable.

2. Heat a thin film of oil in a 12-inch skillet over medium-low heat. Use a ¼ cup measure to drop the batter into the skillet, cooking them in batches until browned on each side, 3 to 4 minutes per side. Add oil as necessary to the skillet. When the pancakes are all done, transfer to a platter and cover with foil to keep warm.

3. **Make the tomato topping:** Melt 1 tablespoon butter in the pan (you don't need to wipe it out first unless there are burned bits sticking to the bottom). Add the sage and cook until crisped, about 2 minutes; use a slotted spoon to transfer to a paper-towel-lined plate; sprinkle with salt.

4. Add the remaining 1 tablespoon butter to the skillet along with the smashed garlic cloves, and cook until they are browned at the edges and softened, about 2 minutes. Add the tomatoes, season with salt and pepper, and cook for 1 minute or so to heat through. Keep warm.

5. Top the warm pancakes with the tomato and garlic mixture, sprinkle with fried sage and coarse salt, and serve with yogurt if you like.

RATATOUILLE

with Crunchy, Meaty Crumbs

Lamb and ratatouille is a classic Provençal combination, though usually one sees them distinct on the plate. Here, I decided to combine the two, adding a lamb-y, crumb-y topping (ground lamb sautéed with garlicky bread crumbs) to a skillet full of ratatouille. It gives the soft, silky, olive oil–imbued vegetables a deeply flavored, meaty crunch that adds heft and textural contrast. Serve this with a bottle of rosé and plates of sliced ripe melon in the waning days of summer.

If you aren't a lamb fan, feel free to make this with ground beef or turkey. You may lose the Provence connection, but you can still serve this with rosé.

6 tablespoons extra-virgin olive oil, plus more for serving

6 ounces ground lamb (or use beef or turkey)

½ cup panko or other dry bread crumbs

4 garlic cloves, grated on a Microplane or minced

2 teaspoons finely chopped fresh rosemary leaves

1¼ teaspoons kosher salt, plus more as needed

Freshly ground black pepper to taste

1 medium onion, cut into 1-inch chunks

1 red bell pepper, seeded and cut into 1-inch chunks

2 medium eggplants (1 pound total), trimmed and cut into 1-inch chunks

2 medium zucchini (1 pound total), trimmed and cut into 1-inch chunks

2 teaspoons finely chopped fresh thyme leaves

2½ cups cherry tomatoes, halved or quartered if large

½ cup chopped fresh basil leaves, plus more for serving

Coarse sea salt, as needed

TOTAL TIME: 1 HOUR
SERVES 4

1. In a 10- to 12-inch skillet, heat 2 tablespoons of the olive oil over medium-high heat. Add the ground meat and cook, breaking up the meat as much as possible with a fork, until it is uniformly golden brown, about 7 minutes. Stir in the panko and cook until the mixture is toasty and crisp, 3 to 5 minutes. For the last minute of cooking, stir in half of the garlic and half of the rosemary. Season with ½ teaspoon of the salt and with black pepper to taste. Scrape the mixture onto a wide plate.

2. Return the skillet to the heat. Add 1 tablespoon of the olive oil, and stir in the onion and bell pepper. Cook, stirring occasionally, until the vegetables are tender, about 7 minutes. Season with ¼ teaspoon of the salt and black pepper to taste. Scrape the mixture into a bowl.

3. Return the skillet to the heat again, and add the remaining 3 tablespoons olive oil. Add the eggplant and zucchini, and cook, stirring frequently, until they are almost tender, about 10 minutes. Season with the remaining ½ teaspoon salt and black pepper to taste.

4. Return the bell pepper mixture to the skillet, and add the remaining garlic, remaining rosemary, and the thyme leaves. Cook for 1 minute. Stir in the tomatoes and basil. Partially cover the skillet, reduce the heat to medium, and cook until the vegetables are completely tender and falling apart, 15 to 25 minutes.

5. To serve, sprinkle the meat crumbs over the surface of the ratatouille. Drizzle with additional olive oil, and top with coarse sea salt and chopped basil.

SPICY BEETS

with Yogurt and Ginger

As much as I appreciate the sweeter side of beets, it's the sassy recipes I gravitate to most. Beets with a shower of vinegar or sour citrus juice, pungent garlic and fresh ginger, fiery chiles—something to tone down all the natural sugars that get even more pronounced when the beets are roasted.

Here I break out a full arsenal of piquant possibilities—chiles, ginger, garlic, lime juice, mustard seeds, black pepper, and yogurt. They help temper the sweetness of the roasted beets without entirely masking it. It's a balanced dish, lively and just sweet enough. A combination of red and golden beets makes this as pretty as it is spunky.

Serve it over Coconut Rice (page 381) if you want to take this back to the sweeter side, or over brown rice (page 276) for an earthier, more savory match.

1. Heat the oven to 375°F.

2. Peel the beets and cut them into 1-inch chunks. In a bowl, toss the beets with the olive oil and season them with ¼ teaspoon of the salt and black pepper to taste. Spread the beets out on a rimmed baking sheet and roast, tossing them occasionally, for 30 minutes.

3. Sprinkle the cumin, mustard, and coriander seeds over the beets, and continue to roast until the beets are tender, about 15 minutes.

4. While the beets roast, prepare the dressing: In a small bowl, whisk together the yogurt, garlic, jalapeño, ginger, remaining ¼ teaspoon salt, and the 1 teaspoon lime juice. Whisk in the chopped cilantro.

5. Scrape the warm beets into a large bowl. Stir in the dressing. Taste, and add more salt or lime juice if needed. Garnish with whole cilantro leaves.

2 pounds beets (a mix of red, yellow, and Chioggia is nice)

2 tablespoons extra-virgin olive oil

½ teaspoon kosher salt, plus more if needed

Freshly ground black pepper to taste

1 teaspoon cumin seeds

¾ teaspoon black or brown mustard seeds

½ teaspoon coriander seeds

⅓ cup plain Greek yogurt

1 fat garlic clove, grated on a Microplane or minced

1 small jalapeño, seeded and finely chopped

1 teaspoon grated peeled fresh ginger

1 teaspoon fresh lime juice, plus more if needed

2 tablespoons chopped fresh cilantro leaves, plus whole leaves for garnish

TOTAL TIME: 1 HOUR
SERVES 4

RICE, FARRO
QUINOA & OTHER

GRAINS

HOW TO COOK GRAINS
FOR YIELDS OF 4

WHITE RICE: Rinse 1½ cups rice. In a medium pot with a tight-fitting lid, combine rice, 2⅞ cups water, and a pinch of salt. Bring to a boil, cover, and reduce to a simmer; cook for 17 minutes. Remove from heat, place a clean dish towel between the top of the pot and the lid, and let stand for 10 minutes longer to steam. Makes about 5½ cups cooked rice.

BROWN RICE: Rinse 1½ cups rice. In a medium pot with a tight-fitting lid, combine rice, 3½ cups water, and a pinch of salt. Bring to a boil, cover, and reduce to a simmer; cook for 40 to 50 minutes. Makes about 6 cups cooked rice.

BARLEY (PEARL): In a medium pot with a tight-fitting lid, combine 1½ cups barley, 5 cups water, and a pinch of salt. Bring to a boil, cover, and reduce to a simmer; cook for 40 to 50 minutes. Remove from heat, and let stand for 5 minutes. Makes about 6 cups cooked barley.

BULGUR (COARSE): In a medium pot with a tight-fitting lid, bring 3 cups plus 2 tablespoons water to a boil. Add 1¾ cups bulgur and a pinch of salt, cover, and simmer until the water is absorbed and bulgur is tender, 15 to 20 minutes. Remove from heat, place a clean dish towel between the top of the pot and the lid, and let stand for 5 to 10 minutes longer to steam. Makes about 5¼ cups cooked bulgur.

FARRO: Fill a medium pot, bring water and ½ teaspoon salt to a boil. Add 2 cups farro, simmer until tender, 15 to 25 minutes. Drain. Makes about 4 cups cooked farro.

POLENTA: In a large pot, bring 6 cups of water and 1 teaspoon salt to a simmer. Slowly whisk in 1½ cups polenta; stir frequently until polenta has thickened enough that it no longer sinks to the bottom of the pot, 5 to 10 minutes. Makes about 6 cups cooked polenta.

QUINOA: In a medium pot with a tight-fitting lid, bring 2 cups water and ½ teaspoon salt to a boil. Add 1½ cups quinoa, cover, and simmer until the water is absorbed and the quinoa is tender, 15 to 20 minutes. Makes about 4½ cups cooked quinoa.

WHEAT BERRIES: Rinse 2 cups wheat berries, then place in a medium pot with enough water to cover and a pinch of salt. Bring to a boil, then cover and reduce to a simmer; cook until the wheat berries are tender, 30 to 60 minutes. Drain. Makes about 4½ cups cooked wheat berries.

SPELT: Rinse 2 cups spelt. In a medium pot with a tight-fitting lid, bring 6 cups water and a large pinch of salt to a boil. Add spelt, cover, and simmer until the water is absorbed and spelt is tender, 65 to 80 minutes. Drain. Makes about 4½ cups cooked spelt.

SUMMER GRAIN BOWL

with Browned Corn, Black Beans, Chiles, and Arugula

Grain bowls should change with the seasons, and this Southwestern-inspired version is suited to the balmy corn-and-tomato days of summer. The browned corn is killer here, with both a sweet juiciness and a caramelized, toasty flavor next to the earthy black beans and pickled chiles. You can use whatever whole grains you've got, but red quinoa is both pretty and gritty, in a good way, and cooks up quickly. Soft and chewy barley is also nice with the corn.

2 to 3 garlic cloves, grated on a Microplane or mashed

1 teaspoon kosher salt

2 teaspoons ground cumin

2 tablespoons fresh lime juice

½ cup extra-virgin olive oil

2 ears corn, shucked (will yield about 2 cups kernels)

4 cups warm, cooked grains (such as quinoa, brown rice, barley, farro, or some kind of combination; see pages 276 to 277)

2 cups arugula

2 cups halved cherry tomatoes

2 cups cooked and drained black beans, either homemade (see page 223) or canned and rinsed

1 ripe avocado, sliced (optional)

¼ cup chopped pickled jalapeño

¼ cup pine nuts, toasted (see page 265), or chopped pecans, toasted

TOTAL TIME: 25 MINUTES
SERVES 4

1. In a small bowl, whisk together the garlic, salt, cumin, and lime juice. Then whisk in the olive oil.

2. Arrange a rack in the position closest to the heat source and preheat the broiler.

3. Place the ears of corn on a small baking sheet and broil, turning them occasionally, until they are well browned all over, 7 to 10 minutes. (Alternatively, you can grill the corn.) Let them cool, and then slice the kernels from the cobs.

4. Spoon the grains into four bowls. Arrange the corn, arugula, cherry tomatoes, black beans, and avocado, if using, on top of the grains. It's pretty to keep them in separate piles, but arrange them as you see fit. Sprinkle each bowl with a tablespoon of the pickled jalapeño and toasted pine nuts. Spoon the dressing over the bowls, or serve it on the side for people to add to taste.

ASIAN GRAIN BOWL

with Roasted Shiitakes, Tofu, Brussels Sprouts, and Miso Dressing

Before I grew into my great love of sushi and sashimi, a trip to a Japanese restaurant when I was a kid meant teriyaki and an iceberg lettuce salad topped with a thick, orange-hued, miso-carrot dressing. The sauce for this wintry grain bowl is a throwback to the pickled flavors of that dressing. And if you've got any dressing left over, it's still pretty great on iceberg—and less traditionally, radicchio. Any whole grain works here, but nutlike farro is a good match with the mushrooms.

1. Heat the oven to 425°F.

2. In a small bowl, combine the carrot, rice vinegar, and sugar. Set aside for at least 10 minutes (and up to an hour) to allow the carrot to pickle slightly.

3. In a large bowl, toss together the Brussels sprouts, sesame oil, 1 teaspoon of the peanut oil, the Sriracha, and salt and pepper to taste. Spread the Brussels sprouts out on a baking sheet and roast until they are browned and crispy, 30 to 35 minutes.

4. Meanwhile, in another large bowl, mix the mushrooms, the remaining 1 tablespoon peanut oil, and salt and pepper to taste. Spread the mushrooms out in one layer on a baking sheet and roast for the last 15 minutes while the Brussels sprouts are in the oven. The mushrooms should be well browned.

5. While the vegetables are roasting, fry the tofu: Cut the block into ½-inch-thick slabs, then cut the slabs in half to make long triangles. Heat ¼ inch of peanut oil in a large nonstick skillet over medium-high heat. Working in batches, add the tofu triangles and fry until they are golden brown, 2 to 4 minutes per side. Try not to move the tofu around while it cooks; this helps it brown better. Transfer each batch of fried tofu to a paper-towel-lined plate and season it immediately with salt.

6. Make the miso dressing: In a blender, combine the grapeseed and sesame oils, miso paste, vinegar, ginger, garlic, lime zest and juice, 1 tablespoon of the pickled carrots, and the honey. Blend until creamy, 1 to 2 minutes.

7. To serve, divide the grains among four bowls. In a large bowl, toss the Brussels sprouts and mushrooms together, and then spoon them over the grains. Add the remaining pickled carrots and the fried tofu. Garnish with the cilantro, chile if using, and sesame seeds, and serve with the miso dressing on the side.

1 large carrot, coarsely grated

¼ cup rice vinegar

1 tablespoon sugar

12 ounces Brussels sprouts (about 3 cups), trimmed and halved lengthwise through the stem

1 teaspoon toasted sesame oil

1 tablespoon plus 1 teaspoon peanut oil, plus more for frying

½ teaspoon Sriracha or other hot sauce, or to taste

Kosher salt and freshly ground black pepper to taste

7 to 8 ounces fresh shiitake mushrooms, stems removed and caps quartered (about 4 cups)

1 package firm tofu (14 to 16 ounces), drained and patted dry

4 cups warm, cooked grains (see pages 276 to 277)

Fresh cilantro leaves, for garnish

Sliced fresh red or green chile, for garnish (optional)

Toasted sesame seeds, for garnish

FOR THE MISO DRESSING
⅓ cup grapeseed, safflower, or other neutral oil

1 tablespoon toasted sesame oil

2 tablespoons white miso paste

2 tablespoons rice vinegar

¼ cup chopped peeled fresh ginger

1 small garlic clove

Finely grated zest of 1 lime

1½ teaspoons fresh lime juice

1 teaspoon honey

TOTAL TIME: 45 MINUTES
SERVES 4

QUINOA EGG BOWL *with*

Steamed Greens, Sugar Snap Peas, and Pecorino

There's more to making an excellent grain bowl than putting, say, a heap of quinoa or brown rice in a bowl and topping it with vegetables. A great grain bowl is all about balancing the chewy whole grains with a variety of textures and flavors. The softness of slow-cooked greens; the richness of egg, avocado, or cheese; the crunch of sesame seeds, toasted seaweed, or very lightly steamed vegetables; the bracing jolt of a pickled element or some kind of tangy dressing. Nestle all these elements in a bowl where they can mingle, and you'll get a thrilling dinner in which each bite is a little different. Yes, you could spread it all out on a plate, but without that cozy proximity for the ingredients to harmonize, it just won't be the same.

Although many a grain bowl takes its cue from Asian cuisines (arguably the tradition evolved from the likes of *bibimbap* and *donburi*), there's no reason to exclude other influences. This version has a similar flavor profile to a Caesar salad—the soft, runny egg; a lemony, cheese-spiked dressing coating crisp green vegetables (here: sugar snap peas and dark, leafy greens). The quinoa adds just enough heft to make it a meal, without weighing it down. Asparagus and green beans or other crunchy vegetables could be substituted for the sugar snap peas.

1. In a medium bowl, whisk together the lemon juice, garlic, and ¾ teaspoon salt. Whisk in the oil and the cheese. Set the dressing aside.

2. Bring a large pot of salted water to a boil over high heat. Add the quinoa and cook until the center of a grain is just opaque and the grains are tender, 12 to 18 minutes. Drain well and keep warm.

3. While the quinoa is cooking, steam the vegetables: Fill a medium pot with 1 inch of water and place a steamer basket in the bottom of the pot. Add the greens and cover the pot; steam until the greens are tender, 5 to 10 minutes. Transfer the greens to a bowl.

4. Add the sugar snap peas to the steamer basket; cover, and cook until they are crisp-tender, about 3 minutes. Remove from the heat.

5. Divide the warm quinoa among four bowls. Arrange the greens, peas, and sliced eggs, if using, on top. Before serving drizzle each bowl generously with the dressing, and shower with more cheese and black pepper.

2 tablespoons fresh lemon juice

3 garlic cloves, grated on a Microplane or mashed

¾ teaspoon kosher salt, plus more as needed

¾ cup extra-virgin olive oil

3 ounces Pecorino Toscano or Manchego cheese, coarsely grated (¾ cup), plus more for garnish

1½ cups quinoa, rinsed well

1 large bunch mustard greens, Swiss chard, or kale, stems and any thick center ribs removed, leaves coarsely chopped (about 8 cups)

8 ounces sugar snap peas trimmed (2 cups)

4 soft-cooked eggs (see page 148), peeled and sliced (optional)

Coarsely ground black pepper to taste

Sliced radishes, for garnish

TOTAL TIME: 30 MINUTES
SERVES 4

KIMCHI GRAIN BOWL
with Kale and Runny Egg

The combination of kimchi and a soft-yolked egg here remind me a little of *bibimbap*—that classic Korean rice and vegetable bowl. But the additions of avocado, steamed kale, and crumbled-up seaweed snacks (for crunchy, salty, umami goodness) make this more of a hybridized mash up than anything authentically Korean. I like to use softer grains such as brown rice or barley here if you're starting from scratch. But as is true with any of the grain bowls in this chapter, you should use what is handy. Convenience should be part of a grain bowl's appeal.

2 tablespoons soy sauce

4 teaspoons finely chopped peeled fresh ginger

1 tablespoon rice vinegar

Pinch of sea salt

¼ cup peanut oil

1 teaspoon toasted sesame oil

1 8-ounce bunch kale, stems and thick ribs removed, leaves torn into large pieces

4 large eggs, at room temperature

4 cups warm, cooked grains (see pages 276 to 277)

1 avocado, pitted, peeled, and sliced

1 cup coarsely chopped kimchi, or to taste

Sliced scallions (white and green parts), for serving

Sesame seeds, for serving

Crumbled dried seaweed snack sheets, for serving (optional)

TOTAL TIME: 30 MINUTES
SERVES 4

1. In a small bowl, whisk together the soy sauce, ginger, vinegar, and salt. Then whisk in the peanut and sesame oils, and set aside.

2. Place a steamer basket in a large pot filled with an inch of water. Place the kale in the basket, cover the pot, and cook over medium heat until the kale is tender, about 7 minutes.

3. Fill a bowl with ice water. Fill a medium saucepan with water and bring it to a boil. Using a slotted spoon, carefully lower the eggs into the water; cook for 6 minutes. Then immediately transfer the eggs to the bowl of ice water to cool. Peel the cooled eggs.

4. Spoon the grains into four bowls. Divide the kale among the bowls, mounding it on top of the grains. Arrange the avocado slices next to the kale. Cut the eggs in half, and place two halves on top of each bowl. Sprinkle each bowl with the kimchi, scallions, sesame seeds, and seaweed. Spoon the dressing over the bowls.

POMEGRANATE QUINOA
with Crunchy Chickpeas

Despite common assumption, quinoa is not actually a grain at all, but a plant related to beets and spinach. Nevertheless, it looks like a grain, acts like a grain, and tastes like a grain, especially when made into this pilaf-like dish, studded with crunchy roasted spiced chickpeas. I like to serve this with a spinach and avocado salad as a light meatless meal. But it also makes an excellent side dish to shrimp or chicken. If you don't have any pomegranate molasses, you can substitute balsamic vinegar, which is a little milder in flavor, but with a similar sweet-tart character.

1. Heat the oven to 400°F. Line a rimmed baking sheet with parchment paper.

2. Spread the chickpeas out in a single layer on a clean dish towel or paper towels, and dry them very well. Once the chickpeas are completely dried, spread them on the prepared baking sheet and roast for 30 minutes, giving the pan a shake halfway through to turn them.

3. While the chickpeas are roasting, bring 2 cups of water to a boil in a medium pot, and stir in the butter and 1 teaspoon of the salt. Stir in the quinoa, reduce the heat to low, cover the pot, and simmer until the water has been absorbed and the quinoa is tender,

12 to 18 minutes. Then fluff the quinoa with a fork.

4. Put the roasted chickpeas in a bowl and toss them with the olive oil, paprika, cumin, and remaining ½ teaspoon salt (or more to taste), tossing until they are well coated.

5. Prepare the dressing: Combine the pomegranate molasses, lemon juice, salt, and pepper in a small bowl, whisking until the salt is dissolved. Then gradually whisk in the olive oil.

6. Spoon the quinoa onto a platter and top it with the chickpeas, cherry tomatoes, parsley, and scallions. Drizzle the dressing over the top, toss gently, and serve.

1½ cups cooked chickpeas, homemade (see pages 232 to 233) or canned, rinsed and drained

1 tablespoon unsalted butter

1½ teaspoons kosher salt, or more to taste

1½ cups quinoa, rinsed well

1 tablespoon extra-virgin olive oil

1 tablespoon sweet paprika

1 teaspoon ground cumin

1 pint cherry tomatoes, halved

1 cup fresh parsley leaves

2 to 3 scallions (white and green parts), sliced

FOR THE DRESSING
2 tablespoons pomegranate molasses (or substitute balsamic vinegar)

2 tablespoons fresh lemon juice

½ teaspoon kosher salt

¼ teaspoon freshly ground black pepper

5 tablespoons extra-virgin olive oil

TOTAL TIME: 35 MINUTES
SERVES 4

FARRO SALAD

with Cherry Tomatoes, Smoked Mozzarella, and Mint

When farro salad replaced pasta salad as the "it" side dish on the picnic-potluck-barbecue circuit, it fell prey to the same problems of bland and starchy mediocrity. Not so this recipe, which combats the potential pitfalls with two simple techniques. The first is to generously salt the cooking water so the farro can thoroughly absorb the seasonings as it softens and swells. The second is to make sure to add in enough diverse, bright, and multitextured ingredients to keep each bite a little different from the last. In this case, ripe cherry tomatoes, cubes of brawny smoked mozzarella, and a handful of fresh green mint do the job with grace, and allow for the salad to be mixed together up to four hours ahead. Just drizzle with a little more good olive oil right before serving.

Naturally, you can break this out at your next picnic-potluck-barbecue. But it's also excellent as a main course with some sliced cucumbers or Green Beans with Caper Vinaigrette (page 377) on the side.

1 teaspoon fine sea salt, plus more as needed

2 cups farro

4 teaspoons sherry vinegar or cider vinegar, plus more to taste

1 pint cherry tomatoes, halved

6 ounces smoked mozzarella, cubed

½ cup torn fresh mint leaves

¼ cup extra-virgin olive oil

Freshly ground black pepper to taste

Lemon wedges, for serving (optional)

TOTAL TIME: 45 MINUTES
SERVES 4

1. Bring a medium pot of heavily salted water to a boil and add the farro. Simmer until tender, usually 15 to 25 minutes, though some varieties can take up to an hour (replenish the water if the level runs low).

2. Drain the farro, and while it is still warm, stir in the vinegar and ½ teaspoon fine sea salt. Let the farro cool to room temperature, about 20 minutes. (Or cook the farro up to 8 hours ahead and keep it at room temperature.)

3. Sprinkle the cherry tomatoes with the remaining ½ teaspoon fine sea salt, and then stir them into the farro along with the mozzarella, mint, and olive oil. Season heavily with black pepper. Taste, and add more salt and/or vinegar if needed, and a squeeze of lemon for brightness if you like.

FARRO & CRISPY LEEKS
with Marinated Chickpeas and Currants

I build this entire salad around the crispy roasted leeks, which are sweet, snappy little morsels on their own, and very hard to stop eating once you start. In addition to using them here, they're also a terrific topping for soups, rice dishes, roasted vegetables, and sautéed fish, where they add both texture and a honeyed, caramelized character. In this unusual salad, their mild sweetness is underscored by the currants, while a lemony, garlicky, chile-spiked dressing zips things up. This salad keeps really well, so feel free to make it in the morning to serve that night. Or make it for your next picnic or cookout—it'll be a ringer with the grilled sausages and barbecued chicken.

4 large leeks, halved lengthwise, cleaned, and cut crosswise into ¼-inch-thick slices

¾ cup extra-virgin olive oil

2 teaspoons kosher salt, plus more to taste

½ teaspoon freshly ground black pepper

3 cups cooked chickpeas, homemade (see pages 232 to 233), or 2 15-ounce cans, rinsed and drained

3 tablespoons fresh lemon juice, preferably from Meyer lemons, plus more to taste

¼ teaspoon red chile flakes

1 garlic clove, grated on a Microplane or mashed

2 cups farro

⅔ cup dried currants or golden raisins

½ cup chopped celery leaves and tender stems (or substitute parsley)

TOTAL TIME: 45 MINUTES
SERVES 8

1. Heat the oven to 425°F.

2. On a large rimmed baking sheet, toss the leeks with ¼ cup of the olive oil, 1 teaspoon of the salt, and the ½ teaspoon pepper. Roast, tossing the leeks frequently, until they are golden brown and crisp at the edges, 20 to 25 minutes. (This might take a little longer, but make sure not to pull the pan from the oven before the leeks are very browned—even a few blackened bits is better than too pale.)

3. In a large bowl, toss the leeks with the chickpeas, 3 tablespoons lemon juice, the remaining 1 teaspoon salt, chile flakes, and garlic. Stir in the remaining ½ cup olive oil. Let the chickpeas marinate while you prepare the farro.

4. Bring a large pot of salted water to a boil. Add the farro and simmer until tender, usually 20 to 25 minutes, though some varieties take as much as an hour (keep an eye on the pot and replenish the water as needed). Drain well.

5. Toss the farro with the chickpea-leek mixture. Stir in the currants and celery. Taste, and add more salt or lemon juice if needed. Serve warm or at room temperature.

POLENTA

with Broccoli Rabe and Fried Eggs

This is one of my go-to, I-don't-feel-like-shopping dinners. Because I always have polenta and eggs in the house, and usually there's something green to sauté, I can make it when it's stormy out, or if I'm working late on a deadline, or if I'd just rather go for a run than run to the store. You can substitute other greens like kale or spinach for the broccoli rabe; I do this often, since they're both regulars in my CSA box. Just note that spinach and kale cook up more quickly than the rabe, so keep an eye on them. Or leave out the sautéed veggies altogether and serve the creamy polenta with a big, crisp green salad—a perfect plan if your CSA leans harder on lettuces than braising greens.

1. In a medium pot, combine 6 cups of water (or use broth if you prefer), 1¼ teaspoons of the salt, and the bay leaf. Bring to a simmer, and then slowly whisk in the polenta. Stir frequently until the polenta has thickened enough that it no longer sinks to the bottom of the pot, 5 to 10 minutes.

2. Reduce the heat to low, cover the pot, and simmer very gently until tender, 15 to 30 minutes (depending on the coarseness of the grind). Remove the bay leaf and stir in the butter.

3. While the polenta is cooking, place a 10- or 12-inch skillet over medium heat. Add 3 tablespoons of the olive oil and heat until it is shimmering. Stir in the smashed garlic and cook until it is golden brown and tender, 3 to 5 minutes.

4. Toss the broccoli rabe and chile flakes into the skillet, and cook until the leaves wilt and the stems just begin to color, about 3 minutes. Season with the remaining ½ teaspoon salt. Stir in ¼ cup of water, partially cover the skillet, and cook until the stems are tender, about 10 minutes. If there's liquid left in the pan, take the cover off, raise the heat, and let it evaporate.

5. Transfer the broccoli rabe to a plate, and wipe out the skillet if necessary. Add the remaining 1 tablespoon olive oil and let it heat up. Crack the eggs into the skillet, and season them with salt and pepper to taste. Fry the eggs sunny-side-up, or flip them over for over-easy (see page 148 for egg frying tips).

6. Spoon the polenta into bowls and top each serving with broccoli rabe and a fried egg. Use a vegetable peeler to shave curls of Parmigiano-Reggiano over the bowl.

1¾ teaspoons kosher salt, plus more as needed

1 bay leaf

1½ cups polenta

4 tablespoons (½ stick) unsalted butter

4 tablespoons extra-virgin olive oil

2 to 3 garlic cloves, smashed and peeled

2 bunches broccoli rabe, thick stems and wilted leaves trimmed

Large pinch of red chile flakes

6 large eggs

Freshly ground black pepper to taste

Chunk of Parmigiano-Reggiano cheese, for shaving

TOTAL TIME: 40 MINUTES
SERVES 6

ASPARAGUS POLENTA

with Burrata

A soft mound of polenta is a blank canvas of a meal, ready to absorb whatever you're in the mood to put on top. I'll often cook up a potful as a landing pad for all kinds of leftovers that aren't quite substantial enough to be called dinner on their own—those couple of tablespoons of last night's braised short ribs, a container of sautéed veggies, that small amount of cooked beans that have no other destination. In this recipe, the polenta is a bed for roasted asparagus and Burrata cheese—a kind of mozzarella that oozes cream when you poke it. It's a meal both comforting and company-worthy, especially if you serve it with a juicy, rare steak or pork chops. I usually make my polenta with water. But if you want a richer flavor and have some good stock in the freezer, feel free to substitute it for all or part of the liquid in any of the recipes in this chapter.

1. Heat the oven to 450°F.

2. In a medium pot, combine 6 cups of water (or use stock if you prefer) with the 1¼ teaspoons salt and the bay leaf. Bring to a simmer, and then slowly whisk in the polenta. Stir frequently until the polenta has thickened enough that it no longer sinks to the bottom of the pot, 5 to 10 minutes.

3. Reduce the heat to low, cover the pot, and simmer very gently until tender, 15 to 30 minutes (depending on the coarseness of the grind).

4. While the polenta cooks, place the asparagus on a large rimmed baking sheet and toss it with the olive oil, salt to taste, and pepper to taste. Roast until tender and browned, 7 to 15 minutes.

5. When the polenta is done, remove the bay leaf and stir in the butter and the ½ teaspoon black pepper.

6. Spoon the polenta onto serving plates and arrange the asparagus on top. Place a portion of the Burrata alongside each serving. Drizzle with olive oil and with balsamic vinegar if you like, and season with flaky sea salt and black pepper.

1¼ teaspoons kosher salt, plus more as needed

1 bay leaf

1½ cups polenta

2 bunches thick asparagus (about 2 pounds), ends trimmed

2 tablespoons extra-virgin olive oil, plus more for serving

½ teaspoon freshly ground black pepper, plus more to taste

3 to 4 tablespoons unsalted butter, to taste

1 whole burrata cheese, about 8 ounces

Balsamic vinegar, for serving (optional)

Flaky sea salt, for serving

TOTAL TIME: 40 MINUTES
SERVES 4 TO 6

BUTTERNUT SQUASH POLENTA *with Ricotta and Fried Sage*

What I love about this recipe is the way the shredded butternut squash absorbs the butter it's sautéed in, increasing the richness of the polenta and making it a little sweet, too. Dollops of ricotta and brittle leaves of fried sage make this a thoroughly luxurious dish on its own, or a seriously special side to braised meats or a simple roast chicken. Or, poach or fry a couple of eggs and plop them on top. All that runny yolk may be overkill, but in the best possible way.

2 tablespoons unsalted butter

8 ounces peeled and seeded butternut squash, grated (about 2 cups)

1¾ teaspoons kosher salt

1 bay leaf

1 cup polenta

4 tablespoons extra-virgin olive oil

1 small bunch fresh sage leaves

½ cup grated Parmigiano-Reggiano cheese

½ teaspoon freshly ground black pepper, plus more for serving

Fresh ricotta, for serving

TOTAL TIME: 40 MINUTES
SERVES 4

1. Melt the butter in the bottom of a medium pot over medium-high heat. Add the squash and sauté until it's golden brown, about 5 minutes. Transfer squash to a bowl.

2. Return the pot to medium heat and add 6 cups of water (or use broth if you prefer), 1¼ teaspoons of the salt, and the bay leaf. Bring to a simmer, and then slowly whisk in the polenta and the squash. Stir frequently until the polenta has thickened enough that it no longer sinks to the bottom of the pot, 5 to 10 minutes.

3. Reduce the heat to low, cover the pot, and simmer very gently until the polenta is tender, 15 to 30 minutes (depending on the coarseness of the grind).

4. While the polenta is cooking, heat 1 tablespoon of the olive oil in a small skillet. Add the sage leaves, in batches if necessary so as not to crowd the pan, and fry until crisp, 1 to 2 minutes. Transfer the leaves to a paper-towel-lined plate and sprinkle with the remaining ½ teaspoon salt.

5. Once the polenta is cooked, remove the bay leaf. Stir in the Parmigiano-Reggiano, remaining 3 tablespoons olive oil, and the black pepper.

6. Heap the polenta into bowls, and serve it topped with dollops of ricotta, the fried sage leaves, and plenty of black pepper.

Turkish BULGUR PILAF
with Yogurt and Pumpkin

The unusual flavors of this pilaf—tangerine zest, chile, and brown butter—come straight from Istanbul, where I learned a similar recipe from Engin Akin, a Turkish food historian and cookbook author. Her version calls for chestnuts instead of pumpkin. But I like the sweetness and velvety texture of the roasted pumpkin flesh against the toasted flavor of bulgur. You can use any kind of winter squash or pumpkin. I like roasting squash with the skin on for this recipe; it makes a more dramatic presentation. And, little known fact: squash skins are not only edible, some of them—particularly from young, tender squashes—are delicious, adding a crisp texture if you oil them up and roast them at high heat. If you're feeling unsure, offer your guests knives to cut off the skin just in case it comes out a bit tough. Delicatas, acorn, red kuri, and dumpling squashes all tend to have tasty thin skins.

This is a substantial and impressive enough dish to serve as a vegetarian entrée at any dinner party, or even Thanksgiving, where it will also go nicely with the turkey. Or in a more Turkish vein, serve it with roasted or braised lamb.

1¼ pounds pumpkin or winter squash (a small whole squash or part of a larger pumpkin), seeded and sliced into 1-inch-thick wedges

1 tablespoon extra-virgin olive oil, plus more for brushing

½ teaspoon kosher salt

Freshly ground black pepper

4 tablespoons (½ stick) unsalted butter

1 medium onion, minced

1¾ cups coarse bulgur

¼ teaspoon ground allspice

3 cups plus 2 tablespoons chicken stock, vegetable stock, or water (or use a combination of broth and water)

Finely grated zest of 1 tangerine or ½ orange

⅛ to ¼ teaspoon ground Turkish red pepper, such as Aleppo pepper, to taste, plus more for garnish

Plain, preferably whole-milk yogurt (if using Greek yogurt, whisk in a little milk to thin it)

Toasted pumpkin seeds or pepitas, for garnish

Chopped fresh dill leaves, for garnish

Coarse sea salt, for garnish

1. Heat the oven to 425°F.

2. Brush the squash wedges with olive oil and season them with the salt and pepper. Spread them out on a rimmed baking sheet and roast, turning them over halfway through, until they are golden brown and tender, 20 to 40 minutes, depending on the variety of squash. Watch them carefully.

3. Meanwhile, heat the 1 tablespoon olive oil with 1 tablespoon of the butter in a 3-quart pot. When the butter has melted, add the onion and sauté until translucent, about 3 minutes. Add the bulgur and allspice, and sauté for 2 minutes.

4. Stir in the stock and bring it to a vigorous boil. Reduce the heat to low, cover the pot, and cook until the bulgur is tender, all liquid has been absorbed, and there appear to be holes in the surface of the bulgur, about 15 minutes. Remove the pot from the heat, place a clean dish towel between the top of the pot and the lid, and let it stand for 5 to 10 minutes longer to steam.

5. Melt the remaining 3 tablespoons butter in a small skillet, and cook until the foam subsides and the butter turns a deep nut-brown, about 5 minutes. Stir in the tangerine zest and Turkish red pepper.

6. To serve, mound the bulgur onto a platter. Arrange the pumpkin on top. Drizzle yogurt and the warm butter mixture over the top. Garnish with the pumpkin seeds, dill, coarse sea salt, and additional Turkish red pepper.

TOTAL TIME: 45 MINUTES
SERVES 4

Middle Eastern
FARRO-LENTIL BALLS
with Tahini

These crunchy orbs hit the same notes as falafel, but with a nubbier texture from the bits of whole-grain farro and lentils, which give these a fabulously uneven, crackling surface. You can form the balls the day before and store them in the fridge, then either broil or fry them just before serving. Frying makes them a little more evenly and thoroughly crunchy, but they broil up extremely well if you're not in the mood for the oil-splattering mess of the skillet. I like to serve these as a main course with a lemony tahini sauce for dipping. But they're also great slipped into a pita with mixed greens, salted yogurt, and some pickles, falafel-style. Or, serve them as an hors d'oeuvres the next time you're throwing a shindig. Added bonus: they're even good at room temperature.

1½ teaspoons kosher salt, plus more as needed

⅓ cup green (French, also called *lentilles du Puy*) or brown lentils

1 bay leaf

1 cup farro

1 small onion, diced

¼ cup fresh parsley leaves

¼ cup fresh cilantro leaves, plus more for garnish

4 garlic cloves: 3 whole, 1 grated on a Microplane or minced

1 fresh red chile or jalapeño, seeded and coarsely chopped

1½ teaspoons ground cinnamon

½ teaspoon ground allspice

1 teaspoon freshly ground black pepper

½ teaspoon sweet paprika

½ cup panko bread crumbs

1 large egg, lightly beaten

2 tablespoons extra-virgin olive oil, plus more for frying and drizzling

⅓ cup tahini

6 tablespoons warm water

Juice of ½ lemon, plus lemon wedges for serving

TOTAL TIME: 1 HOUR
SERVES 4 TO 6 (MAKES 32 BALLS)

1. Bring a small pot of salted water to a boil, and add the lentils and bay leaf. Simmer, partially covered, until the lentils are tender, 25 to 40 minutes.

2. While the lentils are cooking, bring a medium pot of salted water to a boil. Add the farro and simmer until it is very tender (even more tender than you'd want it for salads), about 25 minutes. (Note that this can sometimes take longer depending on the kind of farro you've got—sometimes as much as an hour. Keep an eye on it and replenish the water if needed.) Drain well.

3. When the lentils are tender, remove the bay leaf and drain them well.

4. In a food processor, combine the onion, parsley, cilantro, whole garlic cloves, chile, cinnamon, allspice, black pepper, paprika, and the 1½ teaspoons salt; process until everything is well minced. Add the farro and process, scraping the sides of the bowl as needed, until the grains have broken down and the mixture is a rough, chunky paste, about 2 minutes.

5. Transfer the farro mixture to a bowl and add the lentils, bread crumbs, egg, and the olive oil. Taste, and add more salt if needed. Knead the mixture with your hands until it is well mixed and holds together nicely. Form it into 1¼-inch balls or football shapes and either cook them immediately or cover and refrigerate them for up to 1 day.

6. When you are ready to cook the farro balls, you can either fry them or broil them.

To fry the farro balls, heat a 12-inch skillet over medium-high heat, and then add ¼ inch of olive oil. When the oil is hot, add just enough farro balls to fit in one layer with space between them—if they touch, they won't brown as nicely. Fry the farro balls until they are well browned on all sides, 8 to 10 minutes. Remove them with a slotted spoon and drain them on a paper-towel-lined plate. Add more oil to the skillet and fry another batch or two, as needed.

To broil the farro balls, lay them out in a single layer, not touching, on one or two rimmed baking sheets. Drizzle with olive oil and broil until browned, 6 to 10 minutes, checking them often and shaking the pan occasionally to help them brown all over.

7. In a medium bowl, combine the tahini, grated garlic, warm water, and lemon juice. Serve the farro balls with lemon wedges and the tahini sauce.

Spicy THAI FRIED RICE
with Sausage and Greens

Most of the fried rice you get is more about the rice than the fried. Frying (or really, stir-frying) is merely a convenient way to both heat up the leftover rice and incorporate other ingredients—the egg, the scallion, the splashes of soy sauce—to help stretch it into a meal. But when you do take the time to let the rice really fry and crisp up in enough oil, and at a high enough temperature, you'll get pockets of crunchy grains that can be truly transcendent, adding a gorgeously oily snap and crackle to the usual starchy softness. And it's easy to do—just press the rice into a hot oiled skillet and then don't touch it for a few minutes.

Here, the rice gets seasoned with chiles, fish sauce, and lime, giving it a bright and spicy, Thai-inspired complexity. Not at all traditional, raisins add a bit of sweetness to the mix, while chorizo makes it meaty and substantial. And the greens add color and vegetable matter. It's a piquant and lively dish that, if you've got cooked rice at the ready, comes together fast.

1. Heat a heavy 12-inch skillet or wok over high heat until it is very hot. Pour in the oil and swirl it around the pan (it will probably smoke, and that's okay).

2. Add the onion, scallions, and garlic, give them a quick stir, and cook until they have softened, 1 to 2 minutes. Add the chorizo and jalapeño; sauté until they start to caramelize, 2 to 3 minutes. Add the raisins and the rice, mix well, and spread the mixture out to cover as much of the surface area of the pan as possible; press down on it with a spatula. Cook without moving the mixture until the rice gets a chance to dry out and take on a little color, 1 to 3 minutes; then stir it around a little and toss until it is golden in spots.

3. Add the greens and cabbage, and toss until they are beginning to wilt, 5 minutes. Sprinkle in the soy sauce and fish sauce, coating the contents of the pan. Then push the contents away from the center of the pan and pour the eggs into the center. Cook until the eggs are custardy, 1 to 2 minutes. Then mix everything in the pan, breaking up the eggs. Add the lime juice and season with salt to taste. Serve garnished with sliced scallions and with lime wedges alongside.

3 tablespoons peanut oil or grapeseed oil

1 small onion, diced

2 scallions (white and green parts), sliced, plus more for serving

3 garlic cloves, diced

1 cup diced cured chorizo or spicy salami (6 ounces)

1 jalapeño, seeded and sliced

½ cup black raisins

2 cups cooked white or brown rice

6 cups chopped mixed greens, such as mizuna, baby spinach, or baby greens

1 cup chopped napa cabbage

¼ cup soy sauce

1 tablespoon Asian fish sauce

3 large eggs, lightly beaten

Juice of ½ lime, plus lime wedges for garnish

Kosher salt to taste

TOTAL TIME: 25 MINUTES
SERVES 4 TO 6

SAUSAGE POLENTA

with Red Cabbage and Caraway

Pools of melted butter on your bowl of polenta can be charming, though they're not unexpected. But drips of brawny, porky sausage grease—now that's something special. Here I play up the Germanic theme of the sausages with some quick-roasted red cabbage seasoned with caraway, which you can cook in the same pan as the sausages for easy cleanup later. Plus the mingling of sausage juices with cabbage is exactly the kind of thing that will convert any cabbage doubters at your table. This makes for a pretty complete meal on its own, though it does kind of beg for a lager alongside.

1¾ teaspoons kosher salt, plus more as needed

1 bay leaf

1½ cups polenta

12 ounces (about 4 links) German or Italian sausage, any kind you like

½ head red cabbage, cut into 6 wedges through the core (to keep them intact)

3 tablespoons extra-virgin olive oil

1 teaspoon caraway seeds

1 teaspoon freshly ground black pepper

1 tablespoon cider vinegar

3 to 4 tablespoons unsalted butter, to taste

TOTAL TIME: 40 MINUTES
SERVES 4

1. Heat the oven to 450°F.

2. In a medium pot, combine 6 cups of water (or use broth if you prefer), 1¼ teaspoons of the salt, and the bay leaf. Bring to a simmer, and then slowly whisk in the polenta. Stir frequently until the polenta has thickened enough that it no longer sinks to the bottom of the pot, 5 to 10 minutes.

3. Reduce the heat to low, cover the pot, and simmer very gently until tender, 15 to 30 minutes (depending on the coarseness of the grind).

4. Toss the sausages, cabbage wedges, olive oil, caraway seeds, remaining ½ teaspoon salt, and ½ teaspoon of the pepper together on a rimmed baking sheet. Roast until the sausages are cooked through and the cabbage is tender and slightly caramelized, 25 to 30 minutes.

5. Sprinkle the sausages and cabbage wedges with the cider vinegar, and toss well. Remove the bay leaf from the polenta, and stir in the butter and remaining ½ teaspoon black pepper.

6. To serve, spoon the polenta into a wide bowl. Top with the sausage-cabbage mixture.

TOFU FRIED RICE

with Sugar Snap Peas

Many fried rice recipes stir peas into the pan. In my lighter and more vegetable-forward version, sugar snap peas are a juicier, sweeter addition. You can use any leftover or pre-cooked rice here, brown or white, but delicate jasmine is a personal favorite for its winning aroma. Make sure not to stint on the cilantro or basil leaves for garnish. The sharp herbal notes really help balance out the rich crunch of the rice.

1. In a large bowl, combine the soy sauce and fish sauce; then add the tofu cubes and toss to coat. Let the tofu sit for 5 minutes.

2. Heat a heavy 12-inch skillet or wok over high heat until it is very hot. Pour in the oil and swirl it around the pan (it will probably smoke, and that's okay).

3. Using a slotted spoon, transfer the tofu to the skillet; reserve the marinade. Cook the tofu, without moving it, until it browns on one side. Then stir-fry it so it browns on the other sides, about 10 minutes total. When it's golden all over, transfer the tofu to a bowl.

4. If the pan looks dry, add a little more oil; then add the onion, garlic, ginger, and chiles. Cook, stirring, until the vegetables are fragrant and beginning to turn golden at the edges, about 2 minutes. Add the cabbage and snap peas, and cook until wilted, 2 to 4 minutes. Then add the rice and stir until the ingredients are well combined. Press down on it with a spatula. Cook without moving the mixture until the rice gets a chance to dry out and take on a little color, 1 to 3 minutes; then stir it around a little and toss until it is golden in spots. Add the reserved marinade and mix well; cook to blend the flavors, another 1 to 2 minutes.

5. Make a well in the center of the rice and add the eggs; cook until they are custardy, 1 to 2 minutes. Gently fold the tofu into the rice and eggs, mixing everything together. Sprinkle the lime juice over the fried rice, garnish with the cilantro, and serve with lime wedges alongside.

3 tablespoons soy sauce

3 tablespoons Asian fish sauce

7 ounces firm tofu, patted dry and cut into 1-inch cubes

2 tablespoons peanut oil or safflower oil, plus more if needed

1 medium onion, diced

2 garlic cloves, minced

1 tablespoon grated or minced peeled fresh ginger

3 serrano or Thai chiles, seeded and sliced

2 cups chopped napa cabbage

2 cups sugar snap peas, trimmed

2 cups cooked white or brown rice

3 large eggs, lightly beaten

Juice of ½ lime, plus lime wedges for serving

Fresh cilantro or basil leaves, for garnish

TOTAL TIME: 25 MINUTES
SERVES 4 TO 6

PIZZAS

& PIES

BASIC PIZZA DOUGH

There's a cult around pizza dough making, with self-appointed mavens swearing that unless you seek out "00" flour from Italy and import your water from Naples, you'll never be able to get a good, authentic flavor in your crust. This recipe proves otherwise. Adapted from Franny's Pizza in Brooklyn, the key element here is time. You need to give the dough enough rising time—at least twenty-four hours in the refrigerator—to let it properly ferment and take on a complex, rich, yeasty flavor. This does put the kibosh on trying to whip this up for dinner tonight. But if you can plan ahead, you'll be amply rewarded with a crackling crust with a good chew and plenty of air bubbles that singe in the oven.

I like to make a double batch of the dough and freeze the risen dough balls until I need them. You can pull them out of the freezer in the morning before work, let them defrost in the fridge, and then bring them to room temperature while the oven preheats. On mornings when you think you'll be too stressed or tired or preoccupied to deal with dinner, just get into the habit of defrosting some pizza dough. You'll thank yourself later.

1. Mix the yeast, warm water, and olive oil in the bowl of an electric stand mixer or food processor, and let the mixture sit until the yeast is foamy, about 5 minutes.

2. Using the dough hook or the food processor blade, beat or pulse in the flour and salt, and mix until a smooth, slightly elastic dough forms, 2 to 3 minutes. Oil a bowl with olive oil, place the dough in the bowl, and turn the dough to coat it with oil. Cover the bowl loosely with plastic wrap, and refrigerate it for at least 24 hours and let rise up to 48 hours.

3. Divide the dough in half, and shape each piece into a tight, compact ball. Put the dough balls on a baking sheet and let them rest in the refrigerator for at least 2 hours and up to 12 hours before using.

VARIATION
To make whole-wheat pizza dough, substitute whole-wheat flour for half of the all-purpose flour.

¾ teaspoon active dry yeast

⅞ cup (198 grams) warm (not hot) water

1 teaspoon extra-virgin olive oil, plus more for the bowl

2¼ cups (282 grams) all-purpose flour

1 teaspoon (6 grams) kosher salt

TOTAL TIME: 20 MINUTES + AT LEAST 26 HOURS FOR RISING AND RESTING MAKES 2 8-OUNCE BALLS OF PIZZA DOUGH

PIZZA *with Broccoli Rabe, Ricotta, and Olives*

Bitter broccoli rabe and milky sweet ricotta together are a natural, and in fact make up one of my favorite crostini toppings whenever I have a little leftover sautéed rabe hanging around the fridge. But the combo is even better here, slathered on a black-edged, crispy pizza crust and strewn with olives, which add just the right salty bite. You can substitute other greens for the rabe as long as they have robust character. Mustard greens, kale, and chard all work better than soft baby spinach, which is a little too meek to hold its own here.

2 8-ounce balls pizza dough, white or whole-wheat, purchased or homemade (see page 301)

¼ cup extra-virgin olive oil, plus more for drizzling

4 garlic cloves, smashed and peeled

Pinch of red chile flakes

8 ounces broccoli rabe, trimmed

Kosher salt to taste

Fine cornmeal, for dusting

¼ cup pitted Kalamata olives, thinly sliced

1 cup fresh ricotta

Coarse sea salt to taste

Red chile flakes, for garnish

TOTAL TIME: 1¼ HOURS
MAKES 2 12-INCH PIZZAS

1. Heat the oven to 500°F if your broiler unit is in the oven, or to 450°F if your broiler is in a separate drawer. Place a pizza stone or a rimless baking sheet on the middle rack. Allow the oven to heat for 45 minutes.

2. At the same time, allow the dough to sit at room temperature for 30 minutes.

3. In a large skillet, heat the olive oil over medium-high heat. Add the garlic and brown it all over, about 2 to 3 minutes. Then stir in the chile flakes. Add the broccoli rabe and cook, tossing it frequently, until it is tender, 5 to 7 minutes. Season the broccoli rabe with kosher salt, remove it from the skillet, and coarsely chop it along with the garlic, mixing them together.

4. Turn a rimmed baking sheet upside down (or use a pizza peel if you have one), and dust it generously with fine cornmeal.

Working directly on the baking sheet, stretch and pull one of the pizza dough balls to form a 12-inch round. Scatter half of the broccoli rabe and garlic mixture, and half of the olives over the dough. Dollop half of the ricotta on top. Drizzle with olive oil and sprinkle with coarse sea salt. Jiggle the pizza gently to make sure it is not sticking to the baking sheet or pizza peel, and sprinkle cornmeal under any sticky spots.

5. Slide the crust off the baking sheet or pizza peel onto the hot pizza stone in the oven. Cook the pizza for 3 minutes. Then turn on the broiler and broil the pizza until it is golden, crisp, and blistered in places, 2 to 4 minutes. (If you don't have a broiler in your oven, bake the pizza at 450°F until it's blistered and golden, 10 to 20 minutes.) Using tongs, slide the pizza onto a large platter. Repeat with the remaining dough and toppings.

BUTTERNUT SQUASH
PIZZA *with Sage and Roasted Lemon*

All pizzas are blisteringly appetizing, but this has the added bonus of being one of the prettier pies you can make, too. The orange butternut squash and bright yellow lemon slices caramelize at the edges while the sage leaves add a subtle hint of green. With the acidity of the lemon balancing the sweetness of the squash alongside the woodsy herb, it's a pretty great flavor combination, as well as unexpected. I love this with an arugula or other dark green salad on the side.

1. Heat the oven to 500°F if your broiler unit is in the oven, or to 450°F if your broiler is in a separate drawer. Place a pizza stone or a rimless baking sheet on the middle rack. Allow the oven to heat for 45 minutes.

2. At the same time, allow the dough to sit at room temperature for 30 minutes.

3. Bring a small pot of salted water to a boil. Drop in the lemon slices and cook for 2 minutes; then remove them with a slotted spoon and drain them well. Taste a piece of lemon; if it seems bitter, blanch the slices again. Set them aside.

4. Using a vegetable peeler, remove the squash skin. Then peel away long, thin strips of flesh from the neck. You will need about 3 ounces of squash strips for 2 pizzas. Reserve the remaining squash for another use.

5. Turn a rimmed baking sheet upside down (or use a pizza peel if you've got one) and dust it generously with fine cornmeal.

Working directly on the baking sheet, stretch and pull one of the pizza dough balls to form a 12-inch round. Scatter half of the pecorino over the dough. Top with half of the lemon slices, half of the squash strips, and half of the sage leaves. Drizzle with olive oil and sprinkle with coarse sea salt. Jiggle the pizza gently to make sure it is not sticking to the baking sheet or pizza peel; sprinkle cornmeal under any sticky spots.

6. Slide the crust off the baking sheet or pizza peel onto the hot pizza stone in the oven. Cook the pizza for 3 minutes. Then turn on the broiler and broil the pizza until it is golden, crisp, and blistered in places, 2 to 4 minutes. (If you don't have a broiler in your oven, bake the pizza at 450°F until it's blistered and golden, 10 to 20 minutes.) Using tongs, slide the pizza onto a large platter. Repeat with the remaining dough and toppings.

2 8-ounce balls pizza dough, white or whole-wheat, purchased or homemade (see page 301)

1 small Meyer or regular lemon, sliced paper-thin by hand or with a mandoline

1 small butternut squash

Fine cornmeal, for dusting

½ cup coarsely grated young pecorino (such as Pecorino Toscano) or young Manchego cheese (2 ounces)

2 teaspoons finely chopped fresh sage leaves

Extra-virgin olive oil, for drizzling

Coarse sea salt to taste

TOTAL TIME: 1¼ HOURS
MAKES 2 12-INCH PIZZAS

CHERRY TOMATO PIZZA
with Anchovy and Garlic

As you can see from the recipe lineup in this book, I'm not big on tomato-sauced pizzas, which I think generally cover up the deep yeasty flavor of a good crust. But here, a handful of cherry tomato halves, browned and condensed in the high heat, add just the right sweet juiciness next to the anchovies and slivered garlic. This pie does not stint on the anchovies, which are dissolved into good olive oil and drizzled all over the top. But if you're less of a fan of the funky little fish than I am, you can use fewer than the dozen or so called for. Or, substitute 2 tablespoons of minced capers and make caper oil instead. Less fishy, just as salty. Serve this with a mild-leafed green salad to mellow out the flavors—romaine or butter lettuce work well.

2 8-ounce balls pizza dough, white or whole-wheat, purchased or homemade (see page 301)

¼ cup extra-virgin olive oil, plus more for drizzling

8 to 12 oil-packed anchovy fillets, to taste

Fine cornmeal, for dusting

1 cup halved cherry tomatoes

1 to 2 garlic cloves, to taste, sliced as thin as possible

1 teaspoon dried oregano

¼ cup grated Parmigiano-Reggiano cheese (1 ounce)

Coarse sea salt and freshly ground black pepper to taste

Fresh basil leaves, for serving

TOTAL TIME: 1¼ HOURS
MAKES 2 12-INCH PIZZAS

1. Heat the oven to 500°F if your broiler unit is in the oven, or to 450°F if your broiler is in a separate drawer. Place a pizza stone or a rimless baking sheet on the middle rack. Allow the oven to heat for 45 minutes.

2. At the same time, allow the dough to sit at room temperature for 30 minutes.

3. Heat a small skillet over high heat, and then add the olive oil and the anchovies. Cook, mashing the anchovies with a wooden spoon until they dissolve, about 2 minutes. Set aside and allow to cool.

4. Turn a rimmed baking sheet upside down (or use a pizza peel if you've got one), and dust it generously with fine cornmeal. Working directly on the baking sheet, stretch and pull one of the pizza dough balls to form a 12-inch round. Scatter half of the tomatoes, half of the garlic, and half of the oregano over the dough. Top with half of the cheese. Drizzle with half of the reserved anchovy oil and sprinkle with coarse sea salt and black pepper to taste. Jiggle the pizza gently to make sure it is not sticking to the baking sheet or pizza peel; sprinkle cornmeal under any sticky spots.

5. Slide the crust off the baking sheet or pizza peel onto the hot pizza stone in the oven. Cook the pizza for 3 minutes. Then turn on the broiler and broil the pizza until it is golden, crisp, and blistered in places, 2 to 4 minutes. (If you don't have a broiler in your oven, bake the pizza at 450°F until it's blistered and golden, 10 to 20 minutes.) Using tongs, slide the pizza onto a large platter, drizzle with more oil, and top with basil leaves. Repeat with the remaining dough and toppings.

SPICED LAMB PIE

with Dill, Mint, and Olives

The combination of lamb and puff pastry scented with cinnamon, allspice, and paprika, and laced with fresh mint, may seem like the kind of dinner party dish that you'd want to serve on your fanciest china. And it'd fit in perfectly well there. But it's also got a homey appeal in the pot-pie vein that makes it exactly right for a cozy Sunday supper. Either way, you can assemble this up to four hours in advance, then bake it just before serving. Serve it with something juicy and green—Pan-Fried Asparagus (page 376), Green Beans with Caper Vinaigrette (page 377), or even just some sliced and salted cucumbers will counter some of the puff pastry butteriness.

1. Heat the olive oil in 12-inch skillet over medium heat. Add the leeks and carrots, and sauté until the vegetables have softened but not browned, 8 to 10 minutes. Add the lamb, cinnamon, pepper, paprika, allspice, and salt, stirring to combine. Raise the heat to medium-high and cook until the lamb has browned all over, 10 to 15 minutes. Let the mixture cool completely, and then pour off the fat.

2. While the lamb is cooling, split the puff pastry in half if it's in one piece. Use a floured rolling pin to roll out each piece to roughly 9 × 11 inches. Line an 8 or 9 × 11-inch baking dish, or a shallow 2-quart gratin dish, with one piece of the pastry, pulling the dough up to cover the sides of the baking dish.

3. In a large bowl, whisk 2 of the eggs. Add the drained cooled lamb mixture, along with the olives, parsley, mint, and dill, and mix to combine. Spoon the mixture over the pastry in the baking dish. Top with the remaining piece of pastry, and pinch the edges of both pieces of pastry together to seal them (you're basically making a big sandwich). Chill in the refrigerator for at least 1 hour (and up to 4 hours), or freeze for 15 minutes.

4. Heat the oven to 400°F.

5. Whisk the remaining egg and brush it over the pastry; then sprinkle with the sesame seeds. Bake until the pastry is golden on top, about 35 minutes. (The pie may appear wet when you remove it from the oven, but the pastry will absorb the moisture as it sits.) Allow the pie to cool for 15 to 20 minutes before cutting it into squares. Serve with garlicky yogurt sauce. Leftovers reheat well in a 350°F oven.

NOTE: If your package of puff pastry weighs slightly less than a pound, just roll the dough a little thinner so it will fit the baking dish.

2 tablespoons extra-virgin olive oil

2 leeks (white and light green parts only), finely chopped

2 carrots, finely chopped

2 pounds ground lamb or lean beef

1½ teaspoons ground cinnamon

1½ teaspoons freshly ground black pepper

1 teaspoon sweet paprika

⅛ teaspoon ground allspice

1 tablespoon kosher salt

1 pound puff pastry, thawed if frozen (see Note)

3 large eggs

½ cup sliced pitted, good-quality olives (black or green)

½ cup chopped fresh parsley leaves

½ cup chopped fresh mint leaves

½ cup chopped fresh dill leaves

1 tablespoon sesame seeds

Garlicky Yogurt (page 243), optional

TOTAL TIME: 2½ HOURS
SERVES 8

ROASTED ZUCCHINI PHYLLO PIE

with Herbs and Anchovies

This flaky pie uses the same technique as the greens and feta pie (page 316). But instead of the familiar Greek-inspired combination of feta and dill, I took my cue from my August CSA box and used up some of the zucchini I had in the fridge looking for a home. This is not the kind of dish where the anchovies fade into the background. The salted fish are front and center here, melding with the mild sweet zucchini and garlic in a way that seems somewhat Provençal. This said, you can cut back on them, or replace them with ¼ cup minced black olives.

2½ pounds zucchini, halved lengthwise and sliced into thin half-moons

4 tablespoons extra-virgin olive oil, plus more as needed

Sea salt and freshly ground black pepper as needed

1 large Spanish onion (or 2 smaller onions), halved lengthwise and sliced into thin half-moons

1 2-ounce jar oil-packed anchovies (about 23 anchovies), coarsely chopped

4 garlic cloves, minced

2 tablespoons chopped fresh oregano or marjoram leaves

¼ teaspoon red chile flakes, or to taste

2 large eggs

1 cup fresh mint, parsley, or dill leaves, or a combination, chopped, plus more for serving

2 tablespoons chopped fresh chives

2 teaspoons fresh lemon juice, plus more to taste

6 large sheets phyllo dough, thawed if frozen

TOTAL TIME: 1¼ HOURS
SERVES 4 TO 6

1. Heat the oven to 450°F. On one or two large rimmed baking sheets, toss the zucchini with 3 tablespoons of the oil and a pinch of salt. Roast, tossing the zucchini halfway through, until it is deeply browned, about 40 minutes.

2. Meanwhile, heat a 10-inch ovenproof skillet over medium heat and add the remaining 1 tablespoon oil. Once the oil is hot, add the onion and a large pinch each of salt and pepper. Sauté until golden, about 10 minutes.

3. Add the anchovies, garlic, oregano, and chile flakes to the onion, and sauté until the anchovies melt, 2 to 3 minutes. Scrape the mixture into a large bowl. When the zucchini is done, add it to the same bowl and reduce the oven temperature to 400°F. Let the zucchini mixture cool.

4. In a small bowl, stir together the eggs, mint, and chives. Mix this into the cooled zucchini-onion mixture and then stir in the lemon juice, adding more to taste.

5. Wash out the skillet you used for the onion and brush it all over with olive oil. Cover the bottom of the skillet with 2 pieces of phyllo, overlapping them, with the edges hanging over the sides. Place 2 more pieces of phyllo in the skillet, perpendicular to the others, with the edges hanging over the sides. In the center of the skillet you should have the 4 overlapping pieces, with the overhanging edges on the sides. Drizzle the phyllo lightly with olive oil, and then spoon the zucchini mixture onto the center. Top with the remaining 2 sheets of phyllo, crumpling them so they cover the zucchini but have texture and waves—this will bake up crunchy, as opposed to a smooth, neat top, which is less crunchy. Don't worry if it rips or looks ugly—it will bake up gorgeously browned. Drizzle the top generously with olive oil and sprinkle with salt.

6. Bake until golden brown, 35 to 40 minutes. Serve warm or at room temperature topped with dill.

GREENS & FETA PHYLLO PIE

The first spanikopitas I ever made were straight out of *The Silver Palate Cookbook,* small phyllo triangles laboriously wrought. It wasn't until much later that I realized that a giant greens and feta pie was much easier to make than a bunch of little one-bite hors d'oeuvres. Don't bother fussing with the phyllo here, you don't need to strive for perfection in your layering. Sloppy, messy layers will still bake up into a golden brown and delectable crust holding the mix of creamy cheese and piquant, herb-flecked greens. This makes a terrific brunch dish as well as a comforting and cozy supper.

2 tablespoons extra-virgin olive oil, plus more for drizzling

1 bunch scallions (about 8), trimmed and coarsely chopped

10 ounces Swiss or red chard, leaves and stems sliced separately

Fine sea salt or kosher salt to taste

10 ounces collard greens or kale, stems removed, leaves sliced

Freshly ground black pepper to taste

3 large eggs

6 ounces feta cheese, crumbled (1¼ cups)

½ cup cottage cheese

3 tablespoons unsalted butter, melted

1 cup fresh parsley leaves, chopped

1 cup fresh dill leaves, chopped

½ teaspoon finely grated lemon zest

2 teaspoons fresh lemon juice, plus more to taste

4 large sheets phyllo dough, thawed if frozen

TOTAL TIME: 1¼ HOURS
SERVES 4 TO 6

1. Heat the oven to 400°F.

2. Heat a 10-inch ovenproof skillet over medium heat, and add 1 tablespoon of the olive oil. Once the oil is hot, add the scallions, chard stems, and a pinch of salt. Sauté until the scallions and chard stems are soft, about 10 minutes.

3. Add the remaining 1 tablespoon oil to the skillet, and add the collard greens (in batches if they don't all fit at once). Sauté the greens until they have wilted, 3 to 7 minutes. Then add the chard leaves, seasoning them to taste with salt and pepper. Cook until all the greens have wilted, another 5 minutes or so. Pour everything into a large bowl and let it cool.

4. In a small bowl, stir together the eggs, feta, cottage cheese, 1 tablespoon of the melted butter, and the chopped parsley and dill. Add this mixture to the cooled greens along with the lemon zest and juice, and mix well. Taste and add more lemon juice and salt if needed.

5. Wash out the skillet, and butter the bottom and sides. Cover the bottom of the skillet with 2 pieces of phyllo, overlapping them, with the edges hanging over the sides. Place 2 more pieces of phyllo in the skillet, perpendicular to the others, with the edges hanging over the sides. In the center of the skillet you should have the overlapping 4 pieces, with the edges overhanging the sides. Brush the phyllo lightly all over with melted butter. Then spoon the greens into the center of the skillet where all the phyllo layers overlap. Fold the overhanging phyllo sheets over the filling to partially enclose it, crumpling the phyllo sheets so they have texture (which will bake up crispier than a smooth top). Brush with any remaining melted butter.

6. Bake the pie until the phyllo is golden brown, 40 to 45 minutes. Serve warm or at room temperature.

Rustic EGGPLANT & TOMATO GALETTE

This savory galette, with a hearty whole-grain rye crust, is layered with roasted vegetables, goat cheese, and rosemary. The flavors are a little like ratatouille, baked into a crust. You do need to set aside some time to make this—it will require four baking sheets and take all afternoon to put together. Or, do the work over several days. The dough can be made up to three days ahead, and you can roast the vegetables the day before and store them in the fridge.

1. Make the dough: In a food processor fitted with the steel blade or in a large bowl, pulse or mix together the flours, sugar, and salt.

2. In a measuring cup, lightly beat the egg, and then add just enough heavy cream to get to ⅓ cup. Lightly whisk and set aside.

3. Add butter pieces to the flour mixture, and pulse or use a pastry cutter or your fingers to break up the butter. (Do not overprocess; you want chickpea-sized chunks of butter.) Gradually drizzle up to ¼ cup of the egg mixture over the dough, and combine until the dough just starts to come together. (Reserve the remaining egg mixture.) Mix in the lemon juice and the lemon zest if using.

4. On a lightly floured surface knead the dough into a disk, wrap it in plastic wrap, and refrigerate for 2 hours or up to 3 days.

5. When you are ready to bake, line a rimmed baking sheet with parchment paper. Roll the dough out to form a 12-inch round, transfer it to the prepared baking sheet, and refrigerate it while you prepare the filling.

6. Make the filling: Heat the oven to 425°F.

7. Spread the eggplant and tomato slices in a single layer on three separate baking sheets. Drizzle generously with olive oil, and season with salt and pepper. Roast the vegetables, tossing the eggplant occasionally, until they are golden at the edges, 35 to 40 minutes.

8. Transfer the roasted vegetables to a bowl, add the chiles, and toss.

9. Reduce the oven temperature to 400°F. In a small bowl, combine the goat cheese, garlic, and rosemary. Spread this mixture in a thin layer over the dough, leaving a 1½-inch border all around. Arrange the roasted vegetables evenly over the goat cheese. Fold up the edges of the crust, pleating the edges to hold them in (sloppy is fine). Brush the dough generously with the remaining egg and cream mixture.

10. Bake until the crust is golden brown, about 40 minutes. Let it cool for at least 30 minutes before serving.

FOR THE DOUGH

⅔ cup (80 grams) all-purpose flour

⅔ cup (90 grams) rye flour or whole-wheat flour

1 teaspoon (5 grams) sugar

½ teaspoon (3 grams) fine sea salt

1 large egg

Heavy cream or milk, as needed

8 tablespoons (1 stick) unsalted butter, cut into large pieces

2 teaspoons (10 milliliters) fresh lemon juice

½ teaspoon (4 grams) grated lemon zest (optional)

FOR THE FILLING

2 pounds slender Japanese or baby eggplants, trimmed and thinly sliced

1 pound plum tomatoes, thinly sliced

Extra-virgin olive oil, as needed

Kosher salt and freshly ground black pepper to taste

2 fresh hot chiles, such as cherry peppers, seeded and minced

3 ounces soft and creamy goat cheese (or use cream cheese), at room temperature

1 small garlic clove, grated on a Microplane or minced

1 teaspoon chopped fresh rosemary leaves

TOTAL TIME: ABOUT 4 HOURS
SERVES 8

SOUPS

Quick Southern HAM & NAVY BEAN SOUP

with Spicy Cornbread Croutons

This ham-beans-and-collard-greens soup is excellent by itself, but the cornbread croutons make it outrageous. Cubes of cornbread, toasted until crisp with butter and hot sauce, hold up better than regular soft cornbread served on the side, adding sweetness, a chile burn, and a little crunch all at once. If you happen to have fresh cranberry beans on hand in late summer, you can substitute a cup of the shelled beans (which will weigh 12 ounces still in the pod) for the canned navy beans. They will cook in the soup in fifteen minutes or so. Leftover soup freezes really well, so if you love this classic Southern combination, consider doubling the recipe. Just freeze the croutons separately, then run them under the broiler for a minute or so (watch carefully so they don't burn) after defrosting but before serving.

2 tablespoons unsalted butter, melted

2 teaspoons hot sauce, such as Frank's, plus more for serving

6 ounces cornbread (homemade, page 385, or store-bought), cut into ¾-inch cubes (2 cups)

2 tablespoons extra-virgin olive oil

1 small onion, diced

2 garlic cloves, minced

1 celery stalk, diced

1 pound slab ham, cut into 1-inch cubes

1 15-ounce can navy beans, drained and rinsed

1 red bell pepper, seeded and diced

2 cups sliced collard greens

1 tablespoon paprika

1 teaspoon kosher salt

Freshly ground black pepper

TOTAL TIME: 45 MINUTES
SERVES 4

1. Heat the oven to 300°F.

2. In a small bowl, combine the melted butter with the hot sauce. Brush this over all sides of the cornbread cubes, and place them on a rack set over a half sheet pan. Bake the croutons for 30 minutes. Then remove them from the oven and set them aside, still on the rack.

3. Meanwhile, heat the olive oil in a large pot over medium-high heat. Add the onion, garlic, and celery, and let them sweat and turn golden, stirring occasionally, 10 to 15 minutes.

4. Add 4 cups of water and the ham, beans, bell pepper, and collards. Bring to a simmer and season with the paprika, salt, and black pepper. Take the back of a spoon and mash some of the beans on the inside of the pot (this will help to thicken the soup). Cook for another 15 to 20 minutes.

5. Season the soup to taste, and ladle it into warmed bowls. Add a few dashes of hot sauce to each serving, and top with the cornbread croutons.

GREEK AVGOLEMONO
SOUP *with Greens*

Avgolemono is a classic Greek soup made of chicken stock spiked with lemon and dill and thickened with eggs until it's almost custardy, then ladled over rice or orzo. Here, I add baby greens to the pot to increase the vegetable quotient and add a bit of color. You can also throw in some leftover cooked chicken if you want to make this even more substantial, though it's perfectly satisfying without the added meat. The recipe below makes a small batch of soup because leftovers don't really freeze well (the broth turns grainy from the egg). But with its rich texture and lively flavor, finishing it all in a few days won't be a problem. Tzatziki—cucumbers mixed with yogurt and garlic—goes well here, especially if you really want to Greek out. Or in springtime try the Pan-Fried Asparagus with Lemon Zest (page 376).

1. In a medium pot, bring the stock to a simmer. Add the rice and simmer gently until it is tender, 15 to 20 minutes. Stir in the escarole for the last 5 minutes of cooking.

2. In a medium bowl, whisk together the eggs and 2 tablespoons lemon juice.

3. Whisking constantly, very slowly pour 1 cup of the hot stock into the egg-lemon mixture. Then pour the mixture into the pot of hot soup. Cook gently until the soup begins to thicken, 2 to 3 minutes. Season the soup with the dill, lemon zest, salt and pepper, and more lemon juice if desired.

5 cups chicken or vegetable stock

½ cup white rice or orzo

4 cups coarsely chopped escarole, Swiss chard leaves, or spinach

3 large eggs, at room temperature

2 to 3 tablespoons fresh lemon juice, as needed

¼ cup chopped fresh dill leaves

½ teaspoon finely grated lemon zest

Kosher salt and freshly ground black pepper to taste

TOTAL TIME: 25 MINUTES
SERVES 3 OR 4

Creamy CARAMELIZED BROCCOLI SOUP

with Lemon Zest and Chile

I learned how to make this soup from Andrew Feinberg from Franny's in Brooklyn when I was helping him write his cookbook. The restaurant is justly famous for its amazing pizza, but Andrew also cooks rustic seasonal Italian food brilliantly and simply. Andrew makes this soup in fall when broccoli is at its best. To deepen its flavor, he sears chunks of the vegetable in olive oil until they are dark brown and caramelized on one side, leaving the other bright green to preserve the broccoli's inherent sweetness. The resulting soup is a lot more interesting than your average vegetable puree, with lemon and chile sparking all of the flavors. In my version, I've added a bit of potato to make it thicker and creamier, though feel free to leave it out if you want to keep things on the lighter side. Rye & Cheddar Biscuits (page 380) are an excellent accompaniment.

8 tablespoons extra-virgin olive oil, plus more as needed

2 heads broccoli (about 2 pounds), separated into small florets, stems peeled and diced

2½ teaspoons kosher salt, plus more to taste

2 tablespoons unsalted butter

1 large Spanish onion, diced

5 garlic cloves, chopped

½ teaspoon freshly ground black pepper, plus more for serving

¼ teaspoon red chile flakes

8 ounces potatoes, peeled and thinly sliced

¼ teaspoon finely grated lemon zest

1½ tablespoons fresh lemon juice, plus more to taste

Grated Parmigiano-Reggiano cheese, for serving

Flaky sea salt, for serving

TOTAL TIME: 45 MINUTES
SERVES 4 TO 6

1. In a large soup pot, heat 2 tablespoons of the olive oil over high heat. Add about a third of the broccoli, just enough so that it covers the bottom of the pan in a single layer without crowding. Cook the broccoli without touching it (resist the urge to stir!) until it is dark brown on one side only (leave the other side bright green), 3 to 4 minutes. Transfer the broccoli to a large bowl, and repeat with the remaining broccoli, adding another 2 tablespoons oil for each batch (probably another 2 or 3 batches). When all of the broccoli has been browned, season it with 1 teaspoon salt.

2. Reduce the heat under the soup pot to medium-low. Add the butter and remaining 2 tablespoons oil. When the butter has melted, add the onion, garlic, pepper, chile flakes, and ½ teaspoon of the salt. Cook the onion-garlic mixture until the onions are soft and translucent, about 4 minutes. Then add the potatoes, 4 cups of water, and the remaining 1 teaspoon salt. Bring to a simmer, cover the pot, and cook until the potatoes are just tender, 10 to 15 minutes. Add the broccoli, cover again, and cook until it is tender, another 5 to 10 minutes.

3. Stir the lemon zest into the soup. Using an immersion blender (or working in batches in a blender or food processor), coarsely puree the soup, leaving some small chunks for texture. Stir in the lemon juice. Finish with the grated cheese, a drizzle of olive oil, and a sprinkling of black pepper and flaky sea salt.

BUTTERNUT SQUASH & RED LENTIL SOUP

with Coconut and Spinach

There are many lentil varieties from which to choose, but for me at least, the best ones for soup are the red ones. Actually more of a pale salmon or orange color, these tiny lentils cook quickly and will break down into a puree with only the slightest encouragement from some vigorous stirring. You can also puree them in a blender or food processor into perfect smoothness without the need to strain. Plus, I think they have a lighter and more vegetable-y flavor than super-earthy brown lentils. Here, I've spiced them with cumin and mixed them with sweet butternut squash and coconut milk. It's a thick and almost porridge-like soup with a deep, aromatic flavor and a hit of lime at the end.

6 tablespoons extra-virgin olive oil

2 onions, diced

4 garlic cloves, finely chopped

2 tablespoons tomato paste

2 teaspoons ground cumin

Pinch of cayenne pepper

¾ teaspoon kosher salt, plus more if needed

Freshly ground black pepper to taste

12 ounces butternut squash, peeled, seeded, and diced

1 cup red lentils

2 cups chicken stock

1 13.5-ounce can unsweetened coconut milk

5 ounces fresh baby spinach (optional)

1 teaspoon grated lime zest

Fresh lime juice, as needed

TOTAL TIME: 1 HOUR
SERVES 4

1. In a large pot, heat the olive oil over medium-high heat until it is shimmering. Add the onions and garlic, and cook until they are soft, 5 to 7 minutes. Stir in the tomato paste, cumin, cayenne, the ¾ teaspoon salt, and black pepper to taste; cook for 2 minutes.

2. Stir in the squash and the lentils. Pour in the stock and 4 cups of water, and bring the mixture to a simmer over medium-high heat. Then reduce the heat to low and partially cover the pot; simmer until the lentils and squash are soft, about 30 minutes.

3. Stir the coconut milk into the soup and heat it through. Taste, and adjust the seasoning if needed.

4. Using an immersion blender (or working in batches in a blender or food processor), coarsely puree the soup. Then stir in the spinach if using and the lime zest, and cook until the spinach wilts. Season with lime juice just before serving.

LEEK, TOMATO & FARRO SOUP *with Pancetta*

This comforting winter soup is loaded with tomatoes; salty, porky bits of pancetta; and nubby bits of farro. It's a hearty, rib-sticking kind of soup that's almost stew-like, especially the leftovers, which thicken even more in the fridge. If you'd like something brothier, you can add a bit of water to thin down the soup, but make sure to also add an extra pinch of salt. Or leave it be and eat the warmed-up leftovers with a fork, risotto-style (it will have a similar texture). In any case, the brawny, earthy flavors are sensational. A simple green salad (page 379) on the side is definitely all you'll need to make a meal.

1. Heat a large pot over medium heat. Add the pancetta and cook until it is well browned and crisped, 5 to 10 minutes. Using a slotted spoon, transfer the pancetta to a paper-towel-lined plate. (Leave the rendered fat in the pot.)

2. Add the 2 tablespoons olive oil to the pot, and stir in the leeks, celery, and carrot. Cook, stirring occasionally, until the vegetables have softened, 7 to 10 minutes; stir in the garlic for the last minute. Add the thyme and rosemary sprigs, farro, tomatoes, salt, and a generous grind of black pepper. Bring to a simmer and cook until the farro is almost tender, about 20 minutes. Then stir in the pancetta and simmer for 5 to 10 minutes more.

3. Ladle the soup into warmed bowls, discarding the thyme and rosemary sprigs. Top each one with Parmigiano-Reggiano, a drizzle of olive oil, and a sprinkling of parsley.

5 ounces pancetta or thick-cut bacon, diced

2 tablespoons extra-virgin olive oil, plus more for serving

2 leeks (white and light green parts only), cleaned and thinly sliced

1 large celery stalk, diced small

1 large carrot, peeled and diced small

2 garlic cloves, finely chopped

3 sprigs fresh thyme

1 sprig fresh rosemary

1½ cups farro

1 28-ounce can diced tomatoes with their juices

1 teaspoon kosher salt

Freshly ground black pepper, as needed

Coarsely grated Parmigiano-Reggiano cheese, for serving

Chopped fresh parsley leaves, for serving

TOTAL TIME: 1 HOUR
SERVES 6

RUSTIC SHRIMP BISQUE
with Fennel

If you think that all bisques are creamy, fussy things, this rustic recipe will be a happy surprise. Instead of heavy cream, rice gives the soup body and a nice soft graininess that goes well the succulent bits of shrimp. Pernod and fennel add a hint of licorice complexity, while white wine brings a dose of acid. In order to get the deepest, shrimp-iest flavor, I've simmered the shrimp shells into a quickly made shrimp stock. It does add an extra twenty or so minutes onto the recipe time, but is worth it for the extra-rich flavor. If you have your fishmonger peel the shrimp for you, just ask for the shells for stock.

1. Melt 1 tablespoon of the butter in a large pot set over high heat. Add ½ teaspoon of the salt and the reserved shrimp shells, and cook, stirring frequently, until the shells are lightly browned in spots, about 3 minutes. Add the wine and Pernod, and boil until most of the liquid has evaporated, about 3 minutes. Then add 6 cups of water, the thyme sprigs, and the bay leaf, and simmer, uncovered, for 15 minutes. Strain the shrimp stock into a bowl, pressing on the shells before discarding them.

2. In the same large pot, melt 2 tablespoons of the butter with ½ teaspoon of the salt. Add the shrimp and sauté until they are pink, 2 to 4 minutes depending on their size. Using a slotted spoon, transfer the shrimp to a bowl.

3. Add the remaining 3 tablespoons butter to the pot. When it has melted, add the celery, leeks, garlic, and fennel, and sauté until they have softened, about 5 minutes. Stir in the rice, tomato paste, cayenne, and remaining 1 teaspoon salt, and sauté for 2 minutes. Add the reserved shrimp stock, cover the pot, and simmer until the rice is tender, about 20 minutes.

4. Set aside 4 to 6 nice-looking shrimp and stir the remainder into the bisque; let them cook for 2 minutes. Working carefully and in batches, pour the bisque into a blender and process it to a smooth puree or pulse it to a chunky mixture, as you like. (Or use an immersion blender to puree the soup.) Return the bisque to the pot. Stir in the lemon juice and salt to taste. Reheat the soup if necessary before serving. Serve the soup garnished with the reserved shrimp, the celery leaves, and fennel fronds.

6 tablespoons (¾ stick) unsalted butter

2 teaspoons kosher salt, plus more to taste

1 pound medium or large shrimp, shelled, shells reserved

⅔ cup dry white wine

2 tablespoons Pernod or brandy

3 sprigs fresh thyme

1 bay leaf

2 celery stalks, chopped, leaves reserved for garnish

2 large leeks (white and light green parts only), chopped

2 garlic cloves, chopped

1 fennel bulb, finely chopped, fronds reserved for garnish

¼ cup long-grain rice

2 tablespoons tomato paste

Pinch of cayenne pepper

Fresh lemon juice, to taste

TOTAL TIME: 1 HOUR
SERVES 4 TO 6

SMOKY FISH & POTATO CHOWDER

This homey fish chowder gains its smoky flavor from the combination of bacon and smoked paprika, while vermouth or white wine gives it a lift, and whole milk rounds it all out. Serve it with Rye & Cheddar Biscuits (page 380) if you want to go all out, or with oyster crackers or saltines to take the simpler, tried-and-true New England route. Because the leftovers don't freeze that well, this makes a rather small batch. You can double it if you're feeding a crowd, or if you just want lunch for the next five days, which is as long as it will keep in the fridge.

3 ounces thick-cut bacon (3 to 4 slices), diced

3 tablespoons unsalted butter

2 medium leeks (white and light green parts only), cleaned and thinly sliced

¾ teaspoon kosher salt, plus more as needed

¼ teaspoon hot smoked paprika

⅓ cup dry white vermouth or white wine

2 cups fish stock, good vegetable stock, or clam juice

8 ounces fingerling potatoes, sliced into ¼-inch-thick rounds

3 sprigs fresh thyme

2 cups whole milk

10 ounces flaky white fish, such as hake, cut into 2-inch chunks

Chopped fresh parsley leaves or scallion greens, for garnish (optional)

TOTAL TIME: 40 MINUTES
SERVES 3 OR 4

1. Place a heavy pot over medium-high heat, add the bacon, and cook until it is crisp, about 5 minutes. Use a slotted spoon to transfer the bacon to a paper-towel-lined plate to drain.

2. Spoon off all but 2 tablespoons of the bacon fat in the pot. Add the butter to the pot and let it melt. Then add the leeks and a pinch of salt; cook, stirring frequently, until the leeks are soft, about 5 minutes. Stir in the paprika; cook for 1 minute. Pour in the vermouth and simmer until it has almost completely evaporated, about 2 minutes. Stir in the stock, 1 cup of water, the potatoes, the thyme sprigs, and the ¾ teaspoon salt. Simmer until the potatoes are tender, about 25 minutes.

3. Add the milk and bacon to the pot, and bring the soup to a simmer. Add the fish and cook until it is just opaque, 2 to 4 minutes. Use a fork to flake the fish into large pieces. Taste, and adjust the seasoning if necessary. Remove the thyme sprigs. Serve immediately, with some parsley or scallions for garnish (optional, but it adds a fresh flavor and looks nice, too).

CRISPY CHICKEN-SKIN PHO

FOR THE CHICKEN

1½ pounds skin-on, bone-in chicken thighs (5 to 6 thighs)

Kosher salt, as needed

2 tablespoons Asian fish sauce

1½ tablespoons soy sauce

1½ tablespoons honey

2 teaspoons toasted sesame oil

Finely grated zest of 1 lime

½ to 1 fresh chile, seeded and thinly sliced

FOR THE BROTH

6 cups chicken stock, preferably homemade

6 thin slices peeled fresh ginger

3 whole star anise pods

2 garlic cloves, thinly sliced

½ to 1 fresh chile, seeded and thinly sliced

2 teaspoons light brown or granulated sugar, plus more as needed

2 teaspoons Asian fish sauce, plus more to taste

2 cups sliced Swiss chard leaves

6 ounces rice stick noodles

Boiling water

FOR THE GARNISH

Fresh basil leaves

Fresh cilantro sprigs

Thinly sliced white onion

Bean sprouts

Lime wedges

TOTAL TIME: 45 MINUTES
SERVES 4 TO 6

Making homemade beef pho—the rich Vietnamese noodle soup seasoned with star anise, ginger, and fish sauce—is quite the undertaking, requiring most of a day or more to prepare. This chicken version goes a bit faster and gives you a fantastic garnish of sweet and sticky crispy chicken skin that's potato-chip-like in texture, but with a deeply meaty taste. Frankly the crispy chicken skin is reason enough to make the recipe in the first place. Plus, of course, you'll also get an aromatic broth filled with soft rice noodles, crunchy bean sprouts, shredded chicken, and plenty of fresh wilted Swiss chard, which, while not authentically Vietnamese, has the same lusty, complex flavors of a good pho. If you like, you can make the chicken and broth four or five hours ahead; don't combine them until just before serving. If the chicken skin softens before you serve it, run it under the broiler for a minute to re-crisp it.

1. Heat the oven to 400°F.

2. **Cook the chicken:** Pat the chicken dry and, using your fingers, tug off the chicken skin. Place the skin flat on one half of a large rimmed baking sheet. Sprinkle the skin lightly with salt.

3. In a medium bowl, whisk together the fish sauce, soy sauce, honey, sesame oil, lime zest, and chile. Add the chicken thighs and turn to coat them well. Place the chicken, along with any liquid from the bowl, on the other half of the rimmed baking sheet, next to the skin. Roast, turning the chicken pieces (not the skin) occasionally, until the chicken is cooked through and caramelized, 25 to 30 minutes. If the edges of the chicken skin begin to char before the chicken meat is done, remove the skin with a spatula.

4. Meanwhile, **make the broth:** Combine the stock, ginger, star anise, garlic, and chile in a medium pot, and bring to a simmer. Reduce the heat to medium-low and continue to simmer for 15 minutes. Remove the pot from the heat and stir in the sugar, fish sauce, and Swiss chard, which should wilt on contact with the hot liquid. Taste, and add more fish sauce and/or sugar if needed.

5. Place the rice noodles in a large heatproof bowl and cover with boiling water. Let soak until pliable, 5 to 10 minutes. Drain well.

6. Chop or shred the chicken into bite-size pieces and crumble the crispy skin.

7. Divide the noodles among four to six warmed serving bowls. Ladle the broth into each bowl. Top with the chicken and chicken skin. Scatter the basil, cilantro, onion, and bean sprouts on top. Serve with lime wedges alongside.

MEXICAN TORTILLA
SOUP *with Avocado and Chipotle*

As much as I love a classic Jewish chicken noodle soup, I have to admit that the chile, spices, and a big squeeze of lime in this Mexican version give it a lot more pizzazz than the usual parsley and dill. Plus, with avocados and a dollop of sour cream, it's a rich and satisfying soup without being the least bit heavy. Not to say this replaces my mom's chicken noodle broth in my soup repertoire; I'm just saying it occupies a similarly cozy spot.

Frying your own tortillas here isn't strictly necessary, but they are undeniably more delicious, crisper, and more appealingly rich than anything you can buy. That said, if you don't want to bother, substitute a good brand of purchased tortilla chips.

1. In a medium pot, heat the 1 tablespoon olive oil over medium heat. Add the onion and chile and cook until they are soft, 7 to 10 minutes. Stir in the garlic, cumin, and chipotle; cook for 1 minute. Add the stock, tomatoes, chicken, and salt. Simmer for 20 minutes, breaking up the tomatoes with a spoon.

2. While the soup simmers, prepare the tortillas if you are using them: Slice the tortillas into ½-inch-wide strips; cut any long center strips in half crosswise. Heat the remaining ⅓ cup olive oil in a medium skillet over medium-high heat. Drop in one strip of tortilla to test the oil; if the oil is hot enough, the tortilla strip will sizzle. Fry the tortilla strips in batches, turning them once with tongs, until golden brown, 1 to 2 minutes per batch. Transfer the finished tortillas to a paper-towel-lined plate and immediately sprinkle them with salt.

3. To serve, ladle the soup into warmed bowls and float a handful of tortilla strips in each one. Top with a dollop of sour cream, some diced avocado, sliced scallions, and cilantro. Serve with lime wedges alongside.

⅓ cup plus 1 tablespoon extra-virgin olive oil

1 small onion, diced

1 poblano chile or green bell pepper, seeded and diced

1 garlic clove, finely chopped

1 teaspoon ground cumin

1 chipotle in adobo, seeded and finely chopped

3 cups chicken stock

1 15-ounce can whole peeled tomatoes

2 cups shredded cooked chicken

1½ teaspoons kosher salt, plus more as needed

4 6-inch whole-wheat or corn tortillas (optional)

Sour cream, for serving (optional)

Diced avocado, for serving

Sliced scallions, for serving

Fresh cilantro leaves, for serving

Lime wedges, for serving

TOTAL TIME: 45 MINUTES
SERVES 4

KIMCHI SOUP
with Pork and Tofu

This spicy, heady soup is worth seeking out pork belly for; the pieces simmer up into little soft meaty pillows that melt in the mouth. Butcher shops carry it, as do large supermarkets, and you're sure to find it in Korean or Chinese markets if you happen to have one nearby. This said, using boneless pork loin will also work, though the meat won't be quite as tender as the fatty belly. Try this recipe in place of your more sedate chicken soup next time you have a cold; the fiery Korean chile powder and paste (both available online and at Asian markets) give the broth quite a kick and do wonders to clear up a stuffy head on a bad day.

1 pound pork belly or boneless pork loin, cut into ½-inch pieces

Kosher salt to taste

4 garlic cloves, minced

1 tablespoon grated peeled fresh ginger

2 tablespoons soy sauce

1 teaspoon toasted sesame oil

1 teaspoon Asian fish sauce

8 ounces baby bok choy, stems and leaves separated

2 tablespoons peanut oil

1 medium onion, chopped

3 tablespoons *gochujang* (Korean red chile paste)

½ to 1 teaspoon *gochugaru* (Korean red chile flakes), to taste

2 cups kimchi, chopped, juices reserved

4 cups chicken, pork, or beef stock

12 ounces soft or silken tofu, cut into large cubes

8 scallions (white and green parts), thinly sliced, for serving

Fresh cilantro leaves, for serving

TOTAL TIME: 40 MINUTES + AT LEAST 20 MINUTES MARINATING
SERVES 4 TO 6

1. Put the pork in a bowl and season it all over with salt to taste. Add the garlic, ginger, soy sauce, sesame oil, and fish sauce. Toss well to coat, and then let the pork marinate for 20 minutes at room temperature, or covered overnight in the refrigerator.

2. Thinly slice both the stems and the leaves of the baby bok choy, keeping them separate so you can easily add them at different points in the recipe.

3. Set a heavy-bottomed soup pot over high heat. Add the peanut oil, and when it is hot, add the pork and brown it all over, about 5 minutes. Reduce the heat to medium, add the onion, and cook, stirring, until it has softened, about 5 minutes. Stir in the *gochujang* and *gochugaru*. Cook until the paste darkens in color, 1 to 2 minutes.

4. Add the kimchi and its juices, reserved bok choy stems, stock, 4 cups of water, and a large pinch of salt. Bring to a boil; then reduce the heat to a brisk simmer and cook for 20 minutes. Taste the broth, and adjust the seasoning if necessary.

5. Just before serving, add the bok choy greens and the tofu, and stir gently to combine. When the greens wilt, ladle the soup into warmed bowls and garnish them with the scallions and cilantro.

CHILLED CUCUMBER & CORN SOUP *with Avocado Toasts*

With a garlicky bite and buttermilk tang, this is a vibrant, cooling soup for deep summer. While the pureed cucumber soup is very light on its own, sweet and juicy raw corn kernels and avocado toasts sprinkled with crumbled feta add texture, heft, and a welcome richness. Serve this in teacups or other small bowls as an elegant first course, or pour it into regular bowls to make a light meal.

1. Make the soup: In the bowl of a blender or food processor, combine the cucumbers, buttermilk, garlic, anchovies if you like, scallions, jalapeño, fresh herbs, sherry vinegar, and the ¾ teaspoon sea salt. Blend until smooth. Taste, and adjust the seasoning if needed.

2. Make the avocado toasts: Smash the avocado slices on the toasted bread. Sprinkle the crumbled feta, if using, over the avocado. Squeeze the juice of the lemon half over the top, and finish with a drizzle of olive oil and some black pepper. Transfer the toasts to a plate and set aside.

3. Distribute the soup among four bowls, and serve it garnished with the raw corn kernels, the extra mixed herbs, and a drizzle of olive oil. Serve the avocado toasts alongside.

FOR THE SOUP

1 pound cucumbers, peeled, halved lengthwise, and seeded

2 cups cold buttermilk (or use 1½ cups plain yogurt plus ¼ cup milk or water)

1 large garlic clove, smashed and peeled

2 oil-packed anchovy fillets (optional)

2 scallions (white and green parts), trimmed

½ jalapeño, seeded and chopped

½ cup packed mixed soft fresh herbs (any combination of mint, parsley, dill, basil, and cilantro), plus more for serving

½ teaspoon sherry vinegar or white wine vinegar, plus more to taste

¾ teaspoon sea salt, plus more if needed

FOR THE AVOCADO TOASTS

1 avocado, pitted, peeled, and thinly sliced

4 slices country bread, toasted

2 tablespoons crumbled feta cheese (optional)

½ lemon

Extra-virgin olive oil, for drizzling

Freshly ground black pepper to taste

Kernels from 1 ear fresh corn

Extra-virgin olive oil, for drizzling

TOTAL TIME: 15 MINUTES
SERVES 2 TO 4

WATERMELON GAZPACHO
with Avocado

I make endless batches of gazpacho in the summer. It's a fast and easy lunch, and an ideal way to use up the inevitable pile of overripe, leaky tomatoes piled on the counter (I can never resist buying too many pretty heirlooms in August). Usually I wing it and just throw tomatoes, olive oil, salt, onion, and cucumber into the blender, smoothie-style. It's always good. But when I'm blending gazpacho for guests, I'll break out this tried-and-true recipe, which has added watermelon for sweetness and avocado for a creamy contrast. You can pair this with the Spanish tortilla on page 155 for a tapas-inspired meal. Or for something simpler, serve it with toast covered with sliced hard-boiled eggs (page 148) dressed with mayonnaise or olive oil and maybe an anchovy or two. You can blend the gazpacho up to six hours ahead; just hold the garnishes until just before serving.

1 pound juicy ripe tomatoes, cored and cut into chunks

¼ cup extra-virgin olive oil

1 2-inch-long piece of a day-old crusty baguette (about 2 ounces), torn into pieces

1 cup diced seedless watermelon

1 small cucumber, peeled, seeded, and sliced (1 cup)

2 tablespoons chopped red onion

1 garlic clove, grated on a Microplane or minced

½ teaspoon kosher salt

Freshly ground black pepper to taste

1 ice cube

½ avocado, peeled and diced

TOTAL TIME: 15 MINUTES + AT LEAST
15 MINUTES CHILLING
SERVES 2

1. In a blender, combine the tomatoes, olive oil, bread pieces, ½ cup of the watermelon, the cucumber, red onion, garlic, salt, pepper, and ice cube. Puree until smooth, adding a few tablespoons of water if it seems too thick.

2. Chill the gazpacho in the refrigerator until it is very cold, at least 15 minutes and up to 6 hours. Serve garnished with the remaining chopped watermelon and the avocado.

SALADS
THAT MEAN IT

SPINACH SALAD

with Chickpeas and Sweet Potatoes

There's a lot going on in this hearty salad. It has crunchy, salty chickpeas imbued with spice, which act sort of like croutons, but they are packed with protein. Then, there are sweet potatoes and carrots roasted until exquisitely tender and sweet. The garlic-spiked yogurt dressing is creamy and rich. And finally, there's the spinach, which is earthy, fresh, and, if you use crinkly mature leaves rather than floppy baby spinach, adds another textural element.

If you have time to let the chickpeas air-dry for an additional fifteen to thirty minutes at the end of step 2, they will turn especially crisp in the oven.

1½ cups cooked chickpeas, homemade (see pages 232 to 233) or 1 15-ounce can, rinsed and drained

2 large sweet potatoes (1¼ pounds), peeled and cut into 1-inch cubes

2 medium carrots (8 ounces), cut into ¼-inch-thick rounds

8 tablespoons extra-virgin olive oil

¾ teaspoon kosher salt, plus more as needed

Freshly ground black pepper to taste

2 sprigs fresh thyme

½ teaspoon chili powder

½ teaspoon ground cumin

⅓ cup plain Greek yogurt, preferably whole-milk

2 teaspoons fresh lemon juice

1 garlic clove, grated on a Microplane or minced

5 ounces (5 cups) spinach

2 tablespoons thinly sliced shallots

TOTAL TIME: 20 MINUTES
SERVES 4

1. Heat the oven to 400°F.

2. Line a large baking sheet with a clean dish towel or several layers of paper towels, and spread the drained chickpeas evenly on top. Pat them dry with another dish towel or paper towels.

3. In a large bowl, toss the sweet potatoes and carrots with 2 tablespoons of the olive oil, and season them with the ¾ teaspoon salt and black pepper to taste. Spread them out on a large rimmed baking sheet and top with the thyme sprigs. Roast, tossing the vegetables occasionally, until they are golden brown and very tender, 40 to 50 minutes.

4. Once you have put the vegetables in to roast, toss the chickpeas in a medium bowl with 2 tablespoons of the olive oil, the chili powder, the cumin, and a large pinch of salt. Spread them out on another rimmed baking sheet. Ten minutes after the vegetables have begun roasting, place the chickpeas in the oven and roast until they are crisp and golden brown, 30 to 40 minutes. Let the vegetables and chickpeas cool slightly before dressing. They should be warm or lukewarm, not piping hot and not cold.

5. In a small bowl, whisk together the yogurt, lemon juice, and garlic. Slowly whisk in the remaining 4 tablespoons oil. Season the dressing with salt and pepper to taste.

6. In a large bowl, combine the spinach, roasted vegetables, roasted chickpeas, and shallots. Toss with enough dressing to lightly coat the vegetables and greens, and serve at once.

NIÇOISE SALAD
with Basil Anchovy Dressing

Salade Niçoise, that French bistro staple of potatoes, green beans, olives, and canned or jarred tuna, is given a slightly new flavor profile here. Instead of a classic lemon dressing or vinaigrette, I substitute a piquant and lively mustard-anchovy dressing that's rounded out with lots of herbs. It's got more oomph than usual, which I really like with the saltiness of the tuna. If you prefer fresh fish, you can substitute grilled tuna or even salmon steaks here, which make the whole thing a little more elegant and company-worthy.

1. Using the flat side of your knife on a cutting board, smash the anchovy fillets, garlic, and ¼ teaspoon salt into a paste. Transfer the paste to a small bowl and stir in the lemon juice, lemon zest, and mustard. Stirring constantly with a whisk, slowly pour in the olive oil. Adjust the seasoning if needed. Set aside the dressing.

2. Place the potatoes in a medium pot, add cold water to cover them by 2 or 3 inches, and salt the water generously. Bring the water to a boil, reduce the heat, and simmer until the potatoes are fork-tender, 10 to 15 minutes. If you are using haricots verts, add them during the last 1 minute of cooking; if you are using regular green beans, add them during the last 2 to 3 minutes of cooking, depending upon how thin they are. Drain the vegetables and let them sit until they are cool enough to handle but still quite warm.

3. Halve the potatoes, transfer them to a small bowl, and add the haricots verts. Dress the warm potatoes and beans with some (but not all) of the dressing. When the vegetables are completely cool, toss in the chopped basil.

4. On a large platter or four individual plates, arrange mounds of the potatoes and haricots verts, radishes, tomatoes, and tuna. Scatter the olives over the top, and drizzle with the remaining dressing. Serve garnished with freshly ground black pepper, flaky sea salt, and torn basil leaves.

4 oil-packed anchovy fillets, minced

1 large garlic clove, grated on a Microplane or minced

¼ teaspoon kosher salt, plus more as needed

2 tablespoons fresh lemon juice

¾ teaspoon grated lemon zest

½ teaspoon Dijon mustard

⅓ cup extra-virgin olive oil

4 ounces baby (or micro) red or Yukon Gold potatoes

8 ounces haricots verts or regular green beans

1 tablespoon finely chopped fresh basil leaves, plus torn leaves for serving

8 radishes, cut into wedges, or 1 slender cucumber, peeled and sliced

2 large ripe tomatoes, cut into wedges, or 1 pint cherry tomatoes, halved

2 6- or 7-ounce jars or cans tuna packed in olive oil, drained

½ cup pitted Niçoise or Kalamata olives, sliced

Freshly ground black pepper, for serving

Flaky sea salt, for serving

TOTAL TIME: 25 MINUTES
SERVES 4

SUMMER VEGETABLE
SALAD *with Tapenade and New Potatoes*

In this colorful composed salad, a mix of different vegetables is served alongside a pungent, garlicky black olive tapenade for dipping and slathering—exactly the kind of thing that hits the spot on a steamy summer evening. You can use any vegetables you like here. And feel free to skip the eggplant if it's just too hot to turn on the oven—or try grilling instead of roasting.

If you're a tapenade fan, you'll probably want to use this intensely briny paste everywhere—in sandwiches, on meats, or made into a dip by whisking in some Greek yogurt or sour cream. It will keep for at least a week in the fridge, or even longer if you drizzle the top with a thin coating of olive oil, which will help preserve it.

1. Heat the oven to 400°F.

2. **To prepare the vegetables:** On a large rimmed baking sheet, toss the eggplant with the olive oil, the salt, and black pepper to taste. Spread the cubes out in a single layer and roast, tossing them occasionally, until they are golden brown and tender, 20 to 25 minutes. Let the eggplant cool to room temperature.

3. While the eggplant is roasting, put the potatoes in a large pot and add water to cover; salt the water generously. Place the pot over medium-high heat, bring to a boil, and then reduce the heat; simmer until the potatoes are tender, about 20 minutes. For the last 2 minutes of cooking, drop in the string beans and ear of corn. Drain the vegetables and let them cool. Cut the cooled potatoes, if they are large, into bite-sized chunks, and cut the kernels from the corncob.

4. **Make the tapenade:** In a food processor, combine the olives, basil, capers, olive oil, lemon zest and juice, garlic clove, and anchovy fillet. Pulse until a coarse spread forms. You should have about 1 cup.

5. Arrange the eggplant, potatoes, string beans, cucumbers, and tomatoes on a large platter. Drizzle them very generously with olive oil and sprinkle with lemon juice. Sprinkle with coarse sea salt and black pepper to taste. Serve, with the tapenade alongside for dipping and smearing.

FOR THE VEGETABLES

1 pound eggplant, cut into 1-inch chunks

3 tablespoons extra-virgin olive oil, plus more as needed

½ teaspoon kosher salt, plus more as needed

Freshly ground black pepper, as needed

12 ounces small new potatoes (any variety is fine)

4 ounces string beans, trimmed

1 ear fresh corn, husked

3 Kirby cucumbers, cut into ½-inch-thick rounds

1 cup cherry tomatoes, halved

Juice of ½ lemon

Coarse sea salt, as needed

FOR THE TAPENADE

1¼ cups pitted Kalamata olives

½ cup fresh basil leaves, coarsely chopped

2 tablespoons drained capers

2 tablespoons extra-virgin olive oil

Grated zest and juice of ½ lemon

1 large garlic clove, chopped

1 oil-packed anchovy fillet, chopped

TOTAL TIME: 40 MINUTES
SERVES 4 TO 6

ESCAROLE SALAD *with*

*Crispy Pimentón Chickpeas
and a Runny Egg*

Escarole has a crisp texture and lightly bitter flavor that works well when paired with rich and sharp contrasting notes. Here the runny yolk from a fried egg and the tang of sherry vinegar in the vinaigrette do the trick. And the crispy smoked paprika–dusted chickpeas add a fragrant crunch. Serve this with a baguette to tear apart at the table and dip into the pool of egg yolk and salad dressing on your plate.

If you don't have *pimentón* (smoked paprika), you should probably get some to have on hand (it's easy to find online). But in the meantime, you can use regular paprika instead. It won't have the smokiness, but you'll still have the sweet peppery note to spice things up. Or, substitute garam masala for dusting the chickpeas, which will give the dish more of an Indian slant.

FOR THE DRESSING

1 teaspoon Dijon mustard

2 teaspoons sherry vinegar

½ teaspoon kosher salt, plus more as needed

Freshly ground black pepper to taste

5 tablespoons extra-virgin olive oil

1¾ cups cooked chickpeas, homemade (see pages 232 to 233) or canned, rinsed and drained

4 tablespoons extra-virgin olive oil

1¼ teaspoons sweet *pimentón* (sweet smoked paprika), plus more for serving

4 large eggs

10 cups torn escarole (bite-sized pieces)

TOTAL TIME: 20 MINUTES
SERVES 4

1. Make the dressing: Whisk together the mustard, vinegar, a large pinch of salt, and black pepper to taste in a medium bowl. Slowly whisk in 5 tablespoons of the olive oil until combined. Taste, and adjust the seasonings if necessary. Set the dressing aside.

2. Arrange an oven rack 4 inches from the heat source and preheat the broiler.

3. Spread the chickpeas on a large rimmed baking sheet and toss them with 2 tablespoons of the olive oil, ¾ teaspoon of the *pimentón*, and the ½ teaspoon salt. Broil, tossing them occasionally, until they are golden brown, 6 to 7 minutes.

4. While the chickpeas are cooking, heat the remaining 2 tablespoons olive oil in a 12-inch skillet over medium-high heat. When it is warm, sprinkle in the remaining ½ teaspoon *pimentón*. Crack in the eggs, one at a time, and cook until the edges are firm. Reduce the heat, cover the skillet, and cook until the tops are opaque but the yolks are still runny, about 1 minute.

5. In a large bowl, toss the escarole and chickpeas with the dressing. Divide the salad among four serving plates and top each one with an egg. Sprinkle lightly with additional *pimentón*.

ROASTED CAULIFLOWER SALAD *with Chickpeas, Tahini, and Avocado*

Because I generally subscribe to the what-grows-together-goes-together rule of salad making, combining roasted cauliflower with avocado, tahini, and chickpeas is not something I'd instinctively gravitate toward. But after sampling a similar salad at El Rey Coffee Shop on the Lower East Side, I knew the California–Middle Eastern mashup of elements in fact works really well together. In my version, I balance the creaminess of the sliced avocado and the tahini in the dressing with the sharp and sweet notes of orange and lemon juice while a few drops of honey takes away any rough edges. Use light green Romanesco cauliflower if you can find it—it looks gorgeous here, though regular cauliflower (or broccoli for that matter) tastes just as good. Serve this with slices of grainy bread and more olive oil for dipping. Or for something heartier, broil up a couple of sausages as well.

1 medium head cauliflower, cored and cut into florets

¾ cup extra-virgin olive oil

1¼ teaspoons kosher salt, plus more if needed

Freshly ground black pepper to taste

1 cup cooked chickpeas, homemade (see pages 232 to 233), or two-thirds of a 15-ounce can, rinsed and drained

4 teaspoons fresh lemon juice

1 tablespoon fresh orange juice

1 tablespoon tahini

¾ teaspoon rice vinegar

½ teaspoon honey

¾ cup fresh parsley leaves

¾ cup fresh mint leaves

1 garlic clove, grated on a Microplane or minced

¼ teaspoon ground sumac

⅛ teaspoon crushed Turkish red pepper, such as Urfa or Aleppo

1 bunch watercress

1 avocado, pitted, peeled, and diced, for garnish

Toasted sesame seeds, for garnish

½ teaspoon finely grated orange zest

TOTAL TIME: 45 MINUTES
SERVES 4 TO 6

1. Heat the oven to 425°F.

2. In a large bowl, toss the cauliflower with ¼ cup of the olive oil, 1 teaspoon of the salt, and black pepper to taste. Arrange the cauliflower on two large rimmed baking sheets and roast, tossing it occasionally, until it is well browned and tender, 35 to 45 minutes. Let it cool until it is just a little bit warm or at room temperature.

3. Meanwhile, in a blender combine 2 tablespoons of the chickpeas with the lemon juice, orange juice, tahini, rice vinegar, honey, remaining ¼ teaspoon salt, ¼ cup of the parsley, ¼ cup of the mint, and the garlic, sumac, and Turkish red pepper; puree until smooth. With the motor running, drizzle in the remaining ½ cup olive oil.

4. In a large bowl, combine the roasted cauliflower, watercress, remaining chickpeas, and the remaining parsley and mint. Toss with enough dressing to evenly coat the ingredients; season with additional salt and pepper if necessary. Serve garnished with the avocado, sesame seeds, and orange zest.

ROASTED ACORN SQUASH & BROCCOLI RABE SALAD

with Ricotta Salata

I love putting roasted squashes of all kinds in salads, where they add both sweetness and a velvety texture next to the usual mix of greens and other crunchy elements. You can use any kind of winter squash, but acorn slices up into crescent moons, which roast evenly and are pretty on the plate. You can serve this salad as a light main course. Or, make it a first course or side dish to roast chicken or fish at any autumnal dinner party. And definitely keep it in mind when November rolls around; with its dried cranberries, toasted pecans, and cider-vinegar dressing, it will be a nice new dish for your Thanksgiving table.

1. Heat the oven to 425°F.

2. Place the squash wedges on a rimmed baking sheet and toss them with 2 tablespoons of the olive oil. Sprinkle with ¼ teaspoon of the kosher salt and a few grinds of black pepper. On a separate rimmed baking sheet, toss the broccoli rabe with 2 tablespoons of the oil, the remaining ¼ teaspoon kosher salt, and a few grinds of black pepper.

3. Place the squash in the oven and roast, without moving it, until the undersides are golden brown, about 20 minutes.

4. Flip the squash wedges over and return the pan to the oven. At the same time, place the pan of broccoli rabe in the oven. Roast until the squash is cooked through and the broccoli rabe is tender and lightly colored, about 15 minutes.

5. In a large bowl, combine the squash, broccoli rabe, ricotta salata, pecans, and cranberries. Season with the vinegar, remaining 3 tablespoons olive oil, coarse salt to taste, and black pepper to taste. Toss in the parsley just before serving.

1 small acorn squash (about 1¼ pounds), halved, seeded, and cut into 1-inch wedges (you don't need to peel it)

7 tablespoons extra-virgin olive oil

½ teaspoon kosher salt

Freshly ground black pepper to taste

1 bunch (about 12 ounces) broccoli rabe, trimmed and cut into 2-inch lengths

3½ ounces ricotta salata, crumbled (about ¾ cup)

½ cup pecans, toasted

⅓ cup dried cranberries

2 teaspoons cider vinegar, plus more as needed

Coarse salt, as needed

¼ cup chopped fresh parsley leaves

TOTAL TIME: 45 MINUTES
SERVES 4

HORTA SALAD

with Feta and Olives

If you've ever been to a Greek restaurant or spent any time in Greece and ordered *horta*, a side dish of cool, cooked mixed greens seasoned with lemon juice and plenty of olive oil, you'll instantly understand the reference point for this dish. And even if not, if you love softly cooked greens and salty, creamy feta cheese, you're in for a treat. Here I use Tuscan kale, which has a deep herbal, mineral flavor that's softened by copious amounts of olive oil along with olives and the crumbled feta cheese. Serve this with grilled bread brushed with more olive oil for a very simple meal. It's also nice as a side dish to a simple roast chicken or grilled piece of fish.

If you want to make this ahead, you can boil and dress the kale up to six hours beforehand. Let it rest at room temperature, then garnish it with the feta and olives just before serving.

1. Fill a large pot with water and bring it to a boil. Add a large pinch of salt and the kale, cover the pot, and simmer for 2 minutes. Then drain, and rinse the kale under cold water. Squeeze any remaining water out of the kale.

2. In a large bowl, whisk together the olive oil, lemon juice, ¼ teaspoon salt, and pepper. Add the kale and toss to combine. Garnish with the feta and olives just before serving.

¼ teaspoon kosher salt, plus more as needed

2 large bunches (1½ pounds) Tuscan kale, stems removed, leaves torn into bite-sized pieces

6 tablespoons extra-virgin olive oil

2 tablespoons fresh lemon juice

¼ teaspoon freshly ground black pepper

2 ounces feta cheese, crumbled (½ cup)

¼ cup Kalamata olives, sliced

TOTAL TIME: 15 MINUTES
SERVES 4

BURRATA CAPRESE

with Peaches, Tomato, and Basil

Burrata cheese—that is, mozzarella shot through with cream—is about the richest, creamiest, and most decadent thing you can serve as part of any meal. Here, I've mitigated the richness with juicy tomatoes and sweet peaches, and with a crunchy pine nut and basil dressing on top. This dish also happens to be as stunningly beautiful as it is delicious, not to mention a snap to put together. Serve it with toast or crusty bread to sop up all the creamy juiciness on the plate. Some paper-thin prosciutto, sliced salami, or smoked salmon alongside is a nice salty contrast. And if you can't find good ripe peaches, try nectarines or plums instead, or grapes in the fall. Soft unsalted mozzarella, preferably buffalo mozzarella, makes a good substitute for the burrata.

3 tablespoons pine nuts

⅓ cup packed fresh basil leaves, coarsely chopped

1½ teaspoons fresh lemon juice

½ teaspoon fine sea salt

¼ cup extra-virgin olive oil, plus more as needed

1 whole Burrata cheese (usually about 6 ounces)

2 large or 4 small ripe peaches, pitted and cut into wedges

1 pound ripe tomatoes, cut into wedges (or use cherry tomatoes, halved or left whole)

Flaky sea salt

TOTAL TIME: 20 MINUTES
SERVES 4

1. In a small skillet over medium heat, toast the pine nuts, shaking the skillet occasionally, until they are golden, 3 to 5 minutes. Pour the pine nuts into a small bowl and set them aside.

2. In a blender, combine the basil, lemon juice, fine sea salt, and ¼ cup olive oil. Puree until a chunky dressing forms (you don't want this to be perfectly smooth;

the irregular texture is nice with the creamy cheese).

3. Place the Burrata in the center of a large platter, and arrange the peaches and tomatoes around it. Spoon the dressing over the cheese and the fruit. Drizzle with additional olive oil, and top with the toasted pine nuts and a sprinkling of flaky sea salt.

SPICY THAI SALAD

with Coconut and Crispy Tofu

1 package (14 to 16 ounces) firm tofu, drained

⅓ cup thinly sliced shallots

2 tablespoons soy sauce

1½ tablespoons Asian fish sauce

1½ tablespoons light brown sugar

1 tablespoon grated peeled fresh ginger

Grated zest and juice of 2 limes

2 large garlic cloves, grated on a Microplane or minced

1 serrano chile, seeded and thinly sliced

¼ teaspoon kosher salt, plus more as needed

¼ cup plus 3 tablespoons peanut oil

½ cup cornstarch

1 cup unsweetened coconut flakes

6 cups thinly sliced napa or regular cabbage

1 cup thinly sliced Kirby or Persian cucumbers

1 cup thinly sliced red bell pepper

⅓ cup thinly sliced scallions (white and green parts)

1½ cups fresh cilantro leaves

1½ cups fresh mint leaves

1½ cups fresh basil leaves

1 cup roasted unsalted peanuts, chopped

TOTAL TIME: 25 MINUTES

SERVES 4 TO 6

This salad is as much about the diversity of textures as it is about its Asian-inspired ginger-, soy sauce-, and lime-drenched flavors. Crisp sliced cabbage, cucumber, and bell pepper give it a slaw-like feel, with added crunch from the fried tofu, coconut, and peanuts. The vegetables in this recipe are just suggestions. You can substitute any other crunchy veggies for the cabbage, cucumber, and bell pepper—thinly sliced radishes, turnips, or kohlrabi, grated carrots, chopped raw cauliflower—whatever you have that you love will work.

1. Line a baking sheet with paper towels. Slice the tofu crosswise into ½-inch-thick slabs, and cut each slab in half to make 2 squares. Arrange the squares on the prepared baking sheet and top them with another layer of paper towels.

2. In a small bowl, whisk together the shallots, soy sauce, fish sauce, brown sugar, ginger, lime zest and juice, garlic, chile, and the ¼ teaspoon salt. Whisk in the 3 tablespoons peanut oil.

3. Place the cornstarch in a small bowl.

4. Place a dry 12-inch skillet over medium-high heat. Add the coconut flakes and toast them, stirring frequently, until they are golden, about 5 minutes. Transfer the coconut to a bowl.

5. Add the ¼ cup peanut oil to the same skillet and allow it to heat for a moment. Dip the tofu pieces in the cornstarch, dusting off the excess, and fry them in the hot oil, in batches if necessary, until they are crisp and golden, 4 to 5 minutes per side. Transfer the tofu to a plate and season with salt.

6. Place the cabbage, cucumbers, bell peppers, scallions, and tofu in a large bowl, and toss with the dressing. Gently mix in the cilantro, mint, basil, peanuts, and toasted coconut. Taste, and adjust the seasoning if necessary.

ROASTED WINTER VEGETABLES

with Herbed Buttermilk Dressing

Several types of roasted winter vegetables get tossed together in this wonderfully textured salad. Kale leaves become crunchy and rigid, butternut squash softens into plush cubes, and potatoes split the difference between soft in the center and crispy on the outside. Then everything is coated in a garlicky, creamy yogurt dressing imbued with fresh green herbs, topped with chopped nuts for crunch. Serve this on its own for a light meal, or spoon it on top of some cooked grains—bulgur, brown rice, farro—to bulk it out. It's also tasty with some hard-boiled eggs mixed in if you're looking for more protein.

1. Heat the oven to 450°F.

2. Remove the center ribs of the kale and tear the leaves into large pieces. Place the leaves on a large rimmed baking sheet, drizzle generously with olive oil, and season with salt and pepper to taste. Roast until crisped, 8 to 10 minutes.

3. Remove the kale from the oven, and reduce the heat to 425°F.

4. Place the squash and potatoes, separately, on two large rimmed baking sheets, drizzle them generously with olive oil, and season with salt and pepper. Roast until they are tender, 30 to 40 minutes for the squash and 35 to 45 minutes for the potatoes. Set the squash and potatoes aside.

5. In a small bowl, combine the buttermilk, yogurt, lemon juice, ¼ teaspoon salt, and the garlic. Whisk in 1 tablespoon of olive oil, and then whisk in the herbs.

6. Place the roasted kale and warm vegetables in a large bowl, and toss with enough of the dressing to coat. Just before serving, scatter the nuts, if using, over gently.

1 large bunch kale

Extra-virgin olive oil, as needed

Kosher salt and freshly ground black pepper to taste

2½ cups diced peeled butternut squash (or beets or parsnips)

2½ cups diced potatoes or sweet potatoes

⅓ cup buttermilk

3 tablespoons Greek yogurt, preferably whole-milk

2 teaspoons fresh lemon juice, plus more to taste

1 fat garlic clove, grated on a Microplane or minced

¼ cup chopped soft fresh herbs or bitter greens, such as any combination of arugula, dill, parsley, mint, basil, and tarragon (using several kinds adds complexity but any one will work)

2 tablespoons chopped walnuts or unsalted pistachios, toasted (optional)

TOTAL TIME: 50 MINUTES
SERVES 3 OR 4

Classic Roasted CHICKEN SALAD
with Green Aioli and Chicken Skin Croutons

Adding diced savory chicken skin to a pan of dried bread cubes really ups the crouton ante in this elegant salad, with homemade aioli for an addictive garlicky richness. You can absolutely make this with a rotisserie chicken you've picked up on the way home from work. But if you want something truly magnificent, next time you make the Salt and Pepper Roasted Chicken on page 24, consider roasting two at once, and use the second for this salad a few days later.

1. Heat the oven to 350°F.

2. On a rimmed baking sheet, toss together the bread cubes, chopped chicken skin, 2 tablespoons olive oil, ¼ teaspoon of the salt, and black pepper to taste. Bake, tossing the ingredients occasionally, until the croutons are golden and the chicken skin is crisped, 12 to 15 minutes.

3. Meanwhile, combine the garlic, remaining ¼ teaspoon salt, and 1 teaspoon lemon juice in a blender; let stand for 1 minute to dissolve the salt. Then add the basil, tarragon, egg, and egg yolk, and puree briefly on medium speed. With the motor running, drizzle in the ¾ cup olive oil in a slow, steady stream until the mixture is just combined. Set the aioli aside.

4. Pull the chicken meat off the bones and shred it.

5. In a large bowl, toss the arugula and vegetables together. Dress them to taste with lemon juice, olive oil, salt, and pepper (approximately 2 teaspoons lemon juice to 2 or 3 tablespoons oil, but taste as you go). Arrange the arugula and vegetables on a large platter, top them with the chicken, and drizzle with a little more olive oil. Then garnish the salad with the croutons and crisped chicken skin. Serve the aioli alongside for dipping the chicken.

6 ounces bread, preferably a stale crusty loaf, cut into 1-inch cubes

1 roasted chicken, skin removed and chopped

2 tablespoons plus ¾ cup extra-virgin olive oil, plus more as needed

½ teaspoon kosher salt, plus more as needed

Freshly ground black pepper to taste

1 large garlic clove, grated on a Microplane or minced

1 teaspoon fresh lemon juice, plus more as needed

2 tablespoons fresh basil leaves

1 tablespoon fresh tarragon or mint leaves

1 large egg

1 large egg yolk

8 cups (about 5 ounces) arugula or other greens

1 cup fresh vegetables, such as halved cherry tomatoes, sliced cucumber, or grated carrot, or a combination

TOTAL TIME: 25 MINUTES
SERVES 6

DIPS, SPREADS
& GO-WITHS

Killer HUMMUS *with Whole Chickpeas*

Ultra-creamy and just garlicky enough, of all the hummus recipes I've made over the years, this one is the keeper. Part of the key to its plush, smooth texture is to puree the chickpeas while they are still warm, which encourages them to break down more completely than do cold peas. You'll note that the chickpeas are not peeled here as they are in some more fanatical hummus recipes. That's because they are cooked with baking soda, which helps soften the skins enough to process the beans into a smooth puree. However, if you are using canned chickpeas and want to peel them, or if you just feel like peeling your freshly cooked peas (which is certainly a kind of repetitive therapy), go right ahead.

1. Soak the chickpeas overnight in water to cover and a large pinch of salt. Or quick-soak by covering the chickpeas with boiling water and letting them soak for 2 hours. Either way, drain and rinse the chickpeas before proceeding.

2. Place the chickpeas in a large pot and add enough water to cover them by 4 inches. Add the baking soda and 2 teaspoons of the salt, and bring to a boil. Then reduce the heat and simmer until the chickpeas are very, very soft, 1 to 1½ hours (overcooked chickpeas work well for a smooth hummus). Drain; you'll have about 3 cups. Reserve 3 tablespoons for garnish. Continue with the next step while the chickpeas are still warm.

3. Using a blender or food processor, blend the lemon juice, garlic, and remaining 1¾ teaspoons salt. Let the mixture sit for 10 minutes for the salt to dissolve and the flavors to develop. Then add the tahini and the cumin, and blend, scraping down the sides of the bowl as needed, until a thick paste forms. With the blender running, gradually add the ice water, 1 tablespoon at a time, until the sauce is smooth.

4. Add the warm drained chickpeas and the olive oil to the blender, and blend, scraping down the sides of the bowl, until the mixture is smooth, about 2 minutes. The mixture should be silky smooth. Feel free to add more water if you think the hummus is too thick. Taste for seasoning, and add more salt and/or lemon juice if needed.

5. Spread the hummus out on a flat plate, and garnish it with olive oil and a dusting of paprika.

NOTE: If you like, you can substitute canned chickpeas here, though the flavor won't be quite as sweet and earthy as it is when made with freshly cooked peas, but it will still be quite good. To make the substitution, drain and rinse 2 15-ounce cans of canned chickpeas before starting the recipe at step 3. Microwave the canned chickpeas for 30 to 45 seconds, until warm, before adding them to the blender in step 4, and add 2 to 4 tablespoons warm water; you may need to run the blender for up to 5 minutes. For more information, see pages 232 to 233.

1 cup dried chickpeas (or use canned chickpeas; see Note)

3¾ teaspoons kosher salt, plus more as needed

1 teaspoon baking soda

⅓ cup fresh lemon juice (from 1½ to 2 large lemons)

2 to 3 garlic cloves, to taste, grated on a Microplane or minced

1 cup tahini

¾ teaspoon ground cumin

4 to 6 tablespoons ice water

3 tablespoons extra-virgin olive oil, plus more for drizzling

Sweet or hot paprika, for dusting

TOTAL TIME: 2 HOURS + AT LEAST
2 HOURS SOAKING TIME
MAKES APPROXIMATELY 3½ CUPS/
SERVES 6 TO 8

PEA PESTO *with Ricotta*

Fresh, milky ricotta—the really good stuff that you have to seek out at an Italian deli, gourmet market, or fancy cheese shop—is so delicious that sometimes when I'm in a hurry, I'll just spoon it into a shallow bowl; top it with some excellent olive oil, flaky sea salt, and freshly ground pepper; and call it an appetizer with some crusty bread on the side. It's about as simple as you can get, but is always one of the first things to go when I put it out at a party. More elegant, more satisfying, and prettier than just a scrumptious bowl of ricotta is this dip with a vibrant and garlicky sweet pea and mint pesto swirled into the mellow cheese. You can serve this with crusty bread or whole-grain crackers for dipping, or try it spooned onto toast to make crostini. This is also especially wonderful heaped on top of *pan con tomate*, which is garlicky toast imbued with the guts of a ripe tomato (see sidebar below).

1 cup fresh peas (from about 12 ounces pea pods) or frozen peas, thawed

1 ounce Parmiggiano-Reggiano cheese, grated (¼ cup)

1 cup packed fresh basil or mint leaves, plus more for garnish

1 fat garlic clove, grated on a Microplane or minced

¼ teaspoon fine sea salt

¼ cup extra-virgin olive oil, plus more as needed

1 pound fresh ricotta

Flaky sea salt to taste

Freshly ground black pepper to taste

TOTAL TIME: 15 MINUTES
MAKES APPROXIMATELY 3 CUPS

1. If you are using fresh peas, bring a small pot of salted water to a boil, add the peas, and blanch until they are tender, 1 to 2 minutes. Drain them in a colander and then run cold water over them to stop the cooking. Spread the peas out on a clean dish towel and blot them dry. If you are using thawed frozen peas, simply blot them dry.

2. In a food processor or blender, combine the Parmesan, basil, garlic, and sea salt; process until finely chopped. Add the peas and the olive oil, and process until you have a chunky paste. If the mixture seems very dry, add a little more oil.

3. Spread the ricotta on a plate and top it with dollops of the pea pesto, swirling it so some of the two mixtures combine. Drizzle everything with olive oil, scatter more basil on top, and sprinkle with flaky sea salt and black pepper.

Pan con Tomate

Toast some crusty bread, such as a peasant bread or a sourdough loaf, and then rub it all over with the cut side of a garlic clove. Next, rub the bread with the cut side of a very ripe and juicy tomato; then drizzle good olive oil over the tomato-rubbed bread, and sprinkle with salt. *Pan con tomate* is also excellent draped with Serrano ham or prosciutto before being dolloped with this dip.

CARROT MUHAMMARA
with Toasted Cumin and Walnuts

This recipe comes by way of Yeni Lokanta, a restaurant in Istanbul, where chef Civan Er adds roasted carrots and fresh ginger to *muhammara*, a classic Middle Eastern red pepper and walnut meze. Like everything else on the menu, Civan's twists on a traditional recipe are subtle and are meant to deepen one's appreciation for the original dish, rather than overtake it. Here, the sweetness of the carrots and acidity of the ginger accentuate the flavors already present—caramelized carrots make the peppers even sweeter; zingy ginger bolsters the lemon. His is a masterful touch. Civan's chunky-textured dip skips the usual drizzle of pomegranate molasses, but feel free to add it if you like. Serve this with warm puffy flatbread, pita, or crackers.

1. Heat the oven to 400°F.

2. Place the carrots and bell peppers on separate rimmed baking sheets, and toss each vegetable with enough olive oil to evenly coat each piece. Place both pans in the oven. Roast the peppers until tender, 30 to 35 minutes. Roast the carrots until very tender, 55 minutes to 1 hour or even longer. Let the carrots and peppers cool to room temperature.

3. Once they have cooled, place the carrots, peppers, ½ cup olive oil, lemon juice, garlic, ginger, ground cumin, Turkish red pepper, and half of the walnuts in the bowl of a food processor. Pulse until the mixture is smooth, adding a little water to thin it out if it seems too thick. Season with kosher salt. Stir in the remaining walnuts.

4. In a small dry pan over medium heat, toast the cumin seeds until fragrant, 1 to 2 minutes. Pour them onto a plate to stop the cooking.

5. To serve, spread the *muhammara* on a plate, drizzle it with olive oil, and sprinkle with the toasted cumin seeds and flaky sea salt.

1 pound carrots, cut into ½-inch-thick rounds

1 pound red bell peppers (about 2 peppers), thinly sliced

½ cup olive oil, plus more for roasting and drizzling

⅓ cup fresh lemon juice (from 2 to 3 lemons)

2 garlic cloves, grated on a Microplane or minced

1 tablespoon grated peeled fresh ginger

½ teaspoon ground cumin

¼ teaspoon ground Turkish red pepper

1¾ cups walnut halves, toasted and chopped

Kosher salt to taste

1 teaspoon cumin seeds

Flaky sea salt such as Maldon, for garnish

TOTAL TIME: 1¼ HOURS
MAKES APPROXIMATELY 2½ CUPS

The Controversial
PEA GUACAMOLE

This recipe isn't mine. I got it from Ian Coogan, chef de cuisine of ABC Cocina (one of Jean-Georges Vongerichten's wonderful restaurants in New York), and I published it in the *New York Times,* touting it as a brilliant greenmarket tweak on a classic recipe. What I didn't anticipate was how many guacamole purists there were in the world (and by *world,* I mean on Twitter), who were offended by the idea of peas in guacamole. It became such a thing that both Jeb Bush and President Obama, in a rare moment of solidarity, tweeted about it. Neither had tasted it, but they weren't fans of the concept. This is a shame, because adding peas to guacamole gives it freshness, an intense sweetness, and accentuates the verdant color, helping the guacamole stay green even if you leave it out at a party for a few hours. It really is an excellent and intuitive combination if you happen to be making guacamole in spring.

There's room in the world for more than one kind of guacamole, right? Try it yourself and see.

⅔ cup fresh sweet peas (from about 8 ounces pea pods) or frozen peas, thawed

2 small jalapeños

2 tablespoons packed fresh cilantro leaves, chopped, plus more for garnish

¾ teaspoon kosher salt, plus more if needed

3 small ripe avocadoes, pitted, peeled, and mashed

2 scallions (white parts only), sliced as thin as possible (about ¼ cup)

Finely grated zest and juice of 1 lime, plus more juice if needed

1 tablespoon unsalted sunflower seeds, toasted (see Note)

Flaky sea salt, for serving

Lime wedges, for serving

TOTAL TIME: 45 MINUTES
MAKES APPROXIMATELY 2½ CUPS

1. If you are using fresh peas, fill a bowl with water and ice. Bring a medium pot of salted water to a boil, plunge the peas into the boiling water, and cook until they are al dente, about 1 minute. Drain the peas and immediately transfer them to the ice bath. (If using frozen peas, skip this step.)

2. Heat the broiler to high.

3. Place one of the jalapeños in a small broiler-proof baking pan or skillet and broil, turning it occasionally, until the jalapeño is completely charred, 2 to 3 minutes. Transfer it to a small bowl, cover the bowl with a plate or plastic wrap, and let it sit for 15 minutes. When the jalapeño is cool enough to handle, use a towel to wipe off the charred skin. Cut it in half, and remove the seeds and membranes. Halve, seed, and mince the remaining raw jalapeño.

4. Reserving 2 tablespoons for garnish, place the peas in a blender or a food processor, and add the roasted jalapeño, minced raw jalapeño, cilantro, and ¼ of the teaspoon salt. Process until the mixture is almost smooth but still a little chunky.

5. In a medium bowl, combine the mashed avocadoes, scallions, lime zest and juice, remaining ½ teaspoon salt, and the pea puree. Taste, and add more kosher salt and/or lime juice if needed. Garnish the guacamole with the reserved whole peas and the sunflower seeds and flaky sea salt. Serve it with lime wedges on the side.

NOTE: To toast sunflower seeds, heat a skillet over medium-low heat. Add the seeds to the hot, dry skillet and let toast until fragrant, about 2 minutes. Pour the seeds onto a plate to cool.

Creamy **RED LENTIL DIP**
with Lemon

Vaguely like hummus, but sweeter, lighter, and creamier from the yogurt, this dip features red lentils, which cook up in about twenty minutes instead of two to three hours for chickpeas. This means you can whip it up on a whim whenever you're craving hummus, but would rather not punch open a can (or maybe you've got lentils in the pantry, but no canned chickpeas, or maybe you just like red lentils better than chickpeas, or are in the mood for something differently wonderful—there are many reasons to make this dip). Naturally you can serve this as a dip with all the usual fixings. But it's also really nice dolloped on toasted bread to make crostini. Choose a nubby whole-grain loaf and be generous with the topping of salt, olive oil, and sesame seeds.

2 cups red lentils

4 garlic cloves, smashed and peeled

¾ teaspoon fine sea salt, plus more as needed

Grated zest and juice of 1 lemon, plus more lemon juice if needed

½ cup tahini

¼ cup plain whole-milk yogurt

2 tablespoons extra-virgin olive oil, plus more for drizzling

Flaky sea salt, for serving

Black sesame seeds, for serving (optional)

TOTAL TIME: 30 MINUTES
MAKES APPROXIMATELY 3½ CUPS

1. In a small pot, combine the lentils with just enough water to cover, 2 of the garlic cloves, and a big pinch of fine sea salt. Bring to a simmer and cook, stirring occasionally, until the lentils are very tender and practically falling apart, 15 to 20 minutes. Drain if needed (the lentils might have absorbed all the water) and let them cool for a few minutes.

2. Combine the lemon zest and juice in the bowl of a food processor or blender, and add the lentils (along with the cooked garlic that's mixed in with them) and the remaining raw garlic. Process, scraping down the sides of the bowl often, until you have a very smooth puree. Add the tahini, yogurt, olive oil, and the ¾ teaspoon fine sea salt, and puree until the mixture is very light and creamy, 1 to 2 minutes. If the mixture seems dry and dense, add a little water to lighten it up. Taste, and add more lemon juice and/or salt if needed.

3. Spread the lentil puree on a plate, drizzle it with olive oil, and sprinkle with flaky sea salt and black sesame seeds if desired.

Mediterranean *TUNA & OLIVE SPREAD*

Like the silkiest and most full-flavored tuna mousse imaginable, this dip has a deep savory, briny note from the anchovies and capers. When I first started making it, the idea was to serve it with thinly sliced poached veal breast à la *vitello tonnato*. And it was terrific. But the veal was kind of a pain to make, and really, the best thing about the dish was the complex, fishy, umami sauce. So now I make the sauce all by itself, and serve it as a dip or spread, or drizzled over more simply cooked proteins. Try it dolloped on potato chips, thickly sliced tomatoes, halved boiled potatoes, or soft-cooked eggs—or with your favorite cut-up veggies for dipping.

And do splurge on the best-quality tuna you can get. I really like the kind imported from Spain or Italy that's packed in really good olive oil. If you can't get it and are using regular supermarket tuna, make sure to add the anchovies and even throw in a few extra; the added brininess they contribute will help make up for the less flavorful tuna.

1. In a blender, combine the olive oil, tuna, mayonnaise, basil, capers, lemon juice, anchovies, and garlic, and puree until creamy. Use a spatula to stir in the olives. Taste and add a pinch of salt if needed, but it probably won't need it.

2. Serve the spread in a shallow bowl, garnished with black pepper, a drizzle of olive oil, a squeeze of lemon juice, and a scattering of basil leaves.

5 tablespoons extra-virgin olive oil, plus more for drizzling

1 3-ounce can tuna packed in olive oil, drained

¼ cup mayonnaise

2 tablespoons tightly packed fresh basil leaves, plus more for garnish

1 teaspoon drained capers

2 teaspoons fresh lemon juice, plus more for serving

2 oil-packed anchovy fillets (optional but excellent)

1 fat garlic clove, smashed

1 tablespoon chopped black olives such as Kalamata

Coarse sea salt and freshly ground black pepper to taste

TOTAL TIME: 15 MINUTES
MAKES APPROXIMATELY 1½ CUPS

Israeli BEET LABNEH

Based on a recipe in _Jerusalem_ by Yotam Ottolenghi and Sami Tamimi, this dip is as stunning as it is delicious. When the spiced, roasted red beets are piled into creamy yogurt _labneh_ (drained yogurt that's usually a bit thicker than Greek), they leak magenta and pink juices in the most gorgeous way. I make this often in winter when my CSA is, shall we say, overly generous with the beet rations. To keep up with the rooty onslaught, I like to roast them as I get them, then store the roasted beets in the fridge until I need them for salads, soups, or this creamy dip. They'll last for up to a week if you lightly coat them in oil before piling them into a container, which helps preserve them.

Serve this dip with nubby whole-grain crackers (Wasa crispbread is good) or crostini and a few cut-up raw vegetables (cauliflower, radishes, carrots, and the like). You want something with crunch.

1. Finely dice 1 cup of the beets (about 3 ounces) and place them in a bowl. Grate the zest of half the lemon over the bowl, and add 2½ teaspoons of the lemon juice. Add the cilantro, half of the garlic, half of the jalapeño, ½ teaspoon of the salt, and black pepper to taste. Stir in 2 tablespoons of the olive oil.

2. In a food processor, combine ½ cup of the _labneh_ with the remaining beets, remaining 2 tablespoons oil, remaining jalapeño and garlic, remaining ¼ teaspoon salt, and ½ teaspoon lemon juice. Process until pureed.

3. Spread the remaining 1 cup _labneh_ on a large plate. Spread the pureed beet _labneh_ on top, and scatter the beet relish over the puree. Garnish with the walnuts, cilantro, jalapeños, a drizzle of olive oil, and some flaky sea salt.

NOTE: To roast whole beets, heat the oven to 375°F. Place the unpeeled beets in a small roasting pan, drizzle with olive oil, and season with salt and pepper. Sprinkle 3 tablespoons water into the bottom of the pan. Cover the pan with aluminum foil and roast the beets until they can be easily pierced with a fork, 30 to 60 minutes, depending on the size of the beets. Note that really large older beets might take even longer (up to 2 hours). Try to find small- to medium-sized ones if you're in a hurry. Peel beets with your fingers or a paring knife while they are still warm.

1 pound beets, roasted and peeled (see Note)

1 large lemon

½ cup chopped fresh cilantro leaves

2 small garlic cloves, grated on a Microplane or minced

1 small jalapeño, seeded and finely chopped

¾ teaspoon kosher salt

Freshly ground black pepper to taste

4 tablespoons extra-virgin olive oil, plus more as needed

1½ cups _labneh_ or plain Greek yogurt

⅓ cup coarsely chopped toasted walnuts

Cilantro leaves and sliced jalapeños, for serving

Flaky sea salt, for serving

TOTAL TIME: 15 MINUTES
MAKES APPROXIMATELY 3 CUPS

GREEN TAHINI DIP

I've always made sure to keep a jar of tahini in my fridge for spontaneous hummus making. But until recently, it didn't get much play beyond that. Now, like everyone else who has fallen in love with Israeli and Middle Eastern cuisines, I've been pulling out the tahini jar frequently, using the silky, nutty paste to add body, richness, and non-dairy creaminess to all kinds of dips, dressings, and sauces. In this earthy dip, I've mixed tahini with blanched spinach and fresh herbs to make it as green as possible, along with plenty of lemon and garlic for oopmh. Even die-hard hummus lovers will find this to be a nice change of pace.

Serve this with warm pita bread and whatever cut-up veggies you like. It's also nice with hard-cooked egg halves and potato wedges, or even as a sauce for simply cooked chicken, shrimp, or fish. Just thin it out with a little water if you're using it as a sauce.

2 cups packed spinach leaves (either baby or mature spinach is fine)

¼ cup packed chopped soft fresh herbs, such as a mixture of mint, dill, and/or basil leaves, plus more for garnish

½ cup tahini

¼ cup fresh lemon juice (from 1 to 2 lemons)

2 garlic cloves, grated on a Microplane or minced

½ teaspoon kosher salt

2 to 4 tablespoons ice water

TOTAL TIME: 20 MINUTES
MAKES APPROXIMATELY 1¼ CUPS

1. Bring a kettle of water to a boil. Put the spinach leaves in a colander set in the sink, and pour the boiling water over them (this blanches them and drains them at the same time). Run cold water over the spinach until it is cool enough to handle. Vigorously press and squeeze out as much water as possible from the spinach.

2. Place the spinach in a blender, and add the herbs, tahini, lemon juice, garlic, and salt. Blend until a thick paste forms. With the blender running, add the ice water, 1 tablespoon at a time, until the sauce is smooth and as thick as you want it. Taste for seasoning, and serve in a shallow bowl. Garnish with herbs.

WHITE BEAN DIP
with Charred Scallions

Dense and creamy with a distinct smoky flavor from charring the scallions, this simple, garlicky, crowd-pleasing dip goes with pretty much anything you want to serve it with. Try thick slices of salami or kielbasa for something unexpected. Steamed asparagus, broccoli, and cauliflower are obvious but elegant choices. And good bread is always welcome.

Be sure to get a deep, dark, nearly black color on the scallions when charring them; that's what gives this dip its distinct, smoky-sweet flavor. Without the char, it's just plain old bean dip. Also to note: you can make this with freshly cooked white beans (see page 233) instead of canned beans if you like. It will have an earthier and more intensely beany flavor, which is all to the good.

⅓ cup plus 2 tablespoons extra-virgin olive oil, plus more for drizzling

1 large bunch scallions (about 8 scallions), white and light green parts cut into 2-inch lengths, dark greens thinly sliced

2 garlic cloves, finely chopped

2 15-ounce cans white beans, such as cannellini or Great Northern, drained and rinsed

¼ cup coarsely chopped fresh dill leaves, plus more for serving

4 teaspoons fresh lemon juice

¾ teaspoon kosher salt

Ground Turkish red pepper or hot paprika, as needed

TOTAL TIME: 20 MINUTES
MAKES APPROXIMATELY 3 CUPS

1. Heat the 2 tablespoons olive oil in a 9-inch cast-iron skillet over high heat. Add the white and light green scallion pieces and cook, turning them occasionally, until they are well charred and very tender, 5 to 10 minutes.

2. Transfer the scallions to the bowl of a food processor. Add the garlic, beans, dill, lemon juice, and salt. Pulse to combine. Then, with the motor running, drizzle in the ⅓ cup olive oil. The mixture should be smooth, but with some texture.

3. Scrape the dip into a shallow bowl, drizzle it with olive oil, and sprinkle with Turkish red pepper, the sliced scallion greens, and chopped dill.

SPICED LENTIL DIP

with Fried Leeks and Onions

With all the flavors of a Middle Eastern *mujadara* (spiced lentils and crisp fried onions served over rice), this reinterprets that classic dish as a chunky, aromatic dip. Its dense texture and the sweet fried onions may remind you of vegetarian chopped liver (a staple of the Jewish dairy meals of my childhood), though with a much more complex character from the cumin, allspice, and cinnamon. Feel free to thin this out with a little hot water if it seems too thick for dipping. Or, serve with a butter knife or spoon for spreading on crisp, sturdy crackers, the kind that can stand up to hardy lentils without breaking to bits (Finn Crisps are good). You can also top this dip with some Greek yogurt as a nice bright contrast to the musky lentils.

1. Heat the olive oil in a medium pot over medium heat. Add the onion and cook until it is beginning to color, about 5 minutes. Stir in the leek and cook with the onion until both are tender and darkly golden brown, 5 to 10 minutes. Transfer half of the onion-leek mixture to a bowl to use as a garnish at the end of the recipe.

2. Add the garlic, cumin, allspice, and cayenne to the mixture in the pot; cook until fragrant, 1 minute. Then stir in the lentils, bay leaf, cinnamon stick, and the 1½ teaspoons salt. Add 4 cups of water and bring it to a boil. Reduce the heat, cover the pot, and simmer until the lentils are very tender, 20 to 40 minutes, depending on the age of the lentils; older ones need more cooking time because they will be drier.

3. Remove the pot from the heat, discard the bay leaf and cinnamon stick, and mash the lentil mixture until it becomes a dip with the texture you like. (If you want it smooth, use an immersion or regular blender. I like it chunkier, so I use a potato masher; a fork also works.) Season the mixture with more kosher salt if needed, and with black pepper to taste.

4. Spread the dip out on a plate or in a shallow bowl and drizzle olive oil over it. Scatter the reserved fried onions and leeks over the top, sprinkle with flaky sea salt, and serve.

3 tablespoons extra-virgin olive oil, plus more for drizzling

1 small onion, halved and thinly sliced

1 small leek, halved lengthwise, rinsed, and thinly sliced

2 garlic cloves, grated on a Microplane or minced

1 teaspoon ground cumin

Large pinch of ground allspice

Pinch of cayenne pepper

1½ cups green French lentils (*lentilles du Puy*) or brown lentils

1 bay leaf

1 cinnamon stick, about 2 inches long

1½ teaspoons kosher salt, plus more to taste

Freshly ground black pepper to taste

Flaky sea salt, for garnish

TOTAL TIME: 1 HOUR
MAKES APPROXIMATELY 2 CUPS

Spicy
COCONUT CASHEW DIP

One of the reasons Thai food skyrocketed in popularity in the United States in the '90s is our collective adoration of peanut satay sauce—the peanut-and-coconut-milk concoction that turns regular skewered chicken into a feast, and makes even soggy takeout gone cold taste pretty darn good. A dollop or drizzle of great satay sauce can turn the simplest, plainest of foods into something dazzling. It's just a perfect recipe to have in your repertoire.

My version substitutes mild cashews for more forthright peanuts, which I think makes the whole thing creamier and richer because of the cashews' high fat content. But feel free to use peanuts if you prefer a more classic and toasty flavor profile. Then slather this over everything from grilled chicken and pork to tofu, hard-boiled eggs, rice, and steamed vegetables (crisp-steamed green beans and carrots are especially nice with this). Leftovers, if you have any, will last for a week in the fridge. Feel free to double the recipe.

⅔ cup roasted unsalted cashews (or use peanuts; see Note)

¼ cup unsweetened coconut milk

1 tablespoon tamarind paste or concentrate (optional)

1 tablespoon dark brown sugar

1 tablespoon soy sauce

2 teaspoons Asian fish sauce

Juice of 1 lime, plus more if needed

1 to 2 fresh hot chiles, to taste, seeded and chopped (or substitute cayenne to taste)

1 garlic clove, grated on a Microplane or minced

TOTAL TIME: 15 MINUTES
MAKES APPROXIMATELY 1 CUP

Place the cashews in a food processor or blender, and blend until they begin to form a paste, 1 to 2 minutes. Add the coconut milk, tamarind paste if using, brown sugar, soy sauce, fish sauce, lime juice, chiles, and garlic. Puree until smooth. Taste, and adjust the seasonings if necessary. (If you left out the tamarind paste, you may need to add more lime juice.) If the sauce is too thick, blend in a little water to thin it out.

NOTE: If you don't have either cashews or peanuts on hand, you can make this with ⅔ cup peanut butter. Just add the coconut milk at the end, tablespoon by tablespoon, until the desired consistency is reached; you may not need it all if your nut butter is on the thin side.

CHEDDAR FONDUE
with Irish Whiskey

Who doesn't love a pot full of oozy melted cheese? Fondue is one of those dishes that gets everyone excited, even at the mere mention of it. And it's super easy to make as you don't even need a fondue set—a heavy saucepan and any forks will do the trick. Which means you can whip up a batch even if you haven't inherited your parents' vintage enameled fondue set with matching color-tipped forks like I have (it's one of my most prized possessions).

You can make fondue from a number of different kinds of cheese, as long as they are easily meltable. Here, I use a combination of traditional Gruyère and completely untraditional cheddar, which gives it a slightly grassy, buttery flavor. Gouda, a young pecorino or Manchego, or a stinky raclette would also work well if substituted for the cheddar. I also use a dash of Irish whiskey here instead of the usual kirsch (cherry brandy). Whiskey has a rounder caramel taste, though it's subtle, so feel free to leave it out. Serve this with crusty bread cubes; steamed broccoli or cauliflower; carrot, celery, or fennel sticks; cubed apple; seedless grapes; clementine sections; cubed salami, soppressata, or kielbasa; roasted chestnuts; and/or dried apricots. When it comes to fondue, you have options!

1. Rub the cut side of the garlic halves over the inside of a large Dutch oven or heavy-bottomed saucepan, covering the bottom and halfway up the sides. Add the wine and bring it to a simmer over medium-high heat.

2. Meanwhile, in a large bowl, toss the grated cheeses with the cornstarch.

3. Add a handful of cheese at a time to the simmering wine, stirring until one handful melts before adding the next. Reduce the heat to medium-low and stir constantly until the cheese is completely melted. Add the whiskey, if using, and the lemon juice, and heat until the mixture is bubbling, 1 to 2 minutes. Season the fondue with salt, pepper, and nutmeg if desired. Serve at once. (If the fondue gets cold and starts to congeal, just put it back over low heat for a minute or two, stirring to loosen it up again.)

1 small garlic clove, halved

1 cup dry white wine (anything you like to drink will work as long as it's dry)

12 ounces Gruyère cheese, grated

12 ounces aged cheddar cheese, grated

1½ tablespoons cornstarch

1 to 2 tablespoons Irish whiskey or brandy, to taste (optional)

1 tablespoon fresh lemon juice

Kosher salt and freshly ground black pepper to taste

Freshly grated nutmeg to taste (optional)

TOTAL TIME: 20 MINUTES
SERVES 4 TO 6

Homemade *SEEDY* **CRACKERS**

Homemade crackers taste about a million times better than most anything you can buy—fresher, wheatier, more complex—and are far more economical than the fancy kind you'd get at gourmet shops. Plus, they are ridiculously simple to make and utterly adaptable. If you hate seeds, leave them off and substitute fresh rosemary or thyme leaves or your favorite dried herbs. A sprinkle of grated cheese works well on top, too. Or take a minimalist tack and just sprinkle them with salt. If you want thicker, sturdier crackers, roll them a bit thicker than what is called for. For the thinnest and most delicate crackers, you can roll them a bit thinner. They go with any of the dips in this chapter, and are also excellent served with cheese. At our house, we spread them with salted butter and snack on them before dinner. They are what I reach for when I rush in after work, ravenous and grumpy. A few buttered crackers later and all is well.

You'll notice I added weights to the ingredient list here. I prefer weighing; it's more exact and I find it easier (and there are fewer measuring spoons and cups to wash). But do whatever makes it easy for you.

1½ cups (190 grams) all-purpose flour

1⅓ cups (170 grams) spelt flour or whole-wheat flour or rye flour

1¼ teaspoons (7 grams) fine sea salt

1 teaspoon (5 grams) baking powder

⅔ cup extra-virgin olive oil

Sesame seeds, black onion seeds, or caraway seeds, or a combination, for topping

Flaky sea salt to taste

TOTAL TIME: 30 MINUTES
MAKES ABOUT 1 POUND

1. Heat the oven to 425°F.

2. In a large bowl, whisk together the all-purpose and spelt flours, salt, and baking powder. Add ⅔ cup of water (157 grams) and the olive oil, and stir to combine. Transfer the dough to a clean work surface, knead it a few times, and then divide it in half.

3. Place each portion of the dough on its own large rimless baking sheet. (Don't use insulated cookie sheets if you have other options; they can inhibit crisping). Roll the dough out directly on the baking sheet until it is very thin, ³⁄₁₆ inch or even thinner in areas (it is okay if it's a little uneven; the shape doesn't matter here). Sprinkle your choice of toppings and flaky sea salt to taste over the dough, and use the rolling pin to press them in.

4. Bake for 18 to 20 minutes, or until the edges are deeply browned and the center is pale golden. Make sure that the center is pale golden before you remove these from the oven; otherwise they may not crisp up.

5. Transfer the baking sheets to wire racks to cool. (The crackers will crisp as they cool, but if after cooling they aren't as crisp as you want them to be, put them back in the oven for a few minutes.)

6. Break the cooled crackers into pieces and serve, or store airtight at room temperature for up to 2 weeks.

WINTER VEGETABLE SALAD *with Kale, Cabbage, and Thai Lime Dressing*

An Asian take on the usual kale salad, this one includes slivered cabbage and Brussels sprouts to increase the crucifer content and add sweetness to the bowl. Although the cabbage and kale are crisp and raw here, I sauté the Brussels sprouts for a richer, caramelized flavor. They give the salad a brawny, almost bacon-y depth—but without the meat. And they also add a warm temperature contrast to the cool salad greens.

This is the kind of salad to serve when the rest of your dinner is so elemental (broiled fish or steak, say, or a sautéed chicken breast) that you need something a little unexpected to keep things interesting. Or make this the main dish and pair it with some bread and cheese, or with sesame oil–slicked rice noodles, to round things out. It's also lovely to serve to company when you're looking for an out-of-the-ordinary salad with sparkle and verve.

1. In a medium bowl, whisk together the lime juice, fish sauce, and brown sugar until the sugar is dissolved. Whisking consistently, add the sesame oil, blending until it is emulsified. Set the dressing aside.

2. Heat the olive oil in a large skillet over medium heat. Add the Brussels sprouts and sauté, turning them over once, until they are nicely caramelized, 8 to 10 minutes total. Sprinkle with salt and pepper to taste.

3. In a large bowl, toss together the kale, lettuce, cabbage, basil, and mint. Add dressing to taste, toss, and then top the salad with the Brussels sprouts. Spoon a little more dressing over the salad, and serve.

2 tablespoons fresh lime juice

1½ tablespoons Asian fish sauce

1 teaspoon light brown sugar

2 teaspoons toasted sesame oil

3 tablespoons extra-virgin olive oil

10 large Brussels sprouts, trimmed and thinly sliced through the stem (about 3 cups)

Kosher salt and freshly ground black pepper to taste

2 cups coarsely chopped Russian (purple) kale

2 cups torn red-leaf lettuce

1 cup thinly sliced napa or regular green cabbage

½ cup torn fresh basil leaves

½ cup torn fresh mint leaves

TOTAL TIME: 20 MINUTES
SERVES 4 TO 6

Simplest GREEN SALAD

This is what I make for dinner practically every single night, tossing it with my hands so I can get a feel for the moment when the leaves are nicely coated with the dressing (though use utensils if you want to avoid olive oil on your fingers). You can use any salad greens you like; I tend to go for the dark, slightly bitter ones of the arugula/spinach variety, but this recipe will work with whatever you have in your fridge.

Adding the vinegar, salt, and pepper to the greens before adding the oil gives the salt a chance to start dissolving, and therefore makes for a more evenly seasoned salad. It's a slight but noticeable difference.

When I'm lucky enough to have a ripe avocado, I'll cube that up and add it to the bowl as well. The trick with the avocado is to salt it while it's on the cutting board, before you slide the cubes into the salad. Otherwise it never seems to get seasoned properly. Add the avocado after you've tossed the salad so the cubes don't break down and get mushy.

1. Put the salad greens in a salad bowl, drizzle with the vinegar or citrus juice, and season with fine sea salt and black pepper to taste. Add the garlic if you like, and toss gently.

2. Drizzle the olive oil over the salad, and toss gently again. Top with the avocado if using, and serve.

8 cups salad greens

1 to 2 tablespoons vinegar, fresh lemon juice, or fresh lime juice

Fine sea salt and freshly ground black pepper to taste

1 small garlic clove, grated on a Microplane or minced (optional)

¼ cup extra-virgin olive oil, plus more as needed

1 ripe avocado, pitted, peeled, and cubed, seasoned with salt (optional)

TOTAL TIME: 5 MINUTES
(7 IF YOU'RE ADDING AVOCADO)
SERVES 4

TOMATO SALAD

with Herbs, Shallots, and Lime

Our standard tomato salad technique is to slice up whichever heirlooms are the ripest and juiciest, then sprinkle them with olive oil, flaky sea salt, and freshly ground pepper, along with torn herbs from the deck when I'm feeling particularly festive. It's simple and always delightful. But there are some evenings when I need a little something more—maybe I'm looking to impress a guest or just feel like trying something new. The good thing about tomatoes is that as excellent as they are served plain, they can take a little jazzing up, in this case with shallots and lime. Here I briefly soak the shallot slices in lime juice and salt, which gives them a very light pickled note and mellows their pungency. Scattered over sweet tomatoes, they're a bit tart and a bit crunchy. It's a minor effort for a big result.

1 small shallot, sliced (or use approximately 2 tablespoons sliced red onion)

1 lime

Fine sea salt and freshly ground black pepper to taste

2 pounds ripe tomatoes, preferably a pretty mix of heirloom varieties

Extra-virgin olive oil to taste

¼ cup torn soft fresh herbs (any combination of chives, parsley, basil, tarragon, chervil, fennel fronds, cilantro, and/or mint)

TOTAL TIME: 15 MINUTES
SERVES 4 TO 6

1. Put the shallot slices in a small bowl. Grate the zest from the lime, and add it to the bowl. Cut the bald lime in half and squeeze the juice of one of the halves into the bowl. Season the mixture with fine sea salt and black pepper to taste. Let it sit for 10 minutes while you slice the tomatoes.

2. Slice the tomatoes any which way you like—in thick rounds, large chunks, thin wedges. If your mixture includes cherry tomatoes, halve them. It's nice to have a variety of shapes and textures, so feel free to mix it up. Arrange the tomato pieces on a platter.

3. Sprinkle tomatoes with salt and let sit for 5 minutes. Scatter the shallots, along with a little of the liquid from the bowl, over the tomatoes.

4. Drizzle olive oil all over the tomatoes, and top with the herbs. Season with more salt and pepper and shallot liquid to taste, and serve.

CITRUS SALAD

with Olives

I think of this citrus salad as the winter analogue to a platter of summer tomatoes. It's got the same sweet juiciness and a similar vibrant flavor. And just like that bowl of multihued heirlooms, this is also one of the prettiest and easiest salads you can whip up. Feel free to use whatever sweet citrus you've got. In an ideal world, you'd mix up the colors a bit—choosing deep-red blood oranges, pink Cara Caras, and regular oranges along with some grapefruit. Don't try to make this salad too far ahead. Once cut, the citrus fruit loses juices fast. You've got about a thirty-minute window before your attractive salad turns into a soggy mess.

1. Cut the peels off all the citrus: Using a sharp paring knife, trim a slice off the top and bottom of each piece of fruit. Stand the fruit on a cut end and then trim off all the rest of the skin and pith, wielding the knife so it follows the curve of the fruit. The aim is to remove all of the white pith, but as little of the vibrant flesh as possible.

2. Slice the peeled fruit into rounds, and then use the tip of your knife to pick out any seeds. Arrange the fruit on a platter.

3. Drizzle the olive oil over the citrus, and then season it with flaky sea salt and red chile flakes or black pepper to taste. Top with the olives if you like, and mint, and serve.

3 small oranges or 3 large tangerines

1 white or pink grapefruit

3 tablespoons extra-virgin olive oil

Flaky sea salt to taste

Red chile flakes, Turkish pepper, or freshly ground black pepper to taste

¼ cup chopped pitted good olives (optional; either black or green or a combination)

2 tablespoons fresh mint or cilantro leaves

TOTAL TIME: 10 MINUTES

SERVES 4 TO 6

PAN-FRIED ASPARAGUS

with Lemon Zest

I've gone through so many asparagus phases in my life. First, there was steaming, taught to me by my mother, who used an upright basket that cooked the thicker asparagus ends at a higher temperature than the delicate tips. Then there was stir-frying, a by-product of my early forays into Asian cuisine. Microwaving came and went, quickly replaced by roasting, which remained the go-to method until recently, when pan-frying usurped its golden place. Both roasting and pan-frying give you a similarly charred-on-the-outside, tender-within result. But pan-frying gets you there faster since you don't have to heat up the oven. In this version, I season the seared spears with lemon juice and zest for brightness and tang. But feel free to substitute a drizzle of vinegar and a shower of fresh herbs, or a handful of chopped olives instead. Or to turn a skillet full of asparagus into a meal, a fried egg and/or some crumbled feta or goat cheese on top will get you there quickly and easily.

2 tablespoons extra-virgin olive oil

1 pound asparagus, woody ends trimmed

Fine sea salt and freshly ground black pepper to taste

1 garlic clove, grated on a Microplane or minced

Finely grated zest of ½ lemon

1 tablespoon fresh lemon juice

TOTAL TIME: 10 MINUTES
SERVES 4

1. Heat a 10-inch skillet over high heat, then add the oil and let it get hot for about 20 seconds. Add asparagus, salt, and pepper; cook, shaking the skillet every minute or so, until the asparagus starts to brown, about 5 minutes.

2. Take the skillet off the heat and stir in the garlic, lemon zest, and juice. Toss until asparagus is well coated and garlic is fragrant, about 1 minute, then transfer to serving plates.

GREEN BEANS
with Caper Vinaigrette

The combination of minced capers and red wine vinegar is alchemical—somehow these two staple ingredients magically combine to taste better together than either does on its own. The capers taste herbal and saline and bring out the fruitiness of the vinegar, which makes for a highly nuanced vinaigrette. You can use the vinaigrette on any vegetable or salad you like. Tossed with blanched green beans, it's the kind of side dish that once you start, you just can't stop eating. Don't plan on leftovers.

1. Bring a large pot of heavily salted water to a boil.

2. In a large bowl, whisk together the capers, vinegar, and salt. Stir in the olive oil and dill.

3. Add the green beans to the boiling water and cook until barely tender, 1 to 2 minutes. Drain well, and toss with vinaigrette until well coated. Taste, add salt if needed, and serve.

1 tablespoon minced capers

½ teaspoon red wine vinegar

Large pinch of fine sea salt, more to taste

2 tablespoons extra-virgin olive oil

2 tablespoons chopped fresh dill or parsley

12 ounces green beans, trimmed

TOTAL TIME: 10 MINUTES
SERVES 4

Smashed Sichuan
CUCUMBER SALAD

Mild cucumbers can take a lot of bold seasoning, and here they get it in a dousing of garlic, fresh ginger, chile, and soy sauce. Serve this salad with something mild to soften its bite. I love it with fish (particularly rich salmon or tuna fillets) or with any kind of Asian noodle or grain dish. It also does wonders to perk up a simple plate of fried or scrambled eggs. If you can find thin-skinned Persian cucumbers, they work especially well here, and there's no need to peel them.

You can make the salad up to four hours ahead; store it in the fridge until serving.

1. Arrange the cucumbers on a cutting board. Using a rolling pin, meat pounder, or the flat side of a cleaver or heavy chef's knife, pound the cucumbers until they are broken apart and smashed. Tear them into 1½-inch-long chunks, discarding any seeds that fall out in the process (it's okay to leave some of the seeds). Put the cucumbers in a large bowl.

2. In a small bowl, combine the garlic, ginger, vinegar, sesame oil, soy sauce, salt, brown sugar, and chile slices. Mix well, add this to the cucumbers, and toss.

3. You can serve this straightaway, but it gets better if you chill it for at least 20 minutes and up to 4 hours. Just before serving, taste the salad and adjust the seasonings if needed.

2 pounds cucumbers, peeled if desired

2 garlic cloves, grated on a Microplane or minced

1 teaspoon grated peeled fresh ginger

4 teaspoons Chinese black vinegar or rice vinegar

1½ teaspoons toasted sesame oil

1 teaspoon soy sauce

Kosher salt to taste

Large pinch of light brown sugar

1 small fresh red chile, thinly sliced, seeded if desired

TOTAL TIME: 15 MINUTES
SERVES 4

RYE & CHEDDAR BISCUITS

Rye flour makes these ultra-flaky biscuits hearty and earthy tasting while cheddar makes them rich and savory. I love these with pretty much any soup or salad in this book. And they're terrific for breakfast or brunch. If you don't have rye flour on hand, feel free to substitute whole-wheat flour. And Gruyére or gouda would work well in place of the cheddar. If you've got extra fresh herbs on hand—thyme, dill, or basil—chop up some and add it in. These biscuits take well to embellishments.

2 large eggs

1½ cups (187 grams) all-purpose flour

½ cup (50 grams) rye flour
(or use whole-wheat)

1 tablespoon (12 grams) baking
powder

¼ teaspoon (2 grams) baking soda

1 teaspoon (6 grams) fine sea salt

½ cup (143 grams) cold sour cream
or plain whole-milk Greek yogurt

1 tablespoon (15 grams) light
or dark brown sugar

12 tablespoons (1½ sticks) cold
unsalted butter, cubed

1 cup grated cheddar cheese

TOTAL TIME: 40 MINUTES
MAKES 9 BISCUITS

1. Heat the oven to 450°F. Line a rimmed baking sheet with parchment. In a small bowl, whisk together 1 egg with 1 tablespoon water and reserve.

2. In a large bowl, whisk together the flours, baking powder, baking soda, and sea salt. In a separate bowl, whisk together the sour cream, remaining 1 egg, and brown sugar. Cut the butter cubes into the dry ingredients using a fork or pastry cutter, until the mixture consists of chickpea-sized crumbs. Gently stir in the wet mixture. Fold in the cheese.

3. On a floured work surface, pat the dough into a square that is 1¼-inch tall. Using a sharp, floured knife, cut into 9 equal-sized squares and space the biscuits very close together on the prepared baking sheet. Brush the tops with egg wash. Bake until the biscuits are golden brown and tender, 12 to 17 minutes. Cool for 5 minutes before serving.

COCONUT RICE

Sweet and rich, this mellow rice is a great foil for spicy dishes. You can change the personality of this dish by switching up the grain size. Short-grain will give you stickier rice than will long-grain, which has grains that stay more distinct. Choose either one to suit your taste.

1. Pour the coconut milk into a 2-cup liquid measuring cup, and add enough water to measure 1⅞ cups. Pour the liquid into a medium pot with a tight-fitting lid. Add the rinsed rice and the salt. Bring to a boil, cover the pot, and reduce the heat to a low simmer. Cook for 17 minutes.

2. Remove the pot from the heat, place a clean dish towel between the rim of the pot and the lid, and let the rice stand for 10 minutes to steam.

3. Fluff the rice with a fork, and serve.

VARIATION
To make coconut brown rice, add enough water to the coconut milk to measure 2 cups. Cook for 40 to 50 minutes, until just tender; then let it steam as directed.

1 13.5-ounce can coconut milk

1 cup white rice, either short- or long-grain, rinsed very well

Pinch of kosher salt

TOTAL TIME: 30 MINUTES
MAKES ABOUT 4 CUPS

QUICK-ROASTED BROCCOLI OR CAULIFLOWER

Roasting sturdy broccoli and cauliflower at very high heat crisps their crevices and tenderizes their middles, resulting in a very crunchy-tender vegetable with almost no fuss. The key is to use enough oil to encourage real caramelization. If you use too little, the vegetables steam instead of browning. I make this all the time in the colder months, sometimes serving it as a side dish, and sometimes as an hors d'ouevre at a dinner party. I pile the florets onto a platter and provide napkins on the side (and aioli for dipping when I'm feeling fancy). Guests gobble it up with their fingers. You can give Brussels sprouts the same treatment, though they take a lot less time to roast.

One thing to note: adding the seeds (cumin and/or mustard) halfway through the roasting time ensures they don't burn. Don't be tempted to add them any earlier. Been there, regretted that.

Florets cut from 1 head
(1½ to 2 pounds) broccoli or
cauliflower, broken into
bite-size pieces (about 7 cups)

3 to 4 tablespoons extra-virgin
olive oil

Fine sea salt and freshly ground
black pepper to taste

1 teaspoon cumin seeds (optional)

1 teaspoon black or brown
mustard seeds (optional)

TOTAL TIME: 25 MINUTES
SERVES 4 TO 6

1. Heat the oven to 450°F.

2. Spread the florets out in a single layer on one or two rimmed baking sheets (you want to give them a little breathing room if possible, to help them brown). Drizzle the olive oil over the florets, season with fine sea salt and black pepper, and toss to coat.

3. Roast the florets for about 10 minutes, and then toss them well. If you are using the cumin and/or mustard seeds, add them when you are tossing. Then continue to roast the florets until they are tender and browned at the edges, another 8 to 12 minutes.

4. Serve hot or warm.

Skillet BROWN-BUTTER CORNBREAD

Baking your cornbread in a preheated skillet is more than just a stylish way to present it; it also gives you a nicely crisp crust. When the batter hits the hot pan, it immediately starts to sear, allowing it time to turn brown and very crunchy while the center stays moist. Serve this slathered with butter whenever you want something slightly sweet and crumb-y to give a little more substance to your meal. It's also excellent for breakfast or brunch, and leftovers keep well wrapped in foil and stored at room temperature for at least two days.

1. Heat the oven to 375°F.

2. In a 12-inch ovenproof (preferably cast-iron) skillet, melt the butter over medium heat. Cook, swirling the butter to coat the sides and bottom of the skillet, until the foam subsides and the butter turns a deep nut-brown, about 5 minutes (watch carefully to see that it does not burn). Another clue as to when the brown butter is ready: the frantic bubbling noise will quiet down as the moisture cooks out of the butter. Pour the brown butter into a large bowl. Do not wipe out the pan.

3. Whisk the honey into the brown butter; then whisk in the buttermilk. The butter mixture should be cool to the touch; if not, wait until it is. Then whisk in the eggs. Whisk in the cornmeal, both flours, baking powder, salt, and baking soda. Finally stir in the corn if using.

4. If the skillet is no longer at least somewhat hot (cast iron will retain the heat longer than other metals), heat it on the stove for a few minutes until it's quite hot. Scrape the batter into the hot skillet, place it in the oven, and bake until the top is golden brown and a toothpick inserted into the center emerges clean, 25 to 35 minutes.

5. Dust the top of the cornbread with chile powder if you like. Let it cool in the skillet for 10 minutes before slicing it.

12 tablespoons (1½ sticks) unsalted butter

⅓ cup (113 grams) honey

2¼ cups (550 grams) buttermilk

3 large eggs

1½ cups (180 grams) yellow cornmeal, fine or medium grind (not coarse)

½ cup (65 grams) whole-wheat flour

½ cup (60 grams) all-purpose flour

1½ tablespoons (18 grams) baking powder

1½ teaspoons (9 grams) kosher salt

½ teaspoon (5 grams) baking soda

¾ cup (130 grams) fresh corn kernels (from 1 small ear), optional

Good red chile powder, such as chipotle or New Mexico, for garnish (optional)

TOTAL TIME: 1 HOUR
MAKES 12 SLICES

ACKNOWLEDGMENTS

A book doesn't just spring gracefully out of the heart, head, and soul of its author. It is slowly and sometimes painfully extracted. This takes a team. In other words, I owe lots of thanks to lots of folks. And here they are:

Janis Donnaud, my fearless agent.

The superlative team at Clarkson Potter: Doris Cooper, Marysarah Quinn, Derek Gullino, Aaron Wehner, Amy Boorstein, Kate Tyler, Erica Gelbard, Kevin Sweeting, Carly Gorga, and Danielle Daitch.

Brilliant photographer Eric Wolfinger and his people: Alison Christiana, Alma Espinola, Connor Bruce.

The food styling wizard Alison Attenborough and her lovely assistants Joanna Keohane and Sandy Ta.

I couldn't have done this without my talented recipe testers: Sarah Huck, Adelaide Mueller, Jade Zimmerman, Daniel Bernstein, and Lily Starbuck.

A special thank you to the entire inspiring team at the *New York Times* Food section, including Sam Sifton, Susan Edgerley, Emily Weinstein, Patrick Farrell, Trish Hall, Pete Wells, and everyone else. I wouldn't be here without you!

And, finally, Alice Goldsmith of Brooklyn Peoples Pottery, and Margaret Braun, who lent me much of the fantastically gorgeous handmade pottery that you see as props throughout the book. It was hard to give it back.

INDEX

Note: Page references in *italics* indicate photographs.